PRAISE FOR *WHERE DOES MY STUFF COME FROM*

When I became Secretary of Commerce, I thought I understood supply chains. Then came the semiconductor shortage, and I found myself tracing a single chip's journey through a dozen countries, hundreds of suppliers, and decades of decisions that no one person had made or could fully explain.

In *Where Does My Stuff Come From?*, Willy Shih lays out the principles that shaped modern global production: why manufacturing clustered where it did, why some capabilities are so hard to move once they leave, and why decisions made decades ago now carry consequences for national security and economic resilience.

Professor Shih writes with the authority of someone who has both run manufacturing operations and studied them for decades at Harvard Business School. He explains without oversimplifying. Whether you are a policymaker weighing industrial strategy, a business leader rethinking sourcing, or a citizen who wants to understand what happened when the shelves went empty in 2020, this book gives you the on-the-ground picture you need.

—Gina Raimondo, 40th U.S. Secretary of Commerce

I have spent my entire career in manufacturing, from working on the shop floor to running one of the world's largest manufacturing companies, and I still learn something new every time I walk a factory floor. Reading Willy Shih's book felt much the same.

Willy has seen manufacturing from every angle: Fortune 500 boardrooms, congressional hearings, Harvard classrooms, and countless factories around the world. More importantly, he spent three decades building the systems described in this book and understands how things actually get made. He talks about complex systems the way people who make things do. No jargon. No theory for its own sake. Just a clear explanation of how these systems work and why they matter.

Supply chains touch nearly every aspect of modern life, but not many people understand them. Willy does. He cuts through the noise and explains them in a way anybody can follow.

If you have ever wondered how the thing in your hand got there, and why it matters, read this book. You'll never look at a store shelf the same way again.

—Revathi Advaithi, Chief Executive Officer, Flex

Willy Shih has a rare ability to take the enormous complexity of global supply chains and make it understandable, relevant and engaging. *Where Does My Stuff Come From?* does exactly that.

What makes the book especially valuable is the way that Willy connects the products we use every day to the remarkably intricate networks of companies, transportation systems, and decisions behind them. In doing so, he helps readers understand not only where things come from but why resilient and reliable supply chains matter so much to our economy and daily lives.

From my vantage point at the Port of Los Angeles, I see every day just how interconnected our global economy has become. A decision made thousands of miles away can quickly affect businesses, workers, and consumers here at home. Willy brings those connections to life, explaining not only how goods move around the world but why they are produced and how economics, technology, trade policy, and geopolitics continue to reshape global commerce.

I've long valued Willy's perspective as a friend and trusted colleague. At a time when resilience, sustainability, and adaptability matter more than ever, he has given us a timely and insightful look at how global supply chains work, how we got here, and where we may be headed next.

—Gene Seroka, Executive Director, Port of Los Angeles

Professor Willy Shih is the exceptionally rare scholar of globalization who has spent a career living it in practice rather than just musing on blackboards about how it should work in theory. The economic and political wreckage caused by blind faith in free trade is now visible all around us, so undeniable that the theorists themselves have finally begun to admit their error. Here we finally have the concrete, commonsense answers to the questions of why: Why did the real world depart so dramatically from the textbook? Why was the American industrial base hollowed out? Why did that have such far-reaching consequences for the nation? The stories in this book provide a better economics education than the typical PhD seems to have received.

—Oren Cass, Chief Economist, American Compass

Supply chain management has moved to the center stage since we all experienced the huge disruptions from the COVID-19 pandemic, followed by the almost daily news on how tariffs and trade policies could affect what goods we could get and what prices we may have to pay. Willy Shih's book is no doubt the best book on supply chains in recent years. Shih explains how all the current issues that dominate business and our livelihood these days, such as disruptions, geo-political frictions, logistics challenges, outsourcing, jobs, tariffs, and industrial policies, affect the global supply chains. The underlying theories and concepts came out alive through the rich set of examples in the book. Shih's experience in business and as a government advisor added deeper perspectives to how the global supply chain has evolved from the past and what can be expected in the future. There are also themes that are important but rarely well explained in other outlets. First, this book is really about the interacting forces in a global supply chain, from developing economies to matured ones. Second, Shih provides a clear lens for us to understand how China has become the Factory of the World, with its economic cluster advantage. Third, the diversity of industries covered in the book allows us to appreciate that we must learn to use different paths to effectively manage the supply chain. The lessons that the book provides is a must-read for supply chain professionals, business leaders, and, I venture to say, the general public.

—Hau Lee, The Thoma Professor of Operations,
Information & Technology, Emeritus

WHERE DOES MY STUFF COME FROM?

WHERE DOES MY STUFF COME FROM?

THE POWERFUL ECONOMICS BEHIND GLOBAL SUPPLY CHAINS

WILLY SHIH

WILEY

Published by John Wiley & Sons, Inc., Hoboken, New Jersey.

For general information on our other products and services or for technical support, please contact our Customer Care Department within the United States at (800) 762-2974, outside the United States at (317) 572-3993 or fax (317) 572-4002.

Wiley also publishes its books in a variety of electronic formats. Some content that appears in print may not be available in electronic formats. For more information about Wiley products, visit our web site at www.wiley.com.

Library of Congress Cataloging-in-Publication Data:

Names: Shih, Willy C. author
Title: Where does your stuff come from? / Willy Shih.
Description: Hoboken, New Jersey : Wiley, [2027] | Includes bibliographical references and index.
Identifiers: LCCN 2026030914 (print) | LCCN 2026030915 (ebook) | ISBN 9781394408962 hardback | ISBN 9781394408986 adobe pdf | ISBN 9781394408979 epub
Subjects: LCSH: Supply chain management | Business logistics | International trade | Globalization—Economic aspects
Classification: LCC HD38.6 .S55 2027 (print) | LCC HD38.6 (ebook)
LC record available at https://lccn.loc.gov/2026030914
LC ebook record available at https://lccn.loc.gov/2026030915

Cover Design: Wiley
Cover Images: Michael Burrell/Getty Images, natthanim/Getty Images, Kwangmoozaa/Getty Images, chipstudio/Getty Images
Author Photo: Russ Campbell
Printed and bound by CPI Group (UK) Ltd, Croydon, CR0 4YY

C9781394408962_050926

To all those who have shaped me along the way—the teachers and the mentors, the colleagues who challenged me, and the teams who trusted me to lead them. And especially to those who I have reported to who had enough faith to let me stumble, enough patience to let me find my footing, and enough wisdom to know that both were necessary. You gave me something rarer than knowledge. You gave me room to grow. And finally, to my daughter, Anna, who encouraged me to write this book and who has been an inspiration to me.

Contents

Preface

Say you're with a friend who's excited about a new purchase, like a new gadget or an item of clothing. Perhaps you asked them, "Where did you get it?" The answer may have been, "I bought it on Amazon" or "I picked it up at Walmart," or maybe some other store. But have you ever then thought to yourself, "But wait: Who made that product, and how did it get to the store in the first place?"

Most people probably have no idea how a particular product got to the place where they bought it. And until the COVID-19 pandemic, most didn't think twice about it either. But when all kinds of crazy shortages hit, a lot of people began to wonder. More often than not, they were surprised: "I didn't know that came from China!" Or they had no idea that the car that they wanted wasn't available because the manufacturer was short microcomputer chips that came from Taiwan or Japan. Or that the masks and gowns that healthcare workers depended on also came from China or that bicycles with European-sounding brand names actually came from Taiwan. Sudden shortages have a way of exposing these things.

That's also when people started thinking I was an expert in supply chains. Supply chains refer to the network of people, organizations, and other resources that move a product from raw materials to a final customer. They are supposed to *match* supply with demand. That's when everything is going well, that is.

People Think I'm an Expert in Toilet Paper

My saga as an expert began when an Australian woman who used to work for me sent me an email saying people were hoarding toilet paper down under. I had heard that hoarding was going on in Hong Kong and Seattle as well, so I wrote an article for *Forbes* on the toilet paper supply chain. I admitted up front that I really knew nothing about the toilet paper supply chain, but I argued that we could start with first principles and figure out pretty much what it should look like.

First, the product is relatively inexpensive, but it takes up a lot of space considering how much it weighs. That means its *value density* is relatively low. That means the cost of transporting it from the factory through distribution centers to a store is high as a proportion of its price. Therefore, producers wouldn't want to ship it long distances. Most countries have domestic or near-shore manufacturing, and the largest producers in the world, China, the United States, Japan, Germany, Korea, Brazil, Finland, Canada, Sweden, and Italy are all located inside large markets.

The second important characteristic is that demand for the product is relatively stable. That's just common sense—demand is not seasonal, and consumption should be roughly in line with the size of the population and shouldn't vary much. Granted, hotels and offices use an institutional variety that is different from what is sold for home consumption, but manufacturers optimize their supply chains with all these things in mind.

What happens when shoppers scoop up a lot of toilet paper and hoard it? It sends a demand signal through the supply chain to produce more. Producers might like to ramp up capacity, but that is hard to do instantaneously because the factories likely won't have much slack capacity. Factories are expensive, and for a product with stable demand, you will likely run it at 90% utilization or more, or your chief financial officer (CFO) will accuse you of being wasteful with your capital expenditures. They might eventually run the factory a little hotter and send more into the distribution channel.

Meanwhile, consumers buy a lot more than their immediate needs require and eventually run out of space to store any more, so then they stop buying. Then, as the crisis passes, consumers burn off their "pantry inventory," and that will also take some time, depressing demand. This of course will then lead to overstock in the stores and signals to cut production. At the same time, the manufacturer is trying to figure out what the heck is going on with demand, and a lot of people along the chain get burned. This "bullwhip effect" famously described by my friend Hau Lee will lead to all kinds of troubles across the supply chain (Lee et al. 1997).

That story got picked up by numerous media outlets, starting with the *Los Angeles Times*, the *Wall Street Journal*, BBC, CNN, and others. Even grocery chains started calling me up asking what to do. Sure enough, after about three months, retail sales of toilet paper in the U.S. fell off a cliff, just as I had predicted. In the meantime, people started to think I was one of the world's experts on toilet paper, which I definitely am not.

But people also started to ask me a lot more questions about supply chains, and I realized that I had physically been to and seen a lot of places where stuff actually comes from. Largely this is because I was directly involved in building complex supply chains at a time of rapid globalization. Over the last three decades, I have visited more than 1,000 factories, toured dozens of container ports and air cargo operations, and even followed iron ore from a mine in the Pilbara region of Western Australia all the way to finished steel coming off a cold roll line in Shanghai. I thought by telling some of these stories on how products come into being, I could explain some foundational concepts in trade and supply chains in a more fun and engaging manner than through the more traditional lens of an economist. That was the purpose of writing this book.

I find most supply chain concepts to be quite simple, but somehow when economists explain them it is easy to get lost in the weeds. My focus instead will be on using examples that I have seen during my decades in industry, or ones that I looked at or studied once I joined the faculty at the Harvard Business School. I hope that exploring these examples will be a memorable way to frame these ideas so that next time you see a label on Alaskan salmon that says "Processed in China" or maybe one that says "Designed by Apple in California, Made in China," you will understand the logic of how that came to be. I won't try to offer a complete picture on all the economics of trade and supply chains. People spend their whole careers studying and writing about that. I just want you to look at things differently the next time you go shopping.

"You Actually Read the Labels?"

I'm one of those people who grew up looking at the labels on products, and the boxes they came in. Partly this was because my mother, an immigrant to the United States, always looked to see for herself. That was a legacy of her having lived through World War II and not wanting to buy products from a former enemy. It took her more than four decades to get over that. But it caused me to develop a curiosity about where things came from.

Back in the 1950s and 1960s, we looked for "Made in the USA" a lot, and we did see an increasing number of labels that said, "Made in Japan," mostly on cheap stuff. As I grew older, the things that came from Japan got better and more sophisticated. By the early 1970s, when I was an undergraduate at MIT, some really top-notch consumer products were coming from there. The Sony Trinitron TV was better than anything produced in the United States, and Japanese companies dominated consumer electronics. I would frequently open (as in take the covers off and examine closely) those products when I bought them and study how they were made. Meanwhile, Canon and Nikon cameras took over the photography space, and Toyota Corollas and Honda Civic cars started showing up in force among Californians and college students without a lot of money. Japanese auto imports caused a crisis for the Detroit automakers, just as foreign steel imports had plagued American makers in the 1960s and 1970s, though most people didn't pay attention to this unless you were in the industry and your job was affected.

The cheap stuff shifted to coming from South Korea, Taiwan, Hong Kong, and Singapore—countries I would later learn were referred to as the "Asian Tigers." From the 1960s to the 1990s, these four Asian nations went through rapid industrialization, attracting a lot of foreign investment and becoming export powerhouses in the process. That was a time when the best semiconductor memory chips stopped coming from factories in the United States as they succumbed to competition from Japan. And then the Japanese companies fell by the wayside as Korean companies took over. Meanwhile, computer disk drives shifted from "Made in the USA" to "Made in Singapore" and then "Made in Thailand."

All of these shifts paled in comparison when China opened up to world markets, a process that began in the 1980s and really took off starting in the late 1990s. That was the beginning of an epic stage of globalization when the production of so many goods shifted from the United States and Europe to China. And from Taiwan and Singapore to China. Even from Japan to China. I had a front-row seat for that chapter.

Learning About Trade and Manufacturing on the Job

I started to learn about trade in my first job at IBM, where I started work in late 1979. I worked at a small subsidiary that imported machines manufactured in Germany, Switzerland, and France. I started going to visit those factories after a couple of years, and in the process, I learned to appreciate many of the intricacies of global trade, as well as the risks and opportunities that abounded.

In the late 1980s I moved to one of IBM's mainline divisions, and that's when I started to get serious experience with manufacturing. Roger, my manufacturing guy when I was running workstation development at IBM's Austin, Texas, site, used to tell me how important it was to have manufacturing close to the design team. When you were putting a new computer system into production, you would often have late-breaking design changes or fixes for unexpected problems. Sometimes it was because the designer had little idea of the steps involved in putting a product together, so there might be an awkward assembly sequence or one that was even impossible to execute. That's when we started spending time in factories and understanding a lot more closely how things were done.

That was also a time Asia was really coming into its own in electronics manufacturing. My first trips to Japan, Hong Kong, and Taiwan were with IBM. One of my more memorable early visits was to a large Taiwanese manufacturer of the motherboards that went into personal computers. The motherboard was the main circuit board that almost all of the computer was built upon. That was during the early 1990s when Compaq Computer had started driving down the price of IBM-compatible PCs by sourcing motherboards and entire PCs from Taiwan. As we toured the production line, I asked the plant manager how much they made by assembling each motherboard. "Eight bucks," was his answer. He clarified that this was his entire gross profit above the cost of the components and materials that went into it. Out of that, he had to pay for his factory labor, the cost of depreciation on all the machines on the assembly line, and his overhead for things like electricity and the lease on the building and so on. He didn't have much room for maneuvering on costs.

My next question to him was, "Half the population are boys, and half are girls. How come you only have girls working on the line?" He turned and looked at me and with a wry look on his face said in Chinese, "If we have boys here, they only want to date the girls, and that disrupts production, so we only hire girls."

Reflecting on the eight-buck answer, I said, "Eight bucks is terrible! What are you going to do?" With a smile, he responded, now back in English, "We have a new technology; it's called HMT. See all these surface mount technology (SMT) machines for placing components onto the motherboards? They come from Japan and cost $100,000 each. We're going to move assembly to China and hire 18-year-old girls and have them solder all these components onto the boards by hand. We call it HMT for hand mount technology." That's when I realized that I was entering a whole different world.

Another important lesson for me from those early trips arose from a visit to a vendor in Taiwan who was making the monitor for one of our workstation products whose codename was "Cabeza," Spanish for "head." Cabeza was an all-in-one system with the computer built into the monitor. Somehow, we got on to the topic of freight costs, because this product would be shipped by ocean container, which was one-twentieth the cost of air cargo at the time. We were extremely cost sensitive, and the monitor weighed a lot. They quoted us a price for 670 units, and I naively asked, "What would be the cost if I wanted 671?" The price took a huge jump, because as it turned out, 670 units fit in a single 40-foot shipping container, and if I wanted one additional, it would spill over into another shipping container. For some reason, trivial but important details like this have cluttered my mind for the last three decades.

A Front-Row Seat for Globalization

After leaving IBM, I continued my tour of the computer industry with jobs at Digital Equipment Corporation (DEC) followed by Silicon Graphics Computer Systems (SGI). DEC manufactured systems in Puerto Rico in the late 1960s and 1970s, but by the time I got there a lot of its production was in Albuquerque, New Mexico, and moving across the border into Mexico. SGI, in contrast, still assembled its systems in Mountain View, California, down the street from engineering. But it was when I got to Eastman Kodak in 1997 that I really got immersed in manufacturing, and global manufacturing at that.

Three weeks after arriving at Kodak, I was put in charge of a division called Digital and Applied Imaging, which was the company's nascent consumer digital camera business. Also housed in that division were units that manufactured silicon image sensors with its own semiconductor fab next to Kodak Park in Rochester, a factory in Elmgrove, New York, that was trying to assemble digital cameras, another that assembled slide projectors at the same site, and three factories in New York, Mexico, and Ireland that produced optical discs for data storage. There were other bits and pieces scattered around the world, but these were the big ones that were losing the most money (except for the slide projectors, which weren't really digital). We also owned part of a third-tier camera company in Japan that was a source for a lot of parts as well as having design and assembly capability.

We introduced the world's first one-megapixel digital camera that sold for less than a $1,000 in late 1997. One megapixel was a lot of resolution capability in those days, and under $1,000 meant $999, but it was still a lot of money. It was a great camera for the time, and it made a big splash in the market. We also lost money on every single unit that we sold because even though the industrial design firm IDEO (which did the industrial design for us) won awards for the design, it was just too expensive to manufacture. The designers were more interested in design awards than in our ability to make money.

We struggled with costs for a few years, manufacturing in Japan, continuing to lose money as we sought to grow our market share. Then I made a memorable visit to Walmart in Bentonville, Arkansas, with my global sales manager. We were escorted into a sparse conference room with minimalist (i.e., cheap) furniture and linoleum floors to meet with their buyers. Those buyers told me in no uncertain terms, "If you want to sell in Walmart, you have to manufacture in China." At the time, Walmart had a global sourcing center in Shenzhen, where they bought from an enormous range of suppliers—I think it was many tens of thousands in number. We had already been looking at manufacturing in China, but that nudge (it was more than a nudge, it felt like an ultimatum) really gave us a push.

Looking for potential contract manufacturers in Taiwan and China and then setting up our own factory on the Pudong side of Shanghai gave me the opportunity to see where a huge range of products came from, and it also gave me a lot of insight into the offshoring boom of the early 2000s. When shopping for contract manufacturing capacity, *everyone* was willing to show us nearly everything. They were all trying to impress us with their capabilities. While nobody deliberately told you who was making what products for whom, you could pick these things up by looking at the names on boxes or by looking at parts trays. You could see a lot of products, and you could also see a lot of incoming parts. During these years I typically made as many as 16 trips to Asia a year and could see as many as a half dozen or more different operations on a typical trip.

My stint at Kodak had an unhappy ending, but there was a singular "Kodak moment" for me when we made a front-page story in the March 10, 2005, *Wall Street Journal* (McWilliams 2005). In it, Gary McWilliams wrote, "In Electronics, U.S. Companies Seize Momentum from Japan," recounting how best-selling gadgets like Apple's iPod and Kodak's EasyShare Digital Cameras leveraged outsourcing to beat the Japanese. "The Americans' edge comes from their skill at writing software for new digital chips and from low manufacturing costs. While many Japanese companies spent years debating the merits of outsourcing versus keeping production in-house, U.S. companies have been quick to strike deals with contract manufacturers in China and elsewhere." At the time, I knew Steve Jobs and visited with him occasionally. I'm sure he hated sharing a headline like that with us.

In retrospect, I'm not sure I feel good about leading a race to the bottom, but it put us in a position to finally make money on digital cameras. The choices were about offshoring and surviving as a company or exiting the business. The experience taught me a lot about what was happening in the world of manufacturing and supply chains.

Those years at Kodak were also when I thought a lot about the long-term implications of offshoring production. When I first arrived in 1997, I observed that we had to source essentially every critical component for a digital camera from Japan. Kodak had given up the manufacture of film cameras to Japanese companies in the 1960s and 1970s. It made all its money in film and photofinishing, and some smart consultants (probably trained at the Harvard Business School or some competing business school) must have told Kodak management that since they made all of their profit on film, they would be much more profitable as a company if it abandoned making cameras. They did, and it was. It became a fabulously profitable company. American manufacturers of electronics had meanwhile abandoned the production of things like TVs to the Japanese and Asian countries as well. Suddenly all those things that you needed for making cameras, like zoom lenses and mechanical things like shutters that weren't important in the film era became important in the digital area, but we didn't have any of the skills or capabilities locally to make any of that stuff in volume. Rochester, New York, formerly a great cluster for making optical devices, could no longer support us in the digital age because the supplier base was gone. Writing about this a decade later, we described this as the erosion of the "industrial commons," the network of suppliers for materials, tools, and equipment as well as the capabilities in the workforce that supported an industry (Pisano and Shih 2009). That paper has gotten a lot more interest in the last few years as the urge to "reshore" industries has increased.

Studying Manufacturing and Supply Chains

Since coming to the Harvard Business School in 2007, I have had the opportunity to study a lot more about manufacturing and supply chains. Being on the faculty gave me the privilege of studying a wide range of companies to write cases and conduct research, companies that welcomed the interactions and were gracious in hosting me. I also joined the board of directors of Flex Inc., one of the world's largest contract manufacturers and supply chain specialists. For 15 years, this gave me a window on a wide range of products that the company manufactured for others, ranging from computers, phones, capsule coffee makers, and white goods to industrial equipment and sophisticated manufacturing process tools. It also helped me to get to know manufacturing and supply chains across East and South Asia, Eastern Europe, and Latin America.

As much as anything, this book is a synthesis of things I have learned on my journey of 46 years through the factories and supply chains of the world. And it is an effort to bridge some (but by no means all) of the theories that we teach about supply chains to the reality that is usually a lot messier and more unpredictable. But that's what makes it so interesting.

Introduction

When the COVID-19 pandemic hit in 2020, shortages seemed to come out of nowhere. One week the shelves were full, the next week, there were big gaps where everyday items had vanished. Toilet paper, bicycles, infant formula, microchips—products that people had never worried about suddenly seemed scarce and hard to find. The explanation most often offered was simple: the supply chains were "broken." Yet that frequently raised more questions than it answered. How could systems that usually work so smoothly fail so suddenly? And why did the failures appear in such unexpected places?

Part of the problem is that modern supply chains are complicated and largely invisible. Most of us encounter them only at the very tail end, when we take a finished product off a shelf in a store or it arrives at our door. The long journey that brought it there, often spanning the globe, involving many firms and countless steps that it passed through along the way, is easy to take for granted. Even people who work inside supply chains often see only a small piece of the puzzle. When disruptions occur, they can feel kind of random, because the link to where the problem occurred may be separated by time and distance.

Look a little more closely, however, and the stories become both surprising and at the same time more revealing. The cashew nuts that I bought at my local warehouse club store say on the bottle that they are a product of Vietnam, but they were actually grown in the Côte d'Ivoire (Ivory Coast) in West Africa. Wild-caught salmon and pollock harvested off the coast of Alaska travels to China for processing before returning to Western markets as frozen fillets or fish sticks. These journeys seem crazy until you begin to understand the forces that shaped them. Once you do, the same forces help explain why roses grown in Kenya and Colombia end up in European and American flower shops, why so much clothing is sewn in countries like Bangladesh and Vietnam, and why so many smartphones are assembled in China. It also starts to explain why a disruption in one place far up the chain can take a while before its effects can be felt.

The goal of this book is to make sense of these journeys and to explain some of the basic economic principles that underpin them. We'll use everyday examples to illustrate the sense, or the craziness, behind it all.

Trade and Specialization

To start, we need to step back and ask a deceptively simple question: which goods can be produced in one place and consumed in another, and why? Not everything travels well. Some products are too fragile, too perishable, or too costly to move very far. Others can be shipped halfway around the world with ease, turning distant producers into close economic partners. The ability to separate where something is made from where it is used, which is the essence of trade, is the foundation on which modern supply chains are built. I discuss trade and tradability in Chapter 1.

One of the most important shaping forces is specialization. The famous eighteenth-century philosopher and political economist Adam Smith described a pin factory in which he showed how dividing work into discrete tasks could multiply output many times over—and that logic, it turns out, scales all the way up to the global economy (Smith 1776). Chapter 2 explores how the division of labor within a factory became a division of labor across firms, industries, and continents, producing the tiered supply networks that characterize modern production.

It also confronts an important consequence of all this specialization: tiered supply chains make the sources of disruption nearly invisible until something goes wrong. When a single factory in Japan making a specialty paint pigment went dark after the 2011 earthquake, automakers worldwide discovered they had no idea it existed—until they had to stop taking orders for certain colors of cars.

Labor Arbitrage, Capital, and Contract Manufacturing

Another powerful shaping force is labor arbitrage, which is the subject of Chapter 3. As firms learned they could move tasks across borders, differences in wages became impossible to ignore. Putting numbers to those differences makes clear why manufacturing shifted so rapidly to China in the late 1990s and early 2000s and why the consequences for workers in rich countries were often sudden and severe. But this shift was more than about lower costs; it was about scale, speed, and the reorganization of entire industries.

In Chapter 4 we'll take a look at the trade-off between using more capital (machines and automation) versus using more labor to produce things. This will be particularly interesting in the setting of foods and agricultural products. Many food products travel halfway around the world before they get to the supermarket. And some even travel halfway around the world before turning around and going halfway back again, or even farther. Part of the story is about availability: some agricultural products grow only in tropical climates. But often it is about the trade-off between using more labor versus more capital, or a reflection of what you can do in a high labor-cost country versus a low labor-cost country.

Specialization also leads to a discussion of contract manufacturing, which I discuss in Chapter 5. Over the past half century, companies have increasingly separated the work of designing and marketing products from the work of making them, handing production off to specialist manufacturers that pool demand across multiple customers, invest in expensive equipment, and manage complex multitier supply networks. This transformation reshaped industries from electronics and athletic shoes to pharmaceuticals and personal care products, and it explains why the name on the label so rarely matches the company that actually made what's inside. Henry Ford once owned forests, glassworks, and rubber plantations to supply his factories. Today, your Dell laptop might be assembled by a Taiwanese company you've never heard of, on a line next to one assembling HP laptops, both in the same factory city somewhere in Asia.

Labor-Intensive Assembly

Chapter 6 asks a deceptively simple question: how is it possible that a device as complex as an iPhone, packed with hundreds of components and finished to exacting tolerances, can be assembled by workers with only a few days of training, and why does that work happen in China? The answer turns out to require two separate histories.

The first is the history of assembly process design, tracing a line from French general Jean-Baptiste de Gribeauval's eighteenth-century insight that boring cannon barrels to precise tolerances made weapons both more accurate and more repairable, through the Springfield and Harpers Ferry armories' development of interchangeable parts and the division of labor to Frederick Winslow Taylor's codification of scientific management and Henry Ford's introduction of the moving assembly line at Highland Park in 1913. Ford's essential contribution was not the assembly line itself but the conversion of the overwhelming majority of factory jobs into short, repeatable tasks that required no special skills, what his production superintendent called "farmer tools" because they let farm boys match the output of top mechanics. Toyota's subsequent development of the just-in-time production system added a further layer of efficiency by synchronizing the entire supply chain to the pace of customer demand, eliminating inventory buffers and making disruptions immediately visible. Together, these innovations established the modern template for complex assembly by workers without specialized training.

The second history is about workforce organization. Chapter 6 traces the logic of the self-enclosed factory city from the model industrial villages of the English textile mills and the boarding-house system of the Lowell mills in Massachusetts, where farmers' daughters were recruited, housed, fed, and supervised within a single company-controlled environment, through the Communist-era *danwei*, which bundled employment with housing, healthcare, schools, and political oversight into a walled compound. When Taiwanese and Hong Kong manufacturers moved into China's coastal special economic zones in the 1990s, they reproduced much of this structure: perimeter walls, dormitories, canteens, clinics, and on-site management housing, enabling them to recruit tens or hundreds of thousands of workers from inland provinces and absorb massive demand surges—the kind Apple requires for an iPhone launch—without straining local housing markets or infrastructure. The result is a manufacturing model whose combination of process engineering heritage and workforce organization logic remains extraordinarily difficult to replicate elsewhere.

Industrial Clusters

Chapter 7 examines how industrial clusters shape global supply chains through the unlikely lens of a single question: what do beer, cheese, yogurt, insulin, laundry detergent, and Ozempic have in common? The answer is fermentation—and more specifically, the dense concentration of firms, institutions, and accumulated expertise that grew up around Copenhagen over more than a century and a half.

The chapter traces the cluster's origins to J.C. Jacobsen's founding of the Carlsberg brewery in 1847 and, crucially, his establishment of the Carlsberg Research Laboratory in 1875 with a charter requiring that all scientific results be shared publicly. That commitment to open science seeded the broader ecosystem: Emil Christian Hansen's isolation of pure yeast strains at Carlsberg transformed brewing worldwide, while S.P.R. Sørensen's work on protein chemistry at the same lab attracted a generation of scientists whose knowledge diffused outward into Danish industry. Chr. Hansen, founded in 1874 to produce standardized rennet for cheesemaking, followed a parallel trajectory—expanding from dairy enzymes into yogurt cultures, food colorings, and eventually precision fermentation.

Novo Nordisk's story runs from insulin extracted from pig pancreases in the 1920s, through the development of recombinant DNA production techniques in the 1980s and 1990s, to the launch of semaglutide—the active ingredient in Ozempic and Wegovy—whose manufacture still depends on fermentation using the same *Saccharomyces cerevisiae* yeast that brewers have harnessed for millennia.

Chapter 7 uses this history to illustrate the core economics of industrial clusters: geographic concentration enables knowledge spillovers, supports a specialized labor pool, and creates supplier networks—advantages that explain why a country of six million people has become the world's dominant force in applied fermentation science across industries that on the surface appear to have nothing in common.

Supply Chain Design and Management

Chapter 8 on supply chain design and management starts with three dimensions of the design challenge.

- The first is the fundamental problem of matching supply to uncertain demand and how firms design their supply chains differently depending on whether they are selling predictable staples or fashion-driven products where nobody really knows what will sell until it does.
- The second is the timing of production: whether to make things in advance and hold inventory or wait for an actual order before starting to build. These are more than operational details; they determine whether a product gets made in Texas or Taiwan, in Morocco or Bangladesh.
- The third dimension is coordination: how the many independent firms that make up a supply chain manage to work together, why they so often fail to do so, and what happens when the inevitable lags and information gaps between them cause small disturbances to amplify into costly waves of excess and shortage.

Together, these three themes go a long way toward explaining not just how supply chains are managed, but why the world's production ends up where it does.

Concentrated Nodes and Pricing

Chapter 9 examines a question that standard trade economics tends to sidestep: not just where processing happens but who gets to set the price. The chapter argues that wherever a supply chain has a concentrated node—whether that concentration is in processing capacity, consumption, or control over quality certification—that node acquires the power to determine what the upstream resource is worth to everyone else. Three cases illustrate the argument.

- In Thailand, a diaspora of Burmese gem merchants displaced by the 1962 military coup combined with a homegrown heat-treatment breakthrough to make Bangkok the world's dominant center for colored gemstone processing; today, rough stones from Madagascar, Mozambique, and Sri Lanka travel to Thailand to have their value established, not the other way around.
- In Australia, the Pilbara iron ore industry was built around Japan and priced on Japanese terms for four decades, only to see that pricing power migrate to China as Chinese steelmaking capacity dwarfed everything

that came before—a transition now being institutionalized through state trading companies, futures markets in Dalian, and China's recent investment in the massive Simandou deposit in Guinea, which threatens to give China leverage over Australian supply that financial instruments alone could not provide.

- And in American hardwoods, the offshoring of furniture manufacturing to China after 2001 transferred pricing power from the domestic consumers of timber—the furniture mills of North Carolina and Virginia—to the Chinese buyers who now absorb roughly half of all U.S. hardwood exports so that the price of standing timber in a New Hampshire woodlot is now effectively set in the furniture markets of Guangdong.

Taken together, the three cases show that the geography of pricing power is not determined by geology or comparative advantage alone, but by history, politics, and the cumulative weight of capabilities that, once concentrated somewhere, tend stubbornly to stay.

Tariffs, Nontariff Barriers, and Industrial Policy

Chapter 10 examines how governments use tariffs and nontariff barriers to shape where things come from—often with consequences that are more durable and more dramatic than policymakers intend. Beginning with tariffs, the chapter traces their history from ancient trade routes to the modern era, illustrating through cases such as the "chicken tax" on light trucks, China's auto parts dispute, Australian barley, and the *de minimus* exemption how even narrow or obscure trade rules can redirect entire supply chains.

The chapter then turns to nontariff barriers—cabotage restrictions like the Jones Act, local content requirements, and sanitary and phytosanitary standards—showing how these less visible instruments can be just as powerful. A thread running through all the cases is that trade barriers rarely stop trade; they redirect it, often in ways that persist long after the original rationale has faded, and understanding them is essential for anyone who needs to understand where things come from and why.

Then we will wade into some of the thornier questions that have been making the news of late. How did the United States get so dependent on Asia for semiconductors, especially the high-end ones that go into smartphones and AI datacenters? This will synthesize tradability, labor arbitrage, the role of clusters, and how countless small decisions, each of which made good business sense, taken together placed a critical capability of enormous strategic importance to the United States in a region that is both geologically and geopolitically unstable.

Chapter 11 examines how industrial policy shapes the geography of production through four cases of sustained, strategic state intervention: Airbus in Europe, pharmaceuticals in Ireland, semiconductors in Taiwan, and flat-panel displays in China. The chapter traces how France, Germany, Britain, and Spain pooled resources to create Airbus Industrie in 1970, sustaining the consortium through years of negligible sales before it broke into the American market, deployed fly-by-wire technology with the A320, and ultimately displaced Boeing as the world's largest aerospace company by revenue. It then turns to Ireland, showing how a combination of ultra-low corporate tax rates, targeted FDI recruitment by the Industrial Development Authority, and investment in science and engineering education transformed a stagnant agricultural economy into the world's third-largest pharmaceutical exporter—the source, among other things, of the entire global supply of Botox.

Taiwan's story is one of institutional design: the government used the Industrial Technology Research Institute as a technology incubator, licensing foreign processes, proving them at pilot scale, and spinning them out as public-private ventures—first UMC and then TSMC—that eventually gave a single island nation command of the world's most advanced semiconductor fabrication. Finally, the chapter examines China's BOE Technology Group and the flat-panel display industry, where massive provincial subsidies allowed Chinese manufacturers to climb successive generations of fabrication technology, displace Korean and Japanese producers, and drive down global panel prices.

Across all four cases, the chapter argues that where things are made reflects not comparative advantage alone but deliberate policy choices—and that the institutional form of those choices, not merely their scale, determines whether they succeed.

Looking Forward

The final chapter, Chapter 12, takes stock of where all of this leaves us. A pandemic that exposed hidden fragility, wars that made dependency feel dangerous, a trade war that rewrote the economics of global sourcing, and a rising power that has openly declared its intention to be indispensable have together brought the era of frictionless globalization to something that looks very much like a turning point. The chapter traces the first corporate responses: the trans-shipment schemes, inventory surges, and tariff engineering that allowed companies to preserve existing supply chain relationships, while trade policy was nominally designed to unwind them, and explains why that phase is now exhausting itself.

It then examines the deeper restructuring underway, including the rewiring of trade routes toward geopolitically aligned partners, the genuine but more modest gains from supply chain technology, the physical disruption that climate change is already inflicting on trade infrastructure, and the political contradiction at the heart of reshoring: that the factories coming back will be highly automated and will employ far fewer people than the ones that left.

The chapter closes with four strategic imperatives for navigating this environment and an acknowledgment that the organizations best positioned for what comes next are not those with the most efficient supply chains but those with the most adaptive ones.

Together, these stories are meant to make the global economy feel less abstract and less mysterious. Supply chains are not accidents, nor are they the result of a single grand plan. They are the cumulative outcome of economic logic, technological constraints, and human choices—choices that help explain both their remarkable efficiency and their occasional fragility.

CHAPTER 1

Trade and Tradability

These days when we buy things in a store or online, there is a good chance that most of the items came from far away, often the other side of the world. If you think for a moment why that is, it shouldn't be a surprise. A single Walmart Supercenter might have 140,000 or more different items on its shelves, so it would be impossible for most of those items to be made nearby. Even a small store like a Trader Joe's might have 4,000 different stock-keeping units (SKUs), while a typical grocery store carries anywhere from 30,000 to 50,000 different items (Duffy 2021). How then do shoppers get presented with such variety?

The huge selection in stores is made possible by *trade*, the exchange of goods and services that are produced in one place and consumed in another. Trade can take place across regions or across national borders. It allows the producers of goods and services to specialize and sell beyond their local markets, and it makes it possible for consumers to get access to things that might otherwise be unavailable or prohibitively expensive if they all had to be made nearby.

To understand why trade produces such a remarkable variety at such accessible prices, we need to examine the logic that drives it. At the heart of that logic is the principle of comparative advantage, the idea that regions and countries benefit by specializing in what they produce most efficiently relative to others, and trading for the rest. But not everything lends itself equally to trade, and understanding which goods and services are tradable, and why, turns out to be just as important as understanding trade itself.

Comparative Advantage: A Reason to Trade

Some of the earliest examples of cross-border trade date back to ancient Mesopotamia, an urban civilization that emerged around 3000 BCE in what is now southern Iraq. Merchants exchanged textiles, metals, grains, and other goods along overland and river routes. Archaeological evidence points to long-distance trade networks that linked regions with different natural endowments, enabling people to obtain things that they could not produce locally, such as tin, lapis lazuli, or incense. These early trade routes laid the foundations for specialization and the expansion of economic exchanges across political boundaries (Postgate 1992).

What are the core principles that underlie trade? Much of the early work in the field of economics focused on the trade of goods across borders. Adam Smith, who some saw as the "father" of modern economics and one of the original proponents of capitalism, argued that specialization and exchange, guided by market prices, were the primary sources of economic prosperity (Brown 1997). In his book *The Wealth of Nations*, he described how the division of labor enabled countries to focus on producing goods that they made most efficiently and then to trade with other countries that specialized in other things. This increased overall output and consumer choice (Smith 1776).

Smith argued that *free trade* benefited nations if they focused on expanding the availability of goods rather than just the accumulation of wealth (gold in those days). Said more plainly, the wealth of a nation was measured in how much its people could consume, not how much gold the king or queen had in the treasury. Smith viewed trade as a positive-sum process rooted in productivity rather than national rivalry, a topic that we will come back to in Chapter 11.

When looking at theories behind trade, economists often ask three questions:

1. What goods get exported, and what goods get imported? Said another way, what is the direction or patterns in the trade of goods and services among different countries?
2. What are the prices at which goods and services are exchanged, sometimes referred to as the *terms of trade*?
3. What are the gains from trade, for the world as a whole, but also from the perspective of each country?

The answers to all three are pretty straightforward. David Ricardo, an early nineteenth-century English political economist who helped formalize the economic analysis of trade, refined Smith's notion with his theory of *comparative advantage*. Countries gain from trade by specializing in the goods they can produce most advantageously (at a lower opportunity cost), even if they are less efficient than another country at producing everything. He used as an example England and Portugal. Portugal could produce both cloth and wine with fewer labor hours than England, but it was better at producing wine than cloth, while England was better at producing cloth than wine. If Portugal specialized in wine and England specialized in cloth and the two countries traded, both would end up with more of both goods than if each tried to produce both by themselves. By specializing where they had a comparative advantage and trading for the rest, everybody would produce more in total and enjoy a wider range of goods (Ricardo 1817).

Economists then developed models for supply and demand and predicted some conditions when things should balance out. As more countries specialized, they would all do less and less on their own. Then they needed to trade so that they could have access to the widest selection of goods (Chacholiades 1973). Or that's the theory at least, and it starts to tell us why our stuff comes from such a wide diversity of places.

How Well Does It Travel?

A lot of the concepts of trade are embodied in the idea of the *tradability* of a good—the *degree* to which a product can be produced in one place and consumed in another. For a perfectly tradable good, these locations can be quite far apart, and the costs or restrictions on transporting the goods from where they are made to where they are consumed are negligible compared to their value. This also means, for example, that foreign producers can compete with domestic ones to supply the same customers. This is a core principle to remember when we see some of this stuff coming from the other side of the world.

We typically define the *tradable sector* as industries whose products and services are subject to international competition. In other words, they can come from far, far away. The *nontradable sector* then is those goods and services that are consumed domestically and cannot be easily traded internationally. The key determinants of tradability are as follows:

- **How hard are the goods to transport and store.** Goods that are easy and cheap to ship (like semiconductor chips) are highly tradable; bulky or perishable goods may be limited in their tradability. Perishability can take many forms. Fresh fruits and vegetables can last for some time after they are harvested, if handled properly, so they are tradable. But ready-mix concrete has to be used within two hours after it leaves the batch plant where it is made, so it is not. Location-based services like haircuts and restaurant meals generally aren't tradable. Digitalization has greatly increased the tradability of some types of services, as we will see in some later examples.
- **Barriers found at borders.** Tariffs, quotas, regulations, or controls on the movement of foreign exchange can lower tradability. Countries often

> use labeling requirements on products or different safety inspection standards to make it harder and more expensive for companies who want to import. Most of the time these barriers are designed to protect domestic companies from competition from imports. Sometimes they can be quite creative. When the French wanted to slow the import of Japanese made videocassette recorders in 1982, it required all such imports to pass through an inland customs station at Poitiers, which wasn't really set up to handle a high volume of overseas imports. This caused import volumes to drop from 53,000 units in August across the traditional ports to less than 1,000 units by November (Ohashi 2002).

Economists Rudiger Dornbusch, Stanley Fischer, and Paul Samuelson showed that goods and services are not just purely "tradable" or "nontradable" but lie somewhere along a spectrum from very easy to trade to effectively impossible to trade across borders. In other words, some goods are easily worth shipping and competing over internationally, while others sit on a knife-edge where small differences in transport costs, tariffs, or regulations can tip production in the direction of local versus distant. Their main point was that tradability depends on economics, and as technology, costs, or policies change, the tradability of a good can shift back and forth along this continuum (Dornbusch et al. 1977). Tradability is a matter of degree, rather than a simple dichotomy of tradable or nontradable. This is important to remember these days as countries like the United States erect barriers to trade.

The bottom line on trade then is that if we want more of it, we would like the cost of transporting the goods or services to be low or a small percentage of their value. I like to think of value density as a good measure—high value density is generally more tradable if there aren't other barriers. In this section, we'll work through some examples that both give us a much more concrete feel for how tradability works and illustrate why it makes sense to ship some things from so far away.

Shipping Strawberries from California Is Cheaper than Growing Them Locally in New England

Strawberries are the most popular berry in the United States. They have to be picked by hand, so labor is usually the largest expense and often represents more than half of the variable production costs for growers (Rural Migration News 2020). California produces about 90% of the domestic crop, and Florida around 9% (Yeh et al. 2023). While you can grow strawberries in New England during the summer, try finding people who are willing to pick them. California's climate means a long growing season, and growers there have the ability to mobilize a large agricultural workforce, many of them immigrants.

This makes it an advantageous place to grow them, at least for now, and why the rest of the country trades California for berries.

In Boston in 2025, a one-pound clamshell, typically 15–20 medium-sized berries, cost around $3.99 at the grocery store. Strawberries will stay in pretty good shape for about 10–12 days from the day of harvest if you keep them chilled. Let's say you harvest in California on a Monday and ship that same day for a warehouse arrival on Friday on the East Coast. At that point you should have five to seven days left on their shelf life to get them in the hands of a consumer. It is important to keep them cold as much as possible, at around 35°F. Growers have a two-hour rule in the field because they want each box of berries to be pre-cooled to 33°F pulp temperature as soon as possible after picking. Berries at field temperature lose a day of shelf life for every hour they're not pre-cooled.

How about shipping cost? You can pack eight 1-pound clamshells in a box (a "flat") and stack 120 boxes on a pallet. Twenty-eight pallets fit in a typical refrigerated truck, for a total of 26,880 clamshells. The cost to drive that truck across the country depends on the season and how much demand there is at the moment, but typically that ranges from $8,000 to $12,000. Doing the math, that means it costs between 30–45 cents to ship one clamshell across the country.

Let's say the grower earns around $1.80 per clamshell, and then it costs 40 cents to transport it to New York City. Add some local handling costs in getting them to the store, but you can see why grocery stores can sell them at a pretty healthy profit. They're eminently tradable because when you divide the shipping expense across all those clamshells, the cost is quite reasonable, especially when you can maintain a *cold chain* in which you can control the temperature at which you store and transport the products.

The *economies of scale* that come from picking and shipping a dedicated full truckload justify shipping strawberries 3,000 miles; 70% of agricultural products in the United States are shipped by truck, and some estimates suggest that food items may travel thousands of miles on the way to the store (National Geographic 2014). The same logic applies to those tens of thousands of other SKUs in your local store.

Container Shipping and Why Your Polo Shirts Come from China

Decreasing costs of transportation have always led to an expansion of trade. The growth of railroads in the nineteenth-century United States dramatically lowered the cost and time it took to move goods over land, linking farms and factories with distant markets. By making it economical to ship bulky and low-value goods over long distances, railroads greatly expanded the size of the tradable sector. Railroads also integrated regional economies into one large national market. Large markets that are tradable are attractive to producers.

Moving goods by water has always been one of the most efficient forms of transport. Once a cargo is floating, it is much easier to move than across land. Trade across oceans began at least by the third millennium BCE, when merchants in the Persian Gulf and Indian Ocean exchanged goods such as copper, timber, and luxury items between Mesopotamia, the Indus Valley, and surrounding regions (McLaughlin 2014).

The discovery of the New World and its exploitation by the Europeans made the Atlantic Ocean the central focus of world trade for centuries. By the time of World War II, North America and Europe were the most economically developed parts of the world, and this trade lane was the most important in the world, accounting for approximately 60% of global maritime trade by the 1960s (Slack 1999).

Until the mid-1960s, ocean cargo was handled as break-bulk freight. Goods were packed in boxes, crates, barrels, or sacks and loaded and unloaded piece by piece in a slow, labor-intensive process. Ships spent days or weeks in port while longshoremen manually moved cargo between ships, docks, warehouses, and trucks. Cargo was often damaged, lost, or stolen, and high handling costs often exceeded the cost of the ocean transport leg by itself. That meant if you wanted to trade goods internationally across oceans, it was limited to relatively high-value or non-time-sensitive goods.

Container shipping changed all of this. Goods could be packed into 20 foot long and 8 foot wide standard-sized steel boxes, known as 20-foot equivalents (TEUs), or the 40-foot variant known as a 40-foot equivalent (FEU). Packing the containers became a separate and distinct operation from loading the ship, which meant it was no longer the job of longshoremen and therefore could be done away from the docks. You only loaded the container once at the source, transferred it all at once, and unloaded it at the destination, so the whole shipping process became much cheaper. Containers could be readily transferred between ships, trucks, and trains, and they revolutionized global trade by dramatically reducing the cost, time, and uncertainty of moving goods across distance and borders.

The reduction in handling costs and reduced losses from not having to open containers at ports or interim destinations made long-distance trade economical for a far wider range of products. It also made it a lot faster because ships didn't take weeks to load and unload; port calls of modern container ships can often be as short as 24 hours (see Figure 1.1). Many goods that had once been too bulky, fragile, or low value to ship profitably became tradable, vastly expanding the tradable sector (Levinson 2008).

FIGURE 1.1 The CMA CGM Sorbonne can carry 23,000 TEUs. Docked at Rotterdam World Gateway, circa 2023. *Source:* Willy Shih.

The first trans-Atlantic container ship sailing from New York to Rotterdam was in April 1966, and subsequent adoption was very rapid because of the immense savings in time and money. Ironically, the Vietnam War accelerated the transition. The U.S. military overcame severe logistics bottlenecks supplying troops in Southeast Asia by filling containers at U.S. bases and moving them on commercial carriers. The carriers sent empty containers back via Japan. Japan had modern ports and rapidly growing exports, so they found it efficient to reposition empty containers there, refill them with manufactured goods, and send them onward to U.S. markets (Levinson 2008). Europe-North America container traffic grew rapidly, and Europe-Australasia, North America-Japan, and Japan-Europe all saw rapid adoption (Slack 1999).

How did container shipping affect tradability? Let's look at a typical polo shirt. Checking the Ralph Lauren website, we see that the prices ranged from $69 (on sale) to as much as $145 during the 2025 holiday season. You can fit "1,000 dozen" polo shirts in a 40-foot container (an FEU), and in 2025 it typically cost between $2,000 and $3,000 to ship it from South China to the Port of Los Angeles/Long Beach. Twenty-five cents per shirt, no problem! In the context of the overall supply chain, this is peanuts. Even during the COVID-19 pandemic when the cost to ship that container might have gone up to $10,000, not many people would have complained about the unit cost to ship one shirt.

We'll discuss labor arbitrage in Chapter 3, but it's easy to understand why so many polo shirts and all kinds of imports come by container ship from China or countries with low-cost labor.

Refrigerated Containers and Why Your Frozen Tuna Comes from Thailand

Refrigerated containers (reefers) are insulated containers with their own integral refrigeration unit. They attach to electrical plug points ("reefer points") at special racks in a port or in certain bays on a container ship. They generally can maintain temperatures from −65° to +40°C (−85° to 104°F), and they vastly expanded trade in a wide range of foods.

Let's look at tuna, something that is shipped over very long distances. Thailand-based Thai Union is the largest producer of canned tuna in the world, and when I visited them a few years ago, I learned that they are also a large supplier of frozen tuna to big grocery chains and warehouse clubs like Costco. They catch a lot of tuna in the Indian Ocean and ship it frozen to the United States. Thailand is today the largest source of frozen tuna imports into the United States, followed by Vietnam, Indonesia, and Ecuador. Thailand is also far and away the largest source of canned tuna imports (87 million kg in 2025), although some tuna is imported frozen and then canned (NOAA Fisheries 2026).

Today Thai Union owns the Chicken of the Sea and Genova brands in the United States, as well as John West in the Netherlands and United Kingdom, Parmentier and Petit Navire in France, and King Oscar in Norway, among others. Most of those brands came via acquisitions—that's something that happens when you overfish your own waters and have to sell out your company to someone far away who can still supply the fish. For example, tuna was once the most widely consumed fish in the United States, which once had a significant commercial tuna fishing and canning industry along the West Coast. Tuna was a low-cost high protein food, and the first can of so-called "chicken of the sea" appeared in 1903. Ports like San Diego and San Pedro were home to large tuna fleets during the first part of the twentieth century, and tuna became one of America's most important seafood products, with an industry employing thousands of people. But over time, overfishing and rising environmental concerns, regulations such as the 1972 Marine Mammal Protection Act, and competition from lower-cost foreign fleets led to closures of many U.S. fishing operations and the outsourcing of tuna production and canning (Smith 2012).

Interestingly, the largest source of imports for bluefin tuna, a subspecies that is prized for use in sashimi, was Mexico, followed by Spain and Japan in 2025. And India is the largest source of imported shrimp for the United States,

FIGURE 1.2 The old Tsukiji Fish Market in Tokyo, circa 2005. *Source:* Willy Shih.

thanks to large shrimp farming operations in the state of Andhra Pradesh on the east coast of southern India, which accounts for 82% of the country's production. India has a lot of small-holder shrimp farmers, whereas the second largest exporter to the United States, Ecuador, tends toward large integrated producers (Das et al. 2025).

Some of the finest grades of fish are sent frozen to Tokyo where they are traded at the Tsukiji fish market and then re-exported (see Figure 1.2). Different types of fish are traded all over the world thanks to reefers that can keep them frozen.

Lamb from New Zealand, beef from Brazil and Argentina, and fresh fruit and vegetables from the tropics all can be traded thanks to reefers. During a visit with PSA, the operator of the world's second busiest container port in Singapore, our host told us that the thing that kept them in business was the desire by people everywhere to buy seasonal fruits and vegetables when out of season. In other words, they handled the transshipment of fresh fruits and vegetables from south of the Equator to all over the Northern Hemisphere during the winter months.

Air Cargo and Products with High Time Value

Air cargo has been another driver of growth of the tradable sector. In 2024, air cargo moved about 1% of world trade by weight, but if you looked at the collective value of those shipments, it was around 35% (Felix et al. 2024). What moves by ocean, and what moves by air? Small, light, and valuable is a good fit for air, or things where transit time from the factory to the store matters. Classic polo shirts might not care if they take a 30-day trip by ocean from China, but the latest fashion styles might.

We think of products that have a *high time value* as good candidates to move by air because delays in delivery significantly reduce their value to a customer. A product can have high time value because it spoils, as with perishable agricultural commodities. Or it could be one whose price declines rapidly over time, which often happens with electronics. Uncertain demand is the driver of time value in fashion goods. When a style is hot, you want to get it to market as quickly as possible before tastes shift to something else. You don't want it sitting on a ship somewhere in the middle of the ocean.

Air cargo typically costs 10–15 times as much as ocean container freight, and there are a number of curious aspects of it that affect trade patterns. With an airplane you have to think about both how much weight you can carry as well as volume the cargo takes up. Lower density shipments tend to "cube out," or fill the aircraft volume before reaching maximum weight capacity, rather than "weigh out" or hit the maximum weight before they fill the available volume. Products with a high value density are good candidates for air. Most commodities shipped by air range between 150 and 250 kg/m^3, so if you happen to be shipping pillows urgently, you should think about mixing that with parts for drilling rigs or something heavy (Morrell 2018). This is a little different than ocean container shipping because there if you need more volume, you just get another container. The container shipping lines charge per container and not necessarily the weight of the loaded container, so volume limitations are just a question of how many containers you're spreading your loads across.

There is another reason to use air cargo: the time value of money. Let's say you are making iPhones. Typically, you could stuff around 60,000 of those into a 40-foot container. Let's assume that between delivering the container from the factory in Zhengzhou to a port on the east coast of China like Shanghai, transporting it to Los Angeles/Long Beach, and then trucking it to a distribution center cost $7,000. That amounts to $0.12 per phone and would take about 30–40 days.

I looked on one of my iPhone boxes, and it said the weight was 0.385 kg. If you chartered a 747-8 freighter that can lift 135 metric tons (135,000 kg), that means you can carry approximately 350,650 iPhones (135,000 kg ÷ 0.385 kg). Let's say the charter cost is $750,000; that would lead to a shipping cost of $2.14 per phone. End to end it might take you three or four days. Now let's assume the cost of the phone at the factory door was $400 each. If you sent them the 30-day ocean route, that means you would have ($400) × (60,000) = $24 million tied up for at least a month.

If you said that was worth 1% of the value, it would amount to $4.00 per phone. And that's one reason the most popular loads on air cargo out of Asia for the United States are traditionally electronics like phones, fashion goods, and pharmaceuticals.

Trade in Perishables: Why Do Cut Roses and Fruits Travel So Far?

Just as refrigerated containers enabled trade of many perishable commodities like foods that can keep for the extended shipping time, the ability to maintain a cold chain in air cargo has opened the door to the trading of things you normally wouldn't think of, like cut flowers and different types of fruits.

Flowers Exported from the Netherlands

The Netherlands is the largest exporter of cut flowers, even though it is not the largest grower of cut flowers. I was in a flower market in Lexington, Massachusetts, and they had some blooms that they had grown locally in their own greenhouse, but as I talked to them, they explained that a lot of their roses actually came from Colombia, Ethiopia, and Kenya, often via the Netherlands. As much as 80% of all cut flowers sold in the United States are imported (Utah State University 2024). That seems crazy until you realize that the time it takes to ship them long distances is well within the window in which they stay fresh.

Commercial floriculture got established in the Netherlands during the seventeenth century as growers specialized in high-value crops rather than subsistence farming. By the Dutch Golden Age, flowers, most famously tulips, were being bred, traded, and speculated on as commercial goods (De Vries 1974).

I have visited a large commercial rose grower, Van den Ende Rozen, several times over the last few years. The company is currently in its fourth generation of ownership and is run by the three Van den Ende brothers: Sam, Tim, and Bob. Originally focused on the cultivation of Baby's-Breath flowers, Hans van den Ende shifted the company's focus to roses.

The company currently focuses on the cultivation of two rose varieties: the Red Naomi rose and the Avalanche+® white rose. These two varieties are known for their high-quality characteristics, including high weight, intense color, superior uniformity, and shelf life, and thus they are in high demand on the cut flower market. In total, the company produces 28 million stems of the Red Naomi rose variety each year, mostly for sale all over Europe, but also far beyond.

FIGURE 1.3 Van den Ende Rozen grows roses in greenhouses in Holland; Monster, Netherlands, circa 2024. *Source:* Willy Shih.

FIGURE 1.4 Roses are sorted and cut to length on a semi-automated line; Monster, Netherlands, circa 2024. *Source:* Willy Shih.

Van den Ende Rozen operates in two greenhouses, totaling six hectares (see Figure 1.3). The newest 4.5-hectare greenhouse, located in Monster, Netherlands, was completed in 2008 and contains advanced monitoring and control systems designed to maximize the efficiency of lighting, heat, fertilizer, and water usage during cultivation. In the 3,000 m^2 processing and packaging hall, an automated production line is capable of processing up to 10,000 roses per hour (see Figure 1.4). Roses are stored in cold rooms until they are

FIGURE 1.5 Fresh cut flowers awaiting delivery to buyers at Royal FloraHolland auction; Aalsmeer, Netherlands, circa 2024. *Source:* Willy Shih.

transported. Most of the roses are sold at the Dutch flower auction, but they could go a lot farther from there.

In the late nineteenth and early twentieth century, growers formed cooperatives and introduced centralized auctions, most famously in Aalsmeer near Amsterdam Schiphol Airport, to enable coordinated sales of flowers at large scale. Today the country is a global trading hub for cut flowers, and the Royal FloraHolland flower auction is the largest in the world, occupying a space about the size of 200 football fields. As a lot of flower production shifted to equatorial regions such as Kenya, Ethiopia, Colombia, and Ecuador, air cargo made it possible to harvest flowers one day and sell them at the Dutch auction in next day or two. Today Kenyan rose growers supply around 40% of the roses sold there. The auction buildings are enormous warehouses, where flowers are unpacked and displayed for wholesale buyers who place bids (see Figure 1.5). After they are sold, the boxes of flowers are packed onto trucks for distribution throughout Europe or are shipped by air via Schiphol airport.

Flowers Grown in Kenya I also visited Sian Flowers, a cut flowers company headquartered in Kitengela, Kenya, in the area just south of Nairobi. It is one of the largest growers of roses in Kenya, and it has been exporting almost all its flowers by air cargo. Kenya's proximity to the equator meant typically 12 hours of sunlight per day and a mild tropical climate at higher elevations, so farmers can grow flowers year-round. Higher elevations also meant high levels of ultraviolet radiation that brought out vibrant colors in flowers (see Figure 1.6). And unlike the Netherlands, you don't have to have heated greenhouses, which means your production costs are a lot lower.

FIGURE 1.6 Roses being harvested at Sian Flowers; Kitengela, Kenya, circa 2025. *Source:* Willy Shih.

Cut roses need to have a remaining vase life in the hands of the consumer of at least seven days, and each additional day spent traveling means a loss of around 15% of vase life, so maintaining the cold chain is critical. Flowers harvested early in the morning are placed in buckets of water with a post-harvest solution designed to prevent the growth of bacteria and microorganisms, enhance water uptake, and reduce the pH, and then moved to a cold room to chill. They are sorted, trimmed, and graded and then packed in boxes of 350 stems per box, typically weighing about 17 kg.

Sian sends them to a refrigerated warehouse at Nairobi Jomo Kenyatta International Airport operated by Kuehne+Nagel, a Swiss third-party logistics provider that is an expert in cold-chain handling of agricultural commodities. There they are palletized and put in a vacuum chiller to lower their temperature (see Figure 1.7). Then they are loaded onto a cargo plane for an overnight flight to Amsterdam Schiphol. A Boeing 747 cargo plane typically used on that route can hold up to 90 tons of flowers, and there are a surprisingly large number of dedicated cargo flights every day—with a lot more in the days right before Valentine's Day.

The cost to do all of this depends on the time of year and what other cargo is competing for space on the flight. Typically this ranges from around 13 to 24 cents per stem from the farm all the way to the auction, with the higher price toward Valentine's Day when every grower is trying to get roses to the auction. So your Valentine's Day roses might have traveled halfway around the world!

FIGURE 1.7 Flowers going into the vacuum chiller at Kuehne+Nagel cold-chain warehouse; Nairobi Airport, circa 2025. *Source:* Willy Shih.

Sian Flowers began experimenting with shipping cut roses via container ship. The challenge was how to delay senescence, the plant's natural aging process. The naturally occurring plant hormone ethylene is known to regulate senescence, governing the development of leaves, flowers, and fruits. Dipping cut flowers in a solution containing silver thiosulphate inhibits the plant's generation of ethylene, which forestalls this process. Next, they dip them in a biocide solution to prevent Botrytis Blight, a fungal disease that causes lesions on petals. Then they put the wrapped and boxed cut roses in a controlled atmosphere container—one that not only is refrigerated but also has a built-in scrubber to remove ethylene. The flowers can then survive the transit via truck to the Port of Mombasa; trans-shipment at Salah, Oman; and finally arrival in Rotterdam maybe 30 days later. This was not only a lot cheaper as measured by shipping cost per stem, but the roses also arrived in excellent condition because the cold chain was solid and the extra processing steps extended their life. This worked fine until Houthi attacks on ships in the Red Sea effectively closed the Suez Canal. The transit time around the Cape of Good Hope and Africa was just too long, so they had to go back to using air.

Climacteric Fruits in Controlled Atmospheres Roses are closely related to apples as they both belong to *Rosaceae* family of plants. Like roses, apples are climacteric, which means you can delay their senescence by controlling the atmosphere in which they are stored. That means the fresh

FIGURE 1.8 Connecticut-grown apples for sale in January in Massachusetts, January 2026. *Source:* Willy Shih.

apples you buy in the grocery store might have been picked as much as a year ago and then stored in a controlled atmosphere warehouse. For example, the apples in my local Whole Foods for sale in January say they were harvested in Connecticut (see Figure 1.8). But they couldn't have been harvested recently because there was snow on the ground everywhere and the temperatures were freezing in New England! They were likely picked four to five months ago and stored in a controlled atmosphere warehouse. A friend of mine who runs a grocery chain in Kansas City told me apples can be picked as much as a year before they finally go on sale in the store.

Other climacteric fruits include pears, bananas, melons, apricots, and tomatoes, as well as most stone fruits. And that's why we see so many of these in the store year-round even though the local growing season might be short (or nonexistent). The ability to control shipping conditions vastly increases their tradability.

Reshaping Our Shopping Experiences

Low-cost and efficient transportation have reshaped our shopping experiences, vastly expanding the range of choices available to us as consumers. Add to this the techniques that have been developed to extend the shelf life of perishables, and we see how container shipping and air cargo have been the foundation for making so many more goods tradable.

Together, falling transport costs, standardized logistics, and improved control over temperature and environmental conditions during shipping have dramatically expanded the tradable sector. Goods that were once too fragile, bulky, or time-sensitive to ship over long distances are now routinely moved across continents and oceans. Strawberries, tuna, roses, smartphones, and fashion apparel all travel thousands of miles not because distance no longer matters but because it matters far less than it once did relative to the value of the goods being moved. Tradability, in practice, is the outcome of an economic calculation: whether the cost of moving a product, preserving it, and financing it in transit is small compared with what buyers are willing to pay.

This also helps explain why globalization has affected different parts of the economy unevenly. Activities tied to tradable goods such as manufacturing, agriculture, and resource extraction are exposed to global competition, while many services remain anchored to a place. A haircut, restaurant meals, or a hospital visit cannot be containerized, refrigerated, or flown overnight across an ocean, although the last time I had my head CAT scanned at a hospital in Maine (not a frequent occurrence thankfully), it was interpreted by a doctor in New Zealand.

As we move into the next chapters, we will see how these forces shape where jobs are located, why production moves across borders, and how firms reorganize supply chains to take advantage of differences in costs, capabilities, and technologies around the world.

CHAPTER 2

Specialization and Tiered Supply Chains

In Chapter 1, we saw how specialization enables trade across countries: Portugal makes wine, England makes cloth. But specialization does not operate only at the level of nations. It also occurs within the production of a single good, shaping how work is organized, how firms are structured, and ultimately how modern supply chains function.

Adam Smith offered the classic illustration in *An Inquiry into the Nature and Causes of the Wealth of Nations*, describing how productivity rises when work is divided into discrete tasks. In his famous pin factory example, a worker "not educated to this business" might manage to make only one pin a day. When production was reorganized so that separate workers drew out the wire, straightened it, cut it, sharpened the point, and attached the head, output increased dramatically. Smith reported observing a small, poorly equipped factory with 10 workers could produce roughly 48,000 pins per day simply by dividing the work into specialized steps (Smith 1776).

This logic remains central to modern supply chains. In this chapter, we explore how the division of labor gives rise to a division of firms and how that division produces the tiered structures that characterize many contemporary supply networks. This provides much of the motivation for the field of supply chain management, which looks at the network of organizations, people, resources, activities, and information that connects suppliers to customers. And we examine some of the consequences of complex tiered networks, consequences that help explain what people often mean when they say that a supply chain is "broken."

Harnessing Different Skills and Different Assets

Specialization has always shaped the supply of raw materials for producing finished goods. The person who cuts down a tree is rarely the same one who mills it into lumber, and the craftsperson who turns that wood into furniture brings yet another set of skills. While this division of labor reflects differences in expertise, it has also long been dictated by geography. Iron ore, for example, is mined only where it occurs in concentrations high enough to be worth extracting, such as the Mesabi Range of northern Minnesota or the Pilbara region of Western Australia. The same logic applies to the ultra-pure quartz that is refined into crucibles used to grow monocrystalline silicon ingots for making semiconductors, which comes from a small number of deposits, including one near Spruce Pine, North Carolina (Beiser 2018).

The more compelling driver of specialization is increasing technological complexity. Many modern products often require deep technical knowledge, highly specialized production equipment, and process expertise that no single firm can easily master across all stages of production. Specialization allows firms to narrow their focus, invest in dedicated skills and assets, and rely on markets to supply the other pieces that they need. The result is that complexity pushes production outward, from vertically integrated organizations toward networks of specialized firms, each responsible for a small but critical part of the overall system.

The evolution of the computer industry is a good illustration of this dynamic. Early computers were designed and built as largely monolithic systems, with each model relying on unique, tightly coupled components. IBM transformed the industry in 1964 with the introduction of its System/360 mainframe family, which was organized into modular subsystems such as the central processing unit, disk storage, tape drives, printers, and other peripherals. These modules were connected through standardized interfaces, allowing different development teams to specialize in designing and improving individual components while ensuring that the pieces would work together (Baldwin and Clark 2000).

When IBM introduced the personal computer in 1981, it used a modular approach by defining and publishing interface standards that allowed third parties to produce compatible peripherals and expansion cards. It then relied heavily on components purchased from external suppliers. Each major component such as the processor, memory, storage, display, and operating system was built out of distinct and rapidly advancing technologies. Over time, those technologies became so complex that even IBM could no longer produce all of them internally at world-class levels. Well into the 1980s there were some IBM PCs that had many of the key components like the motherboards and disk drives manufactured by IBM, but the company faced competitors like Dell and Compaq that could buy the best and most advanced disk drives, graphics cards, motherboards, and other key performance-defining components available on the market at any given moment. And IBM usually came up short in that competition, not only on performance but almost always on price.

IBM eventually sold or spun off its printer, disk drive, memory chip, and semiconductor production into separate entities. Most of the component manufacturers grew into large suppliers that could serve a range of customers and applications, led by firms such as Seagate and Western Digital in disk storage; Samsung, SK Hynix, and Micron in memory chips; and Samsung Display, LG Display, and BOE, CSOT, and AU Optronics in flat-panel display screens.

What emerged from this process was a layered industrial structure. IBM defined the system architecture and furnished its brand. Beneath it were Tier 1 suppliers providing complete subsystems like the software, processors, disk drives, memory modules, displays, and other major subsystems. Each of the subsystem suppliers in turn integrated dozens or hundreds of other components from Tier 2 firms that produced controller chips, substrates, specialty chemicals, manufacturing equipment, and other stuff. Each layer specialized in a narrower slice of the value chain, selling primarily to the tier above it rather than directly to the end market.

Technological complexity drove the development of a hierarchy of independent specialists. Standardized interfaces allowed each tier to innovate rapidly within its domain without needing to master the entire system. The modern computer industry thus became a textbook example of a tiered supply chain, in which design, subsystem integration, component production, materials processing, and equipment manufacturing are distributed across distinct but tightly coordinated layers of firms.

Chocolate: A Long Chain of Specialists

The processing of chocolate starting with the harvest and going all the way to making the finished product is another great example of specialization. It harnesses a global network that stretches from small holder farms in tropical climes through traders and exporters to processors primarily located in Europe and the United States, to food companies who turn the processed chocolate into fine chocolates or mass-produced confections. Many others incorporate bulk chocolate into products like ice cream, cakes, pastries, and other prepared foods. The scale of the players at each stage varies, as does the respective shares of the ultimate retail selling prices.

Growing and Harvesting

I had the great fortune to be able to follow the supply chain starting at the tree, and it is quite a journey. Chocolate is made from the fruit seeds of the *Theobroma cacao* (cacao), a member of the *Malvaceae sensu lato* found in the upper Amazon basin that today is part of southern Ecuador. It was introduced into Europe in the sixteenth century following the Spanish colonization of the Americas, and by the eighteenth and nineteenth centuries demand for chocolate was concentrated in countries such as the Netherlands, Switzerland, Belgium, France, and the United Kingdom (Coe 2013). But while a lot of chocolate is still processed in Europe, the largest source of cacao beans today is Côte d'Ivoire—the Ivory Coast in West Africa. Côte d'Ivoire and neighboring Ghana produce around 60% of the global supply, with Ecuador and Peru emerging as major exporters as well.

Cacao trees grow best in lowland tropical forests in a narrow band near the equator. They were introduced into Africa by the Portuguese on the island of San Thome off French Gabon in the nineteenth century, but cultivation was not taken seriously until around 1870 when it started to become valuable commercially (Opoku et al. 2007). Cacao trees were introduced to the Côte d'Ivoire in 1955, where the availability of forest stands and attractive prices for beans fostered large-scale farming of the trees. A government policy that began under French colonial rule—*la terre appartient à celui qui la met en valeur* or "the land belongs to the one who cultivates it"—encouraged local residents and foreign migrants, especially ones from Burkina Faso, to settle and cultivate cacao (Tano 2012). Not surprisingly, most of the farmers are small holders working 2.5–5 hectares (Suh and Molua 2022).

Cacao trees grow up to 30 feet tall. They struck me as a bit unusual the first time I saw one. They have a trait called cauliflory, or flowering and fruiting from the main stem or woody trunks rather than from new growth or shoots. The beans are the fruit seeds, and they grow inside large pods that are shaped like footballs, with each pod holding 30–50 seeds.

The pods are cut from the trees using a sharp blade or pruning hook attached to a pole, or a machete or shear for lower hanging ones. You can see me harvesting a pod in Figure 2.1. The pods are cracked open by hitting them toward the center with a wooden club, and then removing the beans by hand (see Figure 2.2). The farmers spread the husks around and compost them to return nutrients to the soil. The beans are then placed in bags and sent on to someone who handles the fermentation and drying process.

FIGURE 2.1 Cutting cacao pod from tree; Côte d'Ivoire, 2025. *Source:* Willy Shih.

FIGURE 2.2 Removing cacao beans; Côte d'Ivoire, 2025. *Source:* Willy Shih.

Fermentation and Drying

The fermentation process breaks down the viscous pulp surrounding the beans, forms volatile organic compounds that reduce the bitter and astringent taste, and triggers reactions within the beans that release naturally occurring chemicals. The process harnesses naturally occurring yeasts in the air and on the tools and hands of workers. The yeasts feed on the sugar-rich pulp surrounding the beans and convert it to ethanol and CO_2. Amazingly, since different parts of the world have different yeasts floating around in the air, you can get differences in taste of the ultimate chocolate, much like the *terroir* descriptive that the French use to describe environmental conditions associated with making wine and cheese. Like wine, though, you have to have a refined sense of taste, which may not come from wolfing down M&M's. The fermentation process relies on natural heat to help the yeasts metabolize the glucose, fructose, and citric acids in the beans.

I was visiting Côte d'Ivoire with a sourcing manager from Puratos, a mid-size Belgian company that focuses on the premium chocolate market. They have a program called Cacao Trace that promotes sustainable practices in its cacao supply chain, and as part of this they were helping farmers to improve their growing and processing techniques to improve the consistency and flavor of their cacao beans so that the company could pay those farmers more. Often farmers simply pile the beans in heaps by the side of the road and cover them with banana tree leaves. That can have some spotty results, especially when it rains. So, Puratos encourages farmers it works with to bring the beans to cooperatives, where the beans are weighed and then stacked in boxes and covered on the top with banana leaves (see Figure 2.3).

FIGURE 2.3 Fermenting cacao beans in boxes; Côte d'Ivoire, 2025. *Source:* Willy Shih.

FIGURE 2.4 Drying cacao beans under cover; Côte d'Ivoire, 2025. *Source:* Willy Shih.

The first fermentation phase typically lasts around 48 hours, and the next stage starts when the naturally occurring lactic acid bacteria start to consume the glucose, fructose, and citric acid and turn it into lactic acid, acetic acid, and ethanol. The temperature typically rises to 45–50°C, which triggers the switch from alcoholic to acidic fermentation. The acetic acid (the core component of vinegar) is crucial as it destabilizes the cells in the bean cotyledons, releasing important precursor components of the chocolate flavor. These compounds play a crucial role during the subsequent roasting process.

Next comes drying, which leads to the natural dissipation of most of the acetic acid and reduction of the moisture content to 6–8%. Puratos encourages drying under cover (see Figure 2.4), which is preferable to sun drying by the side of the road like a lot of farmers do (see Figure 2.5). The color of the beans is affected by the degradation of polyphenols during the acetic acid fermentation, and the overall quality of the cacao beans and their flavor potential is highly dependent on the rigor applied to the post-harvest process. I'm told the side-of-the-road beans generally find their way into the mass-market brands that we find in vending machines and candy aisles.

FIGURE 2.5 Drying cacao beans by the roadside; Côte d'Ivoire, 2025. *Source:* Willy Shih.

From Roasting to the Final Product

Dried beans are exported, typically to Europe or the United States, where they are roasted. Roasting reduces the level of undesirable components and produces a chocolate aroma and flavor via the Maillard reaction that occurs between reducing sugars and amino acids to produce melanoidins, compounds that confer the brown color and texture to the beans. The roasting also leads to caramelization, which causes the dehydration of sugars and the development of compounds that give chocolate its aroma.

Next comes grinding and mixing all the ingredients. Grinding the beans yields cocoa liquor, and cocoa butter comes out of pressing the cocoa liquor. These are mixed with sugar and milk to make milk chocolate. Modern chocolate making really got going with the invention in 1828 by Coenraad Van Houten in Holland of a hydraulic press that removed most of the cocoa butter from cacao, leaving a cake that can be pulverized into fine powder—which we know as cocoa. That may be a major reason why to this day a lot of the bean processing is still done in the Netherlands, which continues as a big global cacao trading hub (Coe 2013).

Conching is next, a process of mixing and heat treatment that ensures that all solid particles are coated with fat, volatile acids evaporated, and excess moisture removed. This results in a liquid chocolate with the desired viscosity and color. In the last step, the chocolate is tempered to give it stable and consistently sized crystals of cocoa butter when cooled.

I have never seen the movie *Willy Wonka and the Chocolate Factory*, although I did manage to arrange a class visit to the Barry Callebaut factory in Wieze, Belgium, which I suspect was far more visceral. Barry Callebaut is a vertically integrated chocolate manufacturer who also buys beans from West Africa, processes them in Belgium, and supplies major brands like Mondelēz International, Lindt & Sprüngli, Unilever, Hershey, Morinaga in Japan, Groupo Bimbo in Latin America, and GarudaFood in Indonesia, among others. The factory we visited processes about 340,000 metric tons annually. Aside from the conveyor belts carrying streams of chocolate in various stages of production, the things that really stuck with me were the machine that molded 2,000 chocolate chips per second (kerchunk, kerchunk, kerchunk), and the tank trucks filling up at the loading dock with molten chocolate destined for other food manufacturers across Europe. Apparently, the trucks' range is limited by how far you can go before the chocolate cools and solidifies, but I was told they can make it as far as Switzerland. I can't imagine what happens if a truck gets stuck in traffic on the way to the Lindt factory; according to press accounts Lindt buys from Barry Callebaut (Savage and Madeleine Speed 2025). Of course, I had to ask what happens if a tanker full of chocolate solidifies. They told me you had to chip it out by hand. I suspect that's a problem they go to great lengths to avoid.

When the chocolate finally makes it to a retail store somewhere, the key ingredient will have crossed continents and oceans and passed through the hands of multiple specialists who each added some value along the way. In the process it will have been transformed from an agricultural commodity to a widely loved confection or ingredient.

Semiconductor Chips: A Global Sequential Production System

While chocolate chips exemplify geographic specialization, modern semiconductor chip manufacturing takes specialization and geographic spread to new extremes. It's probably the ultimate example of what I call a "global sequential production system," where a little bit of value is added in a country, and then the work is passed on to someone in another country.

Integrated Circuits: Making Transistors in Bulk

The first integrated circuit chips were motivated by the U.S. military's need for greater reliability and compactness in its electronic systems. Two pioneering inventions were the foundation. The first came from Jack Kilby at Texas Instruments, who filed his patent for "Miniaturized Electronic Circuits" in February 1959 (Kilby 1964). The other came from Fairchild Semiconductor, where Robert Noyce (who later co-founded Intel Corporation) invented the first monolithic integrated circuit (IC) in 1959. He described a scheme to make "multiple devices on a single piece of silicon in order to make interconnections between devices as part of the manufacturing process, and thus reduce size, weight, etc. as well as the cost per active element. Instead of making individual transistors and then connecting them with wires, Noyce showed how to make multiple transistor circuits on a single wafer of pure silicon, and then connect them with fine metallic lines that were deposited on top" (Wolff 1976).

From the beginning, there were two big ideas underlying making these integrated circuits (ICs), which these days we often just refer to as "chips."

The first was that transistors and the wiring to interconnect them could be made together in bulk. This was crucial because if you want to make more complicated and sophisticated electronic devices, you use more transistors. And over time if you make each device smaller, you can cram more of them into the same area on a piece of silicon. Noyce's colleague and Intel co-founder Gordon Moore codified this idea in what popularly became known as Moore's law—the number of transistors in an IC doubled approximately every two years (Moore 1965). This reflected the keen insight that if you shrank the linear dimension of a device's features by one half, it would take only a quarter of the space on the same sliver of silicon. That meant in the same area of silicon you could cram four times as many devices, and the amount of power you used would remain roughly constant, a phenomenon that came to be known as Dennard scaling (Dennard et al. 1974).

The second big idea was that there were two distinctive parts of the innovation process: designing the chip and making the chip. This was the beginning of specialization in the chip supply chain.

Designing the Chip Early chips were laid out by hand, by people sitting at drafting tables, who drew pattern masks that would be used in a photolithography process to "print" the transistors and interconnections for the chip. The process was tedious and error-prone, and it was well suited to automation. The first electronic design automation (EDA) tools emerged in the 1970s, and they were the key to moving from chips that contained hundreds of devices (gates) to hundreds of thousands of gates per chip, and today millions or billions per chip.

The earliest programs automated artwork generation and circuit simulation, and with the emergence of powerful computer workstations, software expanded into all phases of the design from capturing circuit schematics, to simulating the logic blocks and placement and routing tools, and eventually into the whole process of synthesizing circuits. Then the challenge was how to get all of this translated into a specification for actually manufacturing the chip.

The U.S. military again provided a key starting point. The Department of Defense's Very High-Speed Integrated Circuit (VHSIC) program created the first hardware-description language, the VHSIC Hardware Description Language (VHDL). VHDL provided a way to describe the behavior and structure of an integrated circuit in a way that it could be modeled on a computer before you translated it into a physical hardware design. This was great because then you could simulate and check your design before turning it into silicon. VHDL provided a foundation for other programs that could read the files and turn them into actual physical designs. The programs collectively generated the instructions for manufacturing a chip, and in those days the computers would write the instructions onto a reel of computer tape. This led to the colloquial expression of "tape out" when a chip design had been completed and sent to the factory (referred to as a "fab" when we are making chips) for manufacture. That term is still used today even though computer tapes have been relegated to the dustbin of history decades ago. Today software companies like Synopsys, Inc.; Cadence Design Systems, Inc.; and the Mentor Graphics unit of Siemens are the major specialist suppliers of EDA tools for this essential front-end design process.

Making the Chip Once the chip has been designed, turning that design into a finished IC involves three groups of manufacturing steps, all carried out in highly specialized fabrication facilities.

- In the first stage, often involving many hundreds of tightly controlled process steps, the transistors are formed on the silicon wafer. This is done by repeatedly depositing thin films, applying light-sensitive chemicals, and using photolithography to print microscopic patterns into the silicon, followed by etching and doping processes that give the transistors their electrical properties.
- In the second stage, the transistors are connected into functioning circuits. Multiple layers of microscopic metal interconnects are deposited and patterned on top of the transistor layer, forming a dense web of wiring (and insulators) that allows signals and power to flow across the chip. Modern chips may contain dozens of metal layers each aligned with extreme precision.

FIGURE 2.6 AMD 3101E memory chip showing wire leads. *Source:* User: Mister rf / CC-BY-SA-4.0 / **https://commons.wikimedia.org/wiki/File:AMD3101E.jpg**

- Finally, the processed silicon wafer is cut into individual chips, known as die, which are then tested, packaged, and connected to the outside world. Packaging protects the fragile silicon chip, provides electrical connections, and helps manage heat, turning each chip into a component that can be handled, shipped, and installed on a circuit board. Each of these stages relies on different equipment and skills.

The pioneers in making ICs, companies like Texas Instruments, Intel, Motorola, and IBM, initially did both their own design and their own manufacturing. In early chips, the die only had a few connections to make to the package and the outside world. This was done by bonding tiny gold wires to the die and attaching them to terminals connected to the pins in the package. Early chips might have had four, eight, or sixteen wires or more to attach (see Figure 2.6). This meant looking through a stereoscopic microscope and attaching the wires with tiny welds. Painstaking work, and a job that would be tough to hire for in the United States, even in the 1970s.

Silicon wafers loaded with chips are very tradable, so it's not a big deal to air freight them to a place like Malaysia and hire armies of workers to package them. Intel opened its first factory in Penang in 1972 to do chip packaging, and by 1975 it had 1,000 people working in a 5-acre factory doing half of the company's chip assembly work. By the early 1980s,

FIGURE 2.7 IC chip packaged in Malaysia. *Source:* Kimmo Palosaari / Wikimedia Commons / Public Domain / **https://commons.wikimedia.org/wiki/File:Three_IC_circuit_chips.JPG**

14 semiconductor firms were doing the same thing (Ahmad 2023). That's why so many early chips had "Malaysia" stamped on the package even if the actual die inside might have been made in the United States or Europe (see Figure 2.7).

The chip packaging industry continued to grow in Southeast Asia, eventually expanding across Taiwan, Vietnam, and China. As automation came to chip packaging, the industry has stayed centered there. Today most semiconductor makers, whether they are located in the United States, Japan, Europe, or Asia, turn to back-end outsourced assembly and test (OSAT) firms located in Malaysia, Vietnam, Taiwan, and China to test and package finished chips in packages suitable for insertion into electronic circuit boards.

Separating Chip Design from Chip Manufacturing

The integration of chip design and chip manufacturing started to change in the 1980s. In January 1981, the U.S. Defense Advanced Projects Agency (DARPA) had a very large-scale integration (VLSI) project that established a facility that could quickly produce prototype ICs. It was the first "foundry" service offering low-cost quick-turnaround fabrication of custom and semicustom IC devices on shared wafers (DARPA n.d.). Economics, and the need to solve a business problem in Taiwan, led to the pure-play foundry model, in which a specialist company could focus exclusively on manufacturing the designs of others.

The Taiwan government's Industrial Technology Research Institute (ITRI) had licensed RCA Corporation's complementary metal-oxide semiconductor (CMOS) process, developing a pilot production capability that it spun out as United Microelectronics Company in 1982. However, it was the desire to offer a "shared kitchen" with a "chef to cook the recipes" for chip design start-ups that didn't have the money to build their own fabs that led to the founding of Taiwan Semiconductor Manufacturing Company (TSMC) as the world's first pure-play foundry (Shih and Wang 2009). Because TSMC took steps early on to isolate and protect the proprietary designs of its customers who turned to it for production, TSMC's business model allowed them to exclusively manufacture designs belonging to other firms. Today TSMC counts companies like AMD, Apple, Intel, MediaTek, Nvidia, and Qualcomm as some of its top customers.

TSMC and other semiconductor makers relied on independent tool makers to make the equipment that they needed for their fabs. I have only been allowed to bring a camera into a major semiconductor fab once, but even then they won't let you take many pictures. Fabs are multi-storied buildings that use enormous amounts of steel and concrete in their construction. The central level is a clean room where the air has been extensively filtered to remove any kind of dust and particulates as these will contaminate the production steps. Above the cleanroom level are interstitial and fan decks that employ huge air handling equipment that pushes filtered air down through the cleanroom through holes in the cleanroom floor to a subfab level that also brings in utilities like power, water, and industrial gases in underneath to all of the equipment (referred to as "tools").

On the cleanroom floor you will see huge tools from companies like ASML, Applied Materials, KLA Tencor, Lam Research, Tokyo Electron, and many others. Many of these are the size of a school bus and sometimes larger, yet on the inside they are using technologies that can shape the chips at the atomic level. The manufacturers of these tools each have their own networks of suppliers spread all over the world. I have toured many of these tool makers, and each has its own complex network of suppliers for components and subsystems.

Let's trace the path of a single chip. It might be designed by teams of engineers working in Silicon Valley together with colleagues in Texas and maybe India, using software from companies based in California who draw on engineers from all over the world. They send the design to a foundry in Taiwan, who then uses tools made in the United States, Netherlands, Japan, Taiwan, Singapore, and Korea to etch tiny circuit patterns onto silicon wafers that were made in Japan and melted in ultra-pure quartz vessels made from material that was mined in Spruce Pine, North Carolina, and then processed using chemicals that came from Japan, Korea, Taiwan, the United States, and elsewhere. The finished wafers are sent to Malaysia or Vietnam for testing and packaging, and then the finished chips go to a circuit assembler in China, Vietnam, or Mexico before finally making it to a server that goes into a datacenter in Virginia. And that would be a simplified version of the journey.

What you see as the chip design gets passed from one step to the next, the one that performs the work associated with that piece of the overall value chain has a tier of suppliers that support them, and each of those suppliers in turn has their own tier supporting them from below. EDA firms, foundries, equipment makers, and OSATs are all effectively links in the chain, and each has its own tiered network.

Lots of Tiers Makes Visibility a Challenge

Many modern products are pretty complicated, with lots of parts. A typical internal combustion engine automobile contains roughly 30,000 individual parts including all the fasteners and small components (Center for Automotive Research 2015). And with all the high-tech features they have today driven by a lot of electronics content, that means a lot of specialization in the supplier network. But there's a big challenge with tiered supply chains, especially ones with lots of layers: visibility. How do I make sure I get the parts I need when I need them?

Until the latter part of the twentieth century, automakers, often referred to as original equipment manufacturers (OEMs), were vertically integrated and produced most of the parts that they used in assembling their vehicles. Sometimes these parts were made by one of their parts divisions; other times they would buy them. Then they would gather and assemble them into larger modules and finally into vehicles on their assembly lines (Klier and Rubenstein 2008).

During the 1990s there was a big shift from vertical integration toward outsourced production of parts from independent suppliers. Partly this reflected increasing adoption of lean production methods across the manufacturing sector (Dyer 2000; Klier and Rubenstein 2008), but it was also a recognition of increasing cost pressures and rising complexity, especially with the incorporation of more digital technologies. GM consolidated most of its parts making operations under a new division called Delphi Automotive Systems in 1995 and spun it off in 1999. Ford did a similar thing, putting its parts operations into Visteon, and then it distributed the shares of it as an independent company to Ford shareholders in 2000.

Instead of producing most components in-house, OEMs like General Motors and Ford joined companies like Toyota in sourcing major systems from large Tier 1 suppliers like Bosch, Denso, Continental AG, Magna, and others. Tier 1 firms, in turn, sourced components and subassemblies from Tier 2 suppliers, which in turn rely on Tier 3 and Tier 4 suppliers for raw materials and more specialized parts. In doing this, the OEMs reduced their fixed costs and narrowed their focus to vehicle design, branding, and final assembly (Helper and Sako 2010; Sturgeon et al. 2008).

OEMs usually can have direct relationships with several hundred Tier 1s, and they might have relationships or knowledge of some or many of the Tier 2s. But it's pretty challenging to even know who all the Tier 3s and more distant suppliers are. It's even harder to keep track of how many parts are in the pipeline coming to you. That's what leads to surprises.

After the March 2011 Tōhoku East Japan earthquake and tsunami, automakers around the world discovered that the only factory for Xirallic pigments used in making certain colors of vehicle paint was out of commission (Park et al. 2013). Xirallic is made of aluminum oxide platelets coated with metal oxides, and it gives paint a crystalline glitter and a sparkling effect that makes it seem to shimmer. It was developed by the Performance Materials division of Merck KGaA in Japan, and there was only one factory in the world that made it—at Onahama in the earthquake zone (Patton 2005; Bennett 2011). The Onahama plant shipped Xirallic to auto paint manufacturers like BASF who mix it with pigments and other chemicals to make the actual paint. Ford had to stop taking orders for "tuxedo black" and limited production to vehicles painted in three shades of red. Chrysler had to limit orders on 10 different colors.

An even bigger problem was that the quake severely damaged the Renesas semiconductor fab in Naka, Japan. At the time, Renesas supplied 30% of all microcontroller chips and 40% of automotive microcontroller chips globally. Those chips were made in Naka, then they had to go somewhere (probably Southeast Asia) to get packaged, and then they probably went to Tier 1s like Bosch or Denso who built them into subsystems. The chip shortage impacted most of the major Japanese automakers, as well as GM, GE Appliance, and some European automakers.

Renesas wouldn't let me visit the damaged fab until August of that year, and as I took the train into Naka, I saw many homes that still hadn't been repaired, with blue tarps covering holes in their roofs. The trains were running, however, and when I got to the fab, there were only a few residual repair projects going on. The Naka campus contained six production and two testing lines housed in separate buildings. The most advanced lines were in the N2 and N3 buildings each of which had two production lines (see Figure 2.8).

FIGURE 2.8 Renesas Naka Fab, August 2011. *Source:* Willy Shih.

What I learned was that the shutdown was so problematic for automakers (especially companies like Toyota, Honda, and Nissan) that the repair and rebuilding effort had become a national emergency and mobilization. They told me that 70,000 people were involved across the country, and a lot of work like the cleaning of the masks used in lithography was farmed out across the country. I had dinner the night before going up to Naka in Tokyo with a friend who was an executive at one of the big semiconductor equipment suppliers. He told me that they had to send a large number of engineers to the clean room to basically rebuild the lithography tools onsite. Apparently 2,500 people per shift worked in the fab on all aspects of repair, three shifts a day, seven days a week, to put things back together.

Several years later I was discussing this with one of my friends at Toyota. He told me after the earthquake and tsunami, they went back and looked at how they defined lead times in the Toyota Production System. Lead time is the elapsed time from when you place an order until when the parts are delivered. He said they realized that they were sourcing semiconductor chips from "geologically and geopolitically unstable parts of the world," so they rethought effective lead time to include disruption risk, which led them to increase inventory buffers for critical semiconductors. Then the COVID-19 pandemic came around, and once again there was a surprise shortage of automotive microcontrollers, but Toyota had a large inventory on hand and was able to keep operating for many months longer than anyone else.

The tiered structure of supply chains has significant economic benefits. It allows automakers to shift capital requirements and technological risk onto suppliers, encouraging specialization and economies of scale at each level. However, it also creates fragility: disruptions in lower tiers can spread upward, as we saw after the earthquake. Increasing digital content and electrification are further reshaping tier boundaries, elevating semiconductor firms and battery manufacturers to quasi–Tier 1 status while reducing the role of some traditional mechanical suppliers (Helper and Sako 2010; Klier and Rubenstein 2008). In short, the auto industry's tiered supply chain reflects an effort to manage growing product complexity through hierarchical specialization.

The Fragmentation of Supply Chains

Technological complexity transformed the division of labor within firms into a division of labor across firms. As products have become more sophisticated, no single organization can master every required capability. Production therefore fractured into layers: designers, subsystem integrators, component specialists, materials suppliers, and equipment makers, each operating at a different tier of the value chain. This tiered structure enables deep specialization, economies of scale, and rapid innovation within domains. But it also stretches production across geographies and across organizations, making visibility harder and disruptions more consequential.

Modern supply chains are not simply long—they are layered. And understanding those layers is essential to understanding both the power and the fragility of the global production system.

CHAPTER 3

Labor Arbitrage

When we talked about Ricardo's model of trade and comparative advantage in Chapter 1, our assumption was that workers in one country (Portugal) could perform certain types of work (producing wine) more productively, while workers in another country (England) could specialize in doing something else (producing cloth), so both countries would benefit by trading with each other.

Often the main advantage one country has over others is significantly lower labor costs. If you can figure out how to harness those lower costs and move the work in a way that you can serve more expensive markets, you can save a lot of money. This is what is called "labor arbitrage," the exploitation of labor cost differentials between countries or regions. Usually that means moving the actual jobs to countries where the cost of labor and of doing business is lower. Labor arbitrage obviously depends on the cost of shipping the goods you're going to produce, but as we saw in Chapter 2, low-cost transportation opened up a world of possibilities.

Labor arbitrage has been the driving force behind the offshoring of manufacturing from the United States and Western European countries over the last 25 years. China has been the primary beneficiary, but so have other emerging markets across East and South Asia, and to some extent Eastern Europe, Turkey, and Africa.

How Labor Arbitrage Works

The core idea behind labor arbitrage is that if I move work to a location where it can be performed more cheaply, I'll save money. This assumes that the work can be specified, and instructions for doing the work can be communicated precisely. In other words, I can produce a spec and ship it to that remote location, and then the workers there can then perform the tasks and produce a comparable level of quality. It also presumes that the cost of communicating with that location is low and that the work product can be shipped back to where you wanted it in the first place. We would also like the transportation cost of the product to be much less than the amount you save in labor costs. Or as we said in Chapter 1, it is easily tradable.

Labor arbitrage plays an important role in any kind of product or service where there is a high *labor content.* That means when the number of person hours invested in producing the product is a high percentage of the total product cost. That typically includes things like sewing clothing or making furniture.

An early example of labor arbitrage in the United States was the migration of textile manufacturing from high-cost New England to the American South beginning in the 1920s and continuing after World War II. Northern mills relocated production to take advantage of the South's lower wages, weaker unions, and longer working hours, moving jobs rather than workers to reduce labor costs while still serving the same national market (Koistinen 2002). This strategy was viable in large part because for much of the twentieth century, U.S. textile and apparel markets were protected by high tariffs and, later, by restrictions that sharply limited imports of foreign-made clothing. Beginning in the 1960s, these protections were gradually converted into quotas under the Multi-Fibre Arrangement (MFA), which tightly controlled but did not eliminate imports from low-wage countries. Trade barriers were then gradually wound down through the Uruguay Round of trade negotiations and ultimately removed with the expiration of the MFA in 2005. This exposed U.S. producers to full global competition and accelerated the shift of apparel production offshore to low-cost countries in what some described as a "race to the bottom" (Anderson et al. 2001).

Cloth and thread are relatively cheap compared to the hourly wages in high-cost countries like the United States, and it is easy to communicate the instructions for making garments. You just supply a pattern to follow, and there are minimal requirements for skills, just cutting and using a sewing machine. Inexpensive transportation made it easy to move large amounts of the work to China (see Figure 3.1). As labor costs in China have increased, garment manufacture has moved to Bangladesh, Cambodia, Indonesia, and Vietnam chasing lower wages.

For mechanical or electronic products, you usually ask, "How many hours of assembly labor does it take?" In 2001 when I was at Kodak, assembly labor in the United States cost around \$20 per hour when you included benefits and overhead. It was around \$9.50 per hour in rural Japan where we had a facility and around \$0.50 per hour in China. That meant if a product like the digital camera in Figure 3.2 had four hours of assembly labor, it would cost us \$80 to do it in Upstate New York, around \$38 in Japan, and around \$2 in Shanghai. Hmmm, I could hire 10 times as many people, and if I could train them to produce the same level of quality, I would be way ahead of the game. The key is what is the relative productivity of the workers in the two locations.

FIGURE 3.1 Sewing women's suit jackets in Tianjin, China, circa 2017. *Source:* Willy Shih.

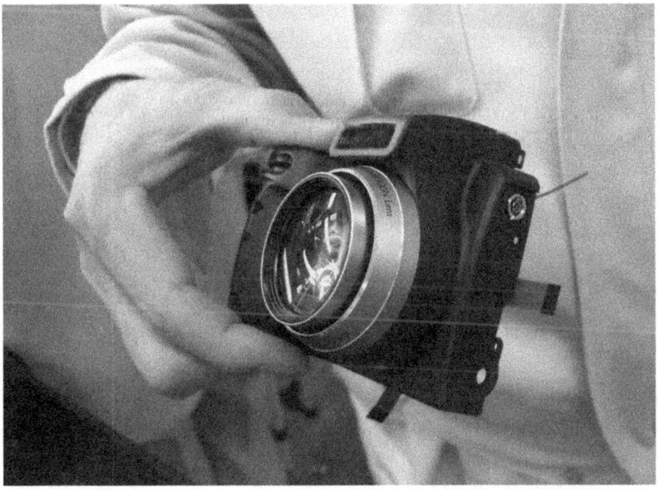

FIGURE 3.2 A Kodak digital camera subassembly at a factory in Japan, circa 2002. *Source:* Willy Shih.

At 50 cents an hour in China, I could tolerate productivity that was one-tenth of what it was in the United States and still be ahead. Way ahead if the product was really labor-intensive.

There aren't a lot of published numbers on comparative labor costs as most manufacturers really don't want you to know stuff like that. But a study conducted by Hong Kong's Christian Industrial Committee that was published in 2008 found that of 50 toys produced for Mattel, Hasbro, McDonald's, and Disney, the direct labor cost for a $16.99 doll was only 56 cents; for a $34.99 play set, 25 cents; for a $44.99 electric toy, 81 cents; and for an $11.99 action figure, 66 cents (Pun and Yu 2008). It's easy to see why so much toy manufacturing moved to China.

"Designed by Apple in California, Made in China"

Anyone who has purchased an Apple product probably has seen these words on the box: "Designed by Apple in California, Made in China" or "Assembled in China." This is probably one of the best-known examples of labor arbitrage. Apple used to assemble its products in the United States. It opened a highly automated factory in Fremont, California, in 1983 to manufacture its original Macintosh computers and opened a plant in Fountain, Colorado, in 1991 among other places. With losses mounting, it sold the Fountain plant to contract manufacturer SCI Systems in 1996, agreeing to purchase assembled Macs for three more years (Prince and Plank 2012).

When Steve Jobs returned to the company in 1997, his first comeback product was the iMac, an all-in-one design that had the computer built into a bright plastic case with a CRT monitor. The product was a real statement, and it was in keeping with the Steve Jobs's mantra at the time of "Think Different." Apple turned to the Korean company LG to manufacture it, which after initial success struggled to keep up with volume demands (McGee 2025).

In 2000, Apple turned to the Taiwanese firm Hon Hai Precision Industries Company, also known as Foxconn, to manufacture the iMac G3 model. The manufacture of IBM-compatible PCs had already largely moved to Taiwan and then China by that point as everyone chased labor arbitrage, so Apple was really following the pack to where high-volume electronic assembly had already moved. It turned to a series of other Taiwanese contract manufacturers for all of its products after that point, companies like Quanta Computer, which eventually assembled notebook computers not only for Apple but for Dell, HP, and most of the other major PC brands. It had much higher standards, though, so it ended up teaching most of these firms a lot about improving their manufacturing capabilities, benefiting all the contract manufacturers' other customers in the process.

We'll talk about some of the unique capabilities for assembling complicated products like iPhones at massive scale that China brings to the table in Chapter 6. But first let's look at other products and services that can benefit from labor arbitrage.

Seeing "Product of USA (Processed in China)" on a Seafood Label

Traditionally most seafood was harvested from wild populations in major fishing grounds along coastal areas like the northeast Atlantic Ocean and the Northwest Pacific off Japan, Russia, and the Bering Sea. The catch was brought to coastal communities and then traded in nearby population centers. But just as efficient transport expanded tradability in so many areas, so too in seafood.

China is the largest seafood producer in the world, and again labor arbitrage comes into the picture. Salmon caught in Alaskan waters need to be deboned before packaging for sale. There are 36 pin bones on the top of the fillet that are best removed by hand using a needle nose or specialized pliers, and that means processing is labor intensive. In 2005 when this was reported in the *Seattle Times*, performing that work in the Pacific Northwest cost about $1 per pound, while processing it in China cost about 20 cents, presumably including the transport cost back and forth (Yeong 2005). So Alaskan salmon traveled frozen all the way to China before being processed, refrozen, packaged, and shipped all the way back to the United States. That's how it can be a "Product of U.S.A." but processed in China.

According to the Food and Agriculture Organization (FAO) of the United Nations, Asian countries produced 72% of aquatic animals, with China ranking first at 36% followed by India and Indonesia at 9% and 7%, respectively (FAO 2025). While China is a major importer of seafood, it is also a large exporter. One estimate was that 74.9% of its imports were re-exported, and of the top 15 species imported, five were reexported almost exclusively (Asche et al. 2022). That tells you a lot of fish come in for processing only to be shipped out to global markets.

China built on this fish processing with its own aquaculture industry. According to the 2024 National Fisheries Economic Statistic Bulletin published by the Chinese Bureau of the Ministry of Agriculture and Rural Affairs, total output was $231.72 billion. That's a *lot* of fish, and while $35.88 billion was marine capture, $69.37 billion was marine aquaculture, and $121.96 billion was inland aquaculture (Aquafeed Media & Aquafeed Media SLU 2025).

Qingdao in the eastern Shandong Province is China's major fish processing hub. It's a beautiful location on the western shore of the Yellow Sea, only about 350 air miles west from Seoul, South Korea. It's probably most famous for Tsingtao beer, which is China's best known export brand, and it also is the home to the appliance company Haier. As Chinese labor costs have risen, companies around Qingdao have invested more in automation, as well as shifting their focus from lower value species like carp and tilapia toward more expensive ones like grouper, sea bass, sea bream, trout, and salmon (Godfrey 2020).

That story about pin bones was from 2005, but the picture has gotten more difficult for the Alaskan industry since then. Labor rates in China and across Asia continue to be far lower than in Alaska, and a high level of Russian exports of pollock, cod, salmon, and crab put a lot of downward pressure on prices received by Alaskan producers (National Marine Fisheries Service, Alaska Fisheries Science Center, Resource Ecology and Fisheries Management, and Stephen Kasperski 2024). This is one reason imports from Asia, China in particular, accounted for such a large part of the seafood consumed in the United States.

Strawberries from Mexico

In Chapter 1 we talked about growing strawberries in California and shipping them to New England. A recent visit to my local Whole Foods market on a cold January morning told an interesting story. In the fresh produce area, there were three different types of strawberries on the stand. There were 1-pound clamshells of Driscoll's organic strawberries imported from Mexico; Astin Farms strawberries from Plant City, Florida; and a 14-ounce box of "Sweetest Batch" Driscoll premium strawberries from California (see Figures 3.3–3.5). Within this roughly 3 × 5-foot space is a story that combines tradability and labor arbitrage.

Strawberry imports increased from 6% of total U.S. consumption in 2002 to around 14% in 2020, with 99% of those coming from Mexico. Certainly, an earlier start to the growing season is an advantage for Mexico, but labor arbitrage also plays a big role. Labor costs are estimated to make up 67% of the wholesale cost of a clamshell of strawberries (Calvin et al. 2022). Labor in California and Florida is much more expensive than Mexico, and that probably explains why the premium strawberries come from California—they're more expensive, and you get two ounces less. But you get a nice box that conveys that premium feel, at least compared to a plastic clamshell.

FIGURE 3.3 One-pound clamshell of Driscoll strawberries, imported from Mexico, January 2026. *Source:* Willy Shih.

FIGURE 3.4 One-pound clamshell of Astin strawberries, from Florida, January 2026. *Source:* Willy Shih.

FIGURE 3.5 14-ounce box of premium Driscoll strawberries from California, January 2026. *Source:* Willy Shih.

Many farm workers who pick domestically come to the United States under the H-2A Temporary Agricultural Program, which allows foreigners to come in to do seasonal farm labor on a temporary basis (Economic Research Service 2025, **USCIS.gov**). This program has grown rapidly, from 94,000 workers participating in 2010 to more than 380,000 in 2024 concentrated in Florida, Georgia, California, and Washington (Valencia and Paulson 2025). Farmers who hire H-2A temporary workers are required to provide transportation, housing, and meals in addition to paying the "Adverse Effect

Wage Rate," which is a minimum set by the U.S. Department of Labor to ensure that foreign guest workers don't impact the pay of U.S. farmworkers. This rate was $19.97 in California in 2025, although there were some rule changes in the middle of the year that changed housing costs from employer paid to an hourly deduction of $3. Growers generally pay a piece rate, so the take-home is generally closer to $25 or more per hour.

I talked to Gary Wishnatzki of Wish Farms in Plant City, Florida. He has been in the berry business since 1974 and is the third-generation owner of Wish Farms in Plant City, Florida. He told me no American citizens want the hard work of picking strawberries, so he is entirely dependent on H-2A workers.

Labor in Mexico is much cheaper, and it can provide more berries during the winter and spring. Workers get paid a lot less than in California or Florida. Rafael Roberto Flores Díaz, the head of the International Trade Practices Unit in the Mexican Ministry of Economy, summarized the problem facing domestic U.S. growers pretty succinctly in a filing that they made with the USITC. "The U.S. domestic industry lacks sufficient productive capacity to supply internal demand for fresh strawberries, particularly during the winter season," he wrote. "Faced with this structural supply limitation, the U.S. market turns to Mexico as a source of supply to meet its internal consumption needs, which have increased steadily over time" (U.S. International Trade Commission 2026).

Interestingly, some Florida strawberry growers and the Florida Department of Agriculture and Consumer Services filed an anti-dumping petition with the U.S. International Trade Commission seeking to impose duties on imports of Mexican strawberries (Janzen et al. 2025). Many of the listed importers were California growers, who apparently used the cheaper Mexican imports to compete with Florida (U.S. International Trade Commission 2026). If you were a California or Florida grower who also imported from Mexico, you probably didn't support the petition, but if you only grew in Florida, you probably did. So, the store shelf at Whole Foods tells a pretty interesting story about the competition between domestic-grown high picking cost berries and imported berries that take advantage of labor arbitrage.

Move the Work, or Move the Workers

Immigrants play a vital role in the U.S. agricultural workforce. According to a survey conducted in 2022, they made up approximately 61% of farmworkers, and a 2022 U.S. Department of Labor survey found 42% were not legally authorized to work in the country (Shih and Chua 2025). I was talking to a gentleman who works at a fresh produce trade association who told me, "Either you are going to import your products or you'll import your labor."

FIGURE 3.6 Assembly line in a Hungarian factory, 2017. *Source:* Willy Shih.

I was visiting a factory in Hungary in 2017. They assembled a variety of consumer and industrial products (see Figure 3.6). While we were looking at one of the lines, I noticed that the standard work instructions were written in Polish. "All the Hungarians went to Austria to work because they get paid more there," my colleague explained. Apparently, there was a shortage of Austrian workers in Austria because many had gone to Germany where they could get paid more. So facing a shortage of workers, the factory recruited workers from Poland. And then of course I was told there was a shortage of workers in Poland because so many workers had come to Hungary, so those jobs were being filled by Ukrainians. Either you import your workers or you import your products.

Call Centers, Back-Office Work, and Offshoring

Offshore call centers are another interesting example of labor arbitrage. They emerged in the financial sector as banks tried to provide computer-assisted services by telephone as they closed branches. They also grew in the travel industry alongside the growth of computerized reservation systems, mail-order sales, and other service operations.

Older people like me still remember when long-distance telephone calls used to cost real money, or I should say the telephone company would bill you (assess a "toll charge") for each individual call. One of the true revolutions in this sector came in 1967 when AT&T introduced the toll-free 800 number, what was officially called Inward Wide-Area Telephone Service (InWATS). This was a way for consumers to essentially "call collect," with the recipient rather than the caller paying for the call. It was also a way of making the transport cost of the product "free," and it made it practical to locate call centers away from the same area code as the caller as consumers wouldn't be afraid of incurring a long-distance toll charge.

AT&T introduced a national 800-number database in 1981, which enabled these toll-free numbers to work nationwide. Number portability came in 1993, which meant businesses could switch carriers and keep their numbers. That was a big deal if you had invested a lot in advertising your number (or had a vanity number like 1-800-FLOWERS), as many airlines, insurance companies, retailers, and service providers had done. It also fueled the trend of putting call centers in lower-cost regions far away from major metropolitan areas. New York City–headquartered Citibank moved its call center and credit card operations to Sioux Falls, South Dakota, in 1981. It could take advantage not only of the much lower cost of labor and office space, but South Dakota also had higher interest rate caps on credit card debt. By incorporating its credit card operations there, Citibank took advantage of not only labor arbitrage but regulatory arbitrage as now it could milk consumers for higher fees on credit card charges that they didn't pay off every month.

Intercontinental telephone calls were still expensive in the 1980s, however, with prices often measured in dollars per minute. The introduction of TAT-8, the first transatlantic submarine optical fiber cable between the United States and Europe, marked the beginning of a massive increase in international calling capacity with commensurate declines in costs (Hochheiser and Hochheiser 2022). The first Transpacific fiber link went into service four months later (Associated Press 2019). New technologies that enhanced the carrying capacity of these fiber links, along with exuberance associated with the buildout of the Internet led to exponential growth of fiber capacity (and the dot-com bubble that popped in 2000). Add to this mix the emergence of new players entering the submarine cable market like Global Crossing, which poured money into international data networks, and the emergence of Voice over IP (VoIP) technology that allowed phone calls to travel over the Internet. International calling quickly went from very expensive to almost free in just a handful of years. That brought a huge labor arbitrage opportunity to the call center market.

That's when we saw offshore call centers start to spring up. If you wanted to service the U.S. market, though, you needed to set up in a place where they spoke English. The obvious candidate was India, and you might remember all the jokes and complaining about Indian call center workers in the press and media those days. But it was cheap, and it was a great way for India to develop its economy, even though it meant many people worked at night. During one of my visits to India in the early 2000s, a former Indian ambassador who was hosting me told me that call centers and back-office outsourcing was a way for India to export labor without having to cope with the nightmares of the country's bureaucracy and poor export infrastructure around its ports.

Offshore call centers were also a great opportunity for the English-speaking Philippines and some poorer parts of the United Kingdom and Ireland. When I was at Kodak, we hired call centers in those locations because we wanted long service and support hours for our customers. The United Kingdom was five hours ahead and the Philippines were 11 hours ahead of New York, so it was a great way to get evening coverage for the West Coast of the United States as well as support across Europe.

Having the world's largest pool of low-cost, scientifically trained, and English-speaking employees was the key to India's boom in information technology outsourcing as well, but it awaited government reforms before being unlocked. Telecom reforms that had begun in the 1980s led to privatization and the lowest cost phone calls within and from India to the world. But it wasn't tapped until a severe macroeconomic and balance-of-payments crisis in 1991 caused the government to really open things up. The Department of Electronics introduced the concept of Software Technology Parks (STPs), kind of an export processing zone that offered tax exemptions, access to reliable power and high-speed telecommunications, along with office space that was ready to move in and use. The government also reduced restrictions imposed by the Monopolies and Restrictive Trade Practices Act which prevented large Indian businesses like the Tata Group from going into IT services. By 2003–04 services exports had grown to $24.9 billion, with software services, the IT outsourcing part, accounting for $12.2 billion. By this time, some people even viewed IT services as the primary engine of the country's economic development for the decades ahead (Srinivasan and Krueger 2005).

Call centers and IT offshoring are great examples of how improvement in and lower cost of communications improved the tradability of services, creating opportunities for labor arbitrage. So, not only did many of your products come from some distant locale, the service and support might as well!

A Central Feature of the Modern Global Economy

Labor arbitrage has been one of the central features of the modern global economy. When transportation and communication costs fall, more activities become tradable. Once they are tradable, firms compare labor costs across locations. If the work can be specified, transmitted, monitored, and shipped back at reasonable cost, it will often migrate to where it can be performed most cheaply and efficiently.

That explains the migration of textile manufacturing from New England to the American South and then from the United States to China and Bangladesh. It explains why salmon caught in Alaska can be processed in Qingdao and why strawberries on a winter shelf in Boston may have been picked in Mexico rather than Florida. It explains why your customer service representative might be in Sioux Falls, Dublin, Manila, or Bangalore.

Labor arbitrage rewards locations that combine low cost with efficiency, scale, and reliability. Over time, these locations build ecosystems and capabilities that go beyond cheap labor. While factories in China started assembling iPhones because wages were low, companies built dense supplier networks and massive scale advantages. India did not merely answer phones; it developed capabilities in software and IT services. What begins as labor arbitrage can evolve into industrial specialization.

If you want to understand where your stuff comes from, start by asking three questions:

1. How labor-intensive is it?
2. Can the work be specified, separated, and transmitted?
3. Are transportation and communication costs low enough to make distance irrelevant?

Where the answer to those questions is yes, labor arbitrage is usually at work.

CHAPTER 4

Capital vs. Labor

Sometimes the products we buy in a store traveled halfway around the world to get to us. And sometimes they start as a raw material and travel halfway around the world to get some processing work done and then back halfway around the world to be sold in a store. If they could collect frequent flyer points along the way, they might not make it into the top tier, but they would be up there in the mileage count.

We looked at labor arbitrage as a big cause of this in Chapter 3. But setting aside the carbon footprint for sending stuff back and forth over vast distances (bad), what's the logic that led to different pieces of a supply chain being so spread far apart? And more significantly, why would someone do things by hand in one place and by machine in another?

For as long as people have made things, they have faced a recurring choice: should I do this work with human hands or using labor-saving tools and machines? Economists describe this as the trade-off between labor and capital, where labor means human effort and skill, and capital means investing money in tools, machines, and technologies that help workers produce more. As early as the Industrial Revolution, people realized that investing in machines could dramatically raise output. But it also changed how many and what types of workers were needed and what kinds of skills mattered.

In the early nineteenth century, David Ricardo recognized that new machinery could increase total production while simultaneously reducing the demand for labor in certain tasks or industries, an insight that has echoed through economic debates ever since (Ricardo 1817). Do I hire more people or buy more machines? As we will see from some examples in this chapter, it can be more complicated and lead to some interesting supply chain layouts. Across these examples, capital does three things: it substitutes for labor when precision is required, it complements labor when tasks are hard to automate, and it determines where labor can be productively deployed.

How Automated Should This Factory Be?

The capital–labor trade-off explains one of the more eye-opening (and educational) experiences I had with manufacturing early in my career. When IBM introduced its personal computer in 1981, it sourced a dot matrix printer from Epson in Japan and rebranded it as the IBM Personal Printer. That was only meant to be interim, although most people (myself included) didn't realize it at the time.

In an effort to be competitive with U.S. manufacturing and sourcing, it designed the ProPrinter (see Figure 4.1), a dot matrix printer that adopted all of the best principles of design for manufacturability—using drop-in parts that would fit only one way and snap-together assembly. In parallel, it set up a highly automated factory in the United States to build it (Marcom 1985; Sanger 1985). The pilot line was a marvel of automation, as robots handled pretty much all of the assembly work. The factory attracted visits from high-level government officials from Washington, as well as all kinds of awards and acclaim (Kaplan 1987).

But not too much later, the factory was quietly shut down and production was moved to Asia, to what I heard was a far less automated factory. That was stunning—here was a product with outstanding design for manufacture built in a factory designed for high labor costs (with high automation) and even then it could *not* be competitive? It turns out that high productivity for this factory also cost a lot of money in the form of capital investment for the equipment, and it was not very flexible if you needed to change to a new model. The setup costs were high compared to a manual assembly operation because you would have to reprogram robots every time you changed the product, and in businesses where products turned over on quick lifecycles, you would never recoup those costs.

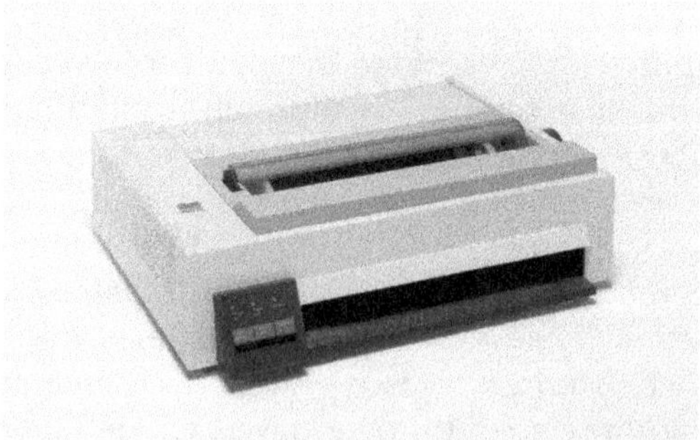

FIGURE 4.1 IBM ProPrinter 4201-001. *Source:* Göran Källvik / CC-BY-SA-3.0 / **https://commons.wikimedia.org/wiki/File:IBM_ProPrinter_4201-001_(1).jpg / https://digitaltmuseum.org/021028863252/skrivare**

This was a replay of the HMT example that I described in the preface. When a lot of manufacturing was offshored from the United States, companies often chose to use less automation because labor was so cheap, and it was much more flexible. I've been in several factories in China where they decide what they will build based on what orders came in overnight. That's really hard to automate.

This is a core decision that managers make when they choose a location: what level of automation to use. Because automation is less flexible, you tend to do the easy things first, like palletizing boxes at the end of an assembly line. Or you prioritize the "dirty and dangerous" things, like painting and welding a car body. That's why the front ends of most car factories, the so-called "body in white" section in which you weld together the unibody and paint it, are highly automated, but most final assembly lines where you install the powertrain and stuff the interiors still tend to use a lot of human assembly workers.

The other driver of automation is when you need precision and repeatability or when it is beyond the capability of humans to perform the process. I have been to many factories that manufacture LCD flat panel displays used in TVs and computer monitors. In these factories you work with sheets of glass that can be larger than a king-sized bed that are only a half millimeter thick. You screen print transistors on one sheet, make tiny cells that you fill with drops of liquid crystal material (a chemical), and then align another sheet of glass that is the same size with other stuff printed on it to make a sandwich—to a precision of one micron. Humans could never do that, let alone handle the glass without breaking it.

The same is true for printed circuit boards and most microelectronic components these days. The precision required today is so high, humans looking through microscopes would struggle to attain the same level of accuracy in assembly, let alone the speed.

Cashew Nuts Travel a Long Way

If you buy a jar of roasted cashew nuts at a warehouse club store like Costco, Sam's Club, or BJ's, there's a very good chance that the labels say they come from Vietnam. They are considered a luxury food, consumed in rich countries like the United States but grown in equatorial climes. But wait, according to the Food and Agriculture Organization (FAO) of the United Nations, the largest grower of cashews in 2025 was Côte d'Ivoire (Ivory Coast), followed by India, and only then Vietnam (Food and Agriculture Organization of the United Nations 2025). You mean they travel around the world to get processed and then back around the world to be sold?

Yes, that's right. French colonial foresters introduced cashew trees to the Ivory Coast in the late 1920s as part of reforestation programs, because at the time the wood was valuable both for use as a construction material and for burning. In the 1950s and 1960s the trees were also used to prevent soil erosion, but it was not until the 1970s that they were recognized for the economic value of the nuts (Bassett et al. 2018). At the time, growing cotton was more appealing to farmers, but this began to change in the 1990s as global market demand heated up and tight supplies of cashews in South Asia led to an influx of Indian traders into the Ivory Coast who were only too happy to buy cashews (Bassett 2001; Bassett et al. 2018).

The cashew fruit (also called a cashew apple) is a yellow-red, oval-shaped "accessory fruit" that grows on the cashew tree (*Anacardium occidentale*) and is a swollen stalk that supports the real fruit—a shell-covered cashew known as a drupe. The ripe cashew apple is sweet and juicy, but it has a very short shelf life, so most of it is not used because most growing areas lack the infrastructure for storing and processing them (Hegde 2022). The cashew apples are separated from the drupes which are then dried, often under the sun. These raw cashew nuts (RCNs) then have to go for further processing, where they are roasted or steamed to make the shell brittle. Then they are cracked open to extract the kernel, and this can be done by hand or by specialized machines. Then the kernels are dried, peeled to remove the inner skins, graded, and packaged.

During the cashew harvest season in Côte d'Ivoire the RCNs are usually put in giant bags and sold to traders. These traders, also called "pisteurs," are independent or semi-independent traders who have cash that they can pay to farmers on delivery. Sometimes they are financed by wholesale traders who might be under contract from an exporter. In neighboring Ghana where the situation is similar, a 100 kg bag of RCNs typically fetches about \$50. This translates to \$500 for a metric ton (1,000 kg) wholesale at export, when the end consumer price for processed nuts typically translates to \$20,000 to \$40,000 per tonne at the retail shelf (Butler 2025).

That means a huge amount of the value is captured by people who ship them around the world and process them. The majority of raw cashew nuts are exported unprocessed from the Ivory Coast and Ghana (often over 80–90% of Côte d'Ivorie's production) to India or Vietnam. The Ivory Coast is the world's largest exporter, and while in principle the nuts could be processed locally, people in West Africa can't get the financing to build the processing plants. Capital is not a problem in India or especially Vietnam, where people have invested in automation to shell and peel the nuts. That also means Vietnamese workers are far more productive on the processing side. And that's why your roasted cashews traveled around the world to get processed and then back around the world to reach your store.

Developing Robots to Harvest Strawberries

We talked about the tradability of strawberries in Chapter 1, and we talked about labor arbitrage in Chapter 3. Gary Wishnatzki reminded me that he is entirely dependent on H-2A labor now, and including piece rate incentives, it costs him around $20–25 per hour to pick berries in Florida. He thinks with labor increasingly hard to get, the only answer is automation, so he has been investing in robots to pick strawberries.

Mechanizing strawberry picking is challenging because the fruit is delicate and plants bear for a whole season. That means fields need to be repicked repeatedly without damaging the plants. Fruit clustering is another significant challenge for a mechanical strawberry harvester, as researchers have tried various methods to separate the clustering of ripe and unripe berries without bruising the unripe ones (Delbridge 2021).

Gary founded a start-up that he named Harvest CROO with partner Bob Pitzer, who had invented a wheel that uses a silicon claw to pick a berry and then rotates to pick another berry at a rapid rate. Once a strawberry is picked, it is rotated to the top of the wheel where it is carefully placed into a cup that will transfer it to a central location in the machine for inspection and then placement in a consumer pack like a box or clamshell (Donnel 2016). Each harvester incorporates 16 robots with the wheel, and the robots are equipped with an AI/machine learning vision system that identifies the ripe berries that are ready to pick (see Figure 4.2). The robots are installed in a large harvester vehicle that straddles the rows and is equipped with a LIDAR system that provides a 360° 3D view of the field. It is fully autonomous and is equipped with a collision avoidance system so that it can work amid people in the fields (see Figure 4.3).

Gary told me the problem is not only the high labor cost he incurs in bringing in H-2A visa holders to pick strawberries (when he can get them), but it's also the competitive pressure from imports. "Strawberries are going to be a luxury item here in not too much longer," he offered. That will be especially true if tariffs get applied to imports.

That makes the robot appealing, but Gary highlighted another challenge: getting funding to continue development of the robot. They have been working on it for nearly a decade, and the robot is not cheap, even though the technology keeps improving. The capital and development costs have to be amortized against the labor cost savings, and as long as inexpensive imports effectively set the market price for strawberries, his investment may or may not be appealing to venture capitalists. "They haven't really caught on to harvesting robotics yet," he told me.

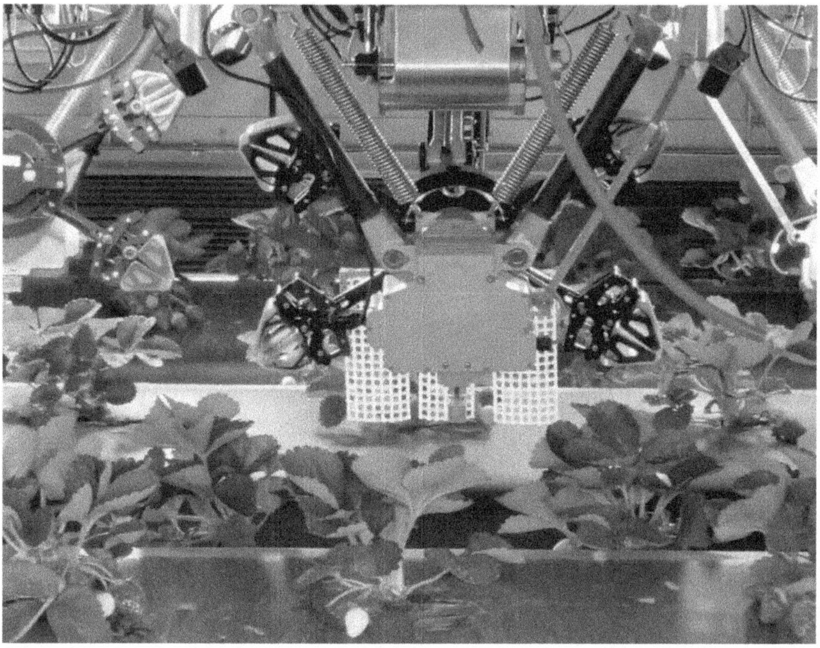

FIGURE 4.2 "Pitzer Wheel" equipped robot inside a Harvest CROO. *Source:* Gary Wishnatzki.

FIGURE 4.3 Harvest CROO operating in a field in Florida. *Source:* Gary Wishnatzki.

I also visited some vegetable growers in the Westland region of the Netherlands, where one company was experimenting with a tomato harvesting robot. Since most of the vegetables are grown in glass houses (greenhouses) there, the tomato plants are supported by three story high trellises. The robot they were testing used a suction arm to pull tomatoes off the vine and into a collector. Most high-cost countries are grappling with how to sustain agricultural production where there is high labor content in harvesting. In the end, it might end up going just like the ProPrinter and cashew nuts. Who can deploy the capital and where, where does it make more sense to use manual labor, and how does it compare to shipping stuff halfway around the world?

Grain, Fruits, and Vegetables in the United States

Gary Wishnatzki's challenge with strawberries is a microcosm of the broader issue with agricultural labor productivity and the U.S. food supply chain. The United States is highly competitive in agricultural products when production can be mechanized. It dominates global production of grains such as corn, soybeans, and wheat because it has large average farm sizes and universal adoption of mechanization ranging from tractors and combines to GPS-guided precision agriculture. Economic historians have long argued that American agriculture's comparative advantage emerged because high wages relative to Europe in the nineteenth century encouraged the development and adoption of labor-saving machinery, reinforcing large-scale, mechanized grain production (Hayami and Ruttan 1985; Allen 1994). U.S. farms are among the most mechanized and productive in the world for major field crops, with very high output per worker, supporting strong export performance in bulk commodities (FAO 2023; USDA Economic Research Service 2024).

By contrast, the United States struggles to compete in more labor-intensive agricultural sectors such as fruits, vegetables, and certain specialty crops where harvesting and handling remain difficult to automate. Not only strawberries, but most berries, lettuce, broccoli, melons, and most tree fruits are more than 90% water and require delicate, selective picking and frequent field passes, making them far more dependent on hand labor. Because U.S. farm wages are high relative to those in Mexico and many developing countries, production costs for these crops are significantly higher unless mechanization can substitute for labor. Yet agricultural economists and policy analysts consistently find that automation in specialty crops has been slower and more technically challenging than in grains, leaving growers heavily reliant on human labor (Martin 2017; Richards 2018). As a result, the United States is a major importer of labor-intensive horticultural products, particularly from Mexico, even while remaining a dominant exporter of capital-intensive grains (USDA Economic Research Service 2024).

This divergence reflects a classic capital–labor trade-off. Where technology allows machines to substitute for workers as in planting, spraying, and harvesting uniform grains, high wages and abundant capital create a competitive advantage for the United States. Where tasks require dexterity, judgment, and crop-by-crop variation and where automation is hard to implement, low-wage countries have a big advantage because as we saw in Chapter 1, transport costs tend to be very low relative to the wage differentials.

In effect, U.S. agricultural competitiveness tracks the elasticity of substitution between capital and labor: high in grains, lower in specialty crops. This pattern is consistent with long-standing theories that predict that countries develop and adopt technologies that economize on their relatively scarce (and expensive) factors of production (Hayami and Ruttan 1985), and with modern trade data documenting the United States' strength in mechanized bulk commodities and relative dependence on imports of labor-intensive produce (FAO 2023; USDA Economic Research Service 2023).

Can Innovation in Choice of Apple Varieties and Harvesting Improve Labor Productivity?

Innovation in apple production over the past two decades has significantly increased labor productivity by changing both which apples are grown and how they are harvested. In Washington State, the largest U.S. apple producer, fresh production rose 38% between the early 2000s and the late 2010s, while bearing acreage increased only 5%; yields per acre rose 29% over the same period. Much of this gain reflects the adoption of new varieties and orchard systems built around dwarf rootstocks and trellises. Dwarf trees concentrate fruiting wood on supported limbs rather than thick trunks, allowing more light penetration and earlier bearing. Trees are planted at higher densities and trained into narrow, two-dimensional canopies that are easier to manage. The result is more apples per acre and per worker hour, as workers can see and reach fruit more easily and spend less time climbing and repositioning ladders (Calvin et al. 2022).

Variety selection has also reshaped labor use and productivity. Traditional varieties such as Red Delicious were typically harvested in one pass, while premium varieties like Honeycrisp may require multiple passes because fruit does not ripen uniformly. Although multiple picks increase labor input per acre, the much higher prices commanded by newer varieties make the additional labor economically viable (Calvin et al. 2022).

Growers increasingly design orchards around these higher-value varieties using trellis systems that facilitate faster and safer harvesting. By aligning orchard architecture with the traits of newer varieties, producers have raised output value per labor hour even when total picking passes increase. Mechanical aids have amplified the productivity of hand labor without fully replacing it. Traditional ladder-based harvesting required workers to spend up to one-third of their time moving and positioning ladders. New self-propelled or tractor-pulled harvest platforms transport workers and bins along the rows, eliminating much of that nonpicking time. Experienced crews who used platforms showed significant efficiency gains. Platforms are now widely used for pruning, thinning, and other orchard tasks, and are increasingly used in harvest operations in appropriately designed orchards.

Together, high-density plantings, premium varieties, and labor-enhancing machinery have increased apples harvested per worker hour, illustrating how biological innovation and mechanical design can complement labor rather than simply substitute for it (Calvin et al. 2022).

Finding the Right Mix of Capital and Labor in Blueberry Production

We grow blueberries at our home in New Hampshire, and as my wife can attest, she does pretty much all of the picking while I sit around and write papers and books like this. I frequently point out to her that the only labor we have is the two of us, so if there is a mechanical solution that I can buy, I will generally favor the use of capital (see Figure 4.4). That has led to a barn full of equipment, and it does enable us to grow much more than we can use.

FIGURE 4.4 We don't have a lot of labor, so we use capital at home in New Hampshire. *Source:* Willy Shih.

We make it a point not to think about how much a particular watermelon or tomato might have cost us, although all of this power equipment has improved my mechanical skills in their operation and associated equipment maintenance.

After strawberries, blueberries are the most popular berry crop in the United States. Fresh-market blueberry production grew 265% from 2000–2002 to 2017–2019. The largest states by production share were Washington, Oregon, and Georgia. Globally, China jumped to the top spot in 2021, passing the United States and Peru (Agrilinkage 2026). Most counter-seasonal imports into the United States come from Peru and Chile.

Blueberry growers have raised labor productivity through planting new varieties that expanded seasonal availability, and growing use of mechanical harvesters. Much of the production increase over the last three decades reflects the development of new cultivated low-chill types that can be grown in warmer regions such as Florida, and varieties that extend the harvest season in both early and late harvest windows. By lengthening the season and improving yields, breeders have increased output per acre and spread fixed labor and capital costs over a larger volume of marketable fruit. Season extension also allows growers to sell when prices tend to be higher, raising revenue per labor hour even when total labor input remains substantial.

As blueberry acreage expanded, growers increasingly planted bushes in uniform rows designed to accommodate mechanical harvesting equipment. Harvesting machines that straddle rows use vibrating rods and air systems to dislodge ripe berries and move them by conveyor to collection bins. These machines, which cost roughly $200,000 to $300,000, dramatically reduce the number of worker-hours required per acre compared with repeated hand picking (Calvin et al. 2022).

While mechanical harvesting was once confined largely to fruit destined for processing, rising labor costs and improved sorting technology have encouraged some growers to use machines for part of the fresh crop as well. Even when machines result in lower fresh "pack-out" rates, sometimes by up to 20% due to bruising or because they picked immature fruit, the reduction in labor costs can offset the losses. Many growers now use a hybrid strategy that maximizes labor productivity across the season. They hand harvest the first pass, when fruit quality and fresh-market prices are highest, and then switch to mechanical harvesting for later passes as yields thin and more berries are diverted to processing.

This approach matches labor intensity to marginal revenue: scarce, high-value fruit receives labor-intensive hand-picking, while lower-value fruit is gathered with capital-intensive machinery. In combination with variety innovation and expanded acreage, these technological adjustments have allowed the U.S. blueberry industry to scale output rapidly despite rising wages and strong import competition (Calvin et al. 2022). The result is a great example of using a mix of capital and labor to raise output per worker in a crop that remains partially dependent on hand harvesting.

Combining Capital with Labor

Over time, economists developed a more systematic way to think about the trade-off between capital and labor. In the mid-twentieth century, models of economic growth treated production as the result of combining labor with capital, allowing firms to substitute one for the other as relative costs changed. If wages rose, firms had a stronger incentive to invest in machines; if machines were expensive or unreliable, firms depended more on people. The idea that capital and labor are to some degree substitutes became a foundation of modern economics, formalized in growth models and production functions that remain popular today (Solow 1956; Arrow et al. 1961). These models help explain why richer economies with higher hourly labor costs tend to use more machinery and automation and why capital investment is such a powerful driver of productivity growth.

More recently, economists have refined this picture by focusing not on jobs as a whole but on the tasks that make up those jobs. Modern machines and software tend to replace workers most easily in routine, well-defined tasks, while complementing workers in tasks that require judgment, creativity, or more complicated interactions. As a result, capital often substitutes for some kinds of labor while increasing the productivity and wages of others. Studies of computers, automation, and industrial robots show that this task-by-task substitution helps explain both rising productivity and growing inequality within labor markets (Autor et al. 2003; Acemoglu and Restrepo 2020). In plain terms, the capital–labor trade-off is not about whether machines replace people entirely but about which parts of production are handed over to machines and which remain in the hands of people.

Capital rarely eliminates labor outright. More often, it determines *which labor*, *where*, and *under what conditions* human work becomes economically the most competitive. Cashews are processed in Vietnam not because machines replace workers but because machines make workers productive enough, consistent enough, and financeable enough to dominate global trade.

CHAPTER 5

Outsourcing and Contract Manufacturing

One of the biggest sources of confusion on where a product comes from arises from the practice of outsourcing. Until the 1980s, most companies were vertically integrated. A company made all the bits and pieces of the product itself, assembled it, and then put its brand on it and sold it.

But that has all changed. This chapter examines how and why outsourcing and contract manufacturing became central to modern production. It begins with the historical shift away from vertical integration, tracing how competitive pressures in the 1970s and 1980s led companies to separate brand ownership from manufacturing. It then explores the economic logic behind outsourcing: cost reduction, asset specificity, demand pooling, and the concentration of firms on their core competencies.

The chapter also describes the rise of contract manufacturers in electronics, with the emergence of large supply chain service organizations such as Flextronics (later renamed Flex), Foxconn, and Jabil that coordinate procurement, production, and logistics on behalf of branded goods firms. It also shows how the contract manufacturing model has spread far beyond tech, into sectors like athletic footwear, personal care products, food and beverages, and pharmaceuticals. Throughout, we highlight a distinction between original equipment manufacturers (OEMs) and original design manufacturers (ODMs), and examine the challenges that arise when contract manufacturers begin competing with their own customers.

From Vertical Integration to Outsourcing

When Henry Ford built the Ford Motor Company during the first half of the twentieth century, he ensured that it not only made its own steel but that it also owned timberland in Michigan's upper peninsula to supply wood, it had a glassworks to make windows, and it even attempted to secure rubber supplies through plantations in Brazil (Henry Ford Heritage Association 2016). The River Rouge complex (my first factory tour, which I took at age six) literally had coal and iron ore coming in one end and cars coming out the other. AT&T owned its own telecommunications network and produced its own telephones and network switching equipment. IBM not only produced its own computer systems starting with the semiconductors, but it also developed and manufactured its own peripherals: data storage subsystems, displays, printers, card punches, and terminals.

Some researchers assert that during the 1970s and 1980s, the failure of many American companies to successfully respond to rising competition from Asia led to serious questioning about whether vertical integration was the right business model (Sturgeon 2002). This coincided with companies starting to ship work off to Asia, as we pointed out with semiconductor packaging in Chapter 2. This became especially prevalent in electronics assembly for products like radios and TVs. The assembly work went to companies in Japan, Hong Kong, Korea, and Taiwan. That also marked the eventual decline of U.S. companies' brand share in the late 1970s and 1980s as foreign manufacturers like Sony rose to prominence (see Table 5.1). That's when it started to become clear that the brand on the label wasn't necessarily the name of the company who manufactured the product.

TABLE 5.1 U.S. Firms' Brand Share and Manufacturing Share in Television Receivers

Year	1960	1970	1978	1990
U.S. firms' brand share in black-and-white television receivers	98%	72%	65%	
U.S. firms' manufacturing share in black-and-white television receivers	98%	48%	12%	
U.S. firms' brand share in color television receivers	100%		81%	55%
U.S. firms' manufacturing share in color television receivers	100%		57%	12%

Source: Willy Shih based on Bettis et al. (1992).

The usual motivation to outsource is to reduce costs compared to doing it in-house. If the manufacturing operation is capital intensive, this gets fixed assets like factory buildings and production equipment off the books and improves a company's return on invested capital (ROIC). It also facilitates competition among suppliers and in theory should promote higher quality as the outsourcer can choose among suppliers—in other words, harness the market to provide the best choices rather than be locked in to your own internal production capabilities. This can be especially valuable if newer technologies become available that make existing ones obsolete. You don't really want to own an apparel factory that specializes in making polyester fabric when that goes out of style. You bear all the downside risk if tastes shift because it might be hard to redeploy the specialized cutting and sewing systems overnight.

Economists describe this problem as one of *asset specificity*. Let's say you need an expensive machine to produce some part of your product, but you don't have enough volume to justify buying it on your own because you won't use it that much. In such circumstances, it makes sense to buy that part from an outside supplier that can manufacture and sell the same or similar versions to multiple customers, *pooling the demand*, and reaping the associated economies of scale. The marginal cost savings generated by increasing volume from one customer to multiple customers gets shared in the form of a lower price for everybody (Klein et al. 1978; Riordan and Williamson 1985).

Scale also helps more broadly in cost reduction. It increases the utilization of fixed assets, and it can aggregate fluctuations in the demand across different customers. It can also increase the bargaining power for procurement of raw materials and other inputs in the upstream supply chain. This is why less profitable or commoditized components and subsystems, which are likely to use a common design, and processes requiring expensive equipment are often outsourced to independent manufacturers who can take advantage of economies of scale and scope by pooling demand.

Another claim is that outsourcing noncore work allows the allocation of more resources and management attention to the core tasks that a company does (or should do) best. C. K. Prahalad and Gary Hamel popularized the theory that the core competencies of a company were the roots of its competitive advantage, so firms should focus their energies on these and redeploy assets that support the rest (Prahalad and Hamel 1990). Some even suggest that firms should outsource activities in which they cannot excel and focus on those activities where they can be the best (Quinn et al. 1990). More broadly, outsourcing facilitates quicker responses to changes in the marketplace because you aren't saddled with potentially obsolete assets. Those problems end up in the lap of the outsource provider.

Supply Chain Tiering and the Rise of Contract Manufacturing

As we saw in Chapter 2, specialization meant that it became more natural to divide up the work and outsource part or all of it. For example, one of the things IBM did when it introduced its PC was to turn to a contract manufacturer, SCI systems in Huntsville, Alabama, to manufacture the printed circuit boards. IBM had used SCI earlier in the 1970s to manufacture parts for its mainframe computer terminals, but for the PC it needed surface-mount printed circuit board capacity, which was expensive and time-consuming to implement. Contracting it out gave IBM a lot of flexibility, and SCI's labor costs were half of IBM's (SCI Systems—Company History n.d.).

IBM's use of SCI Systems did not mark the invention of contract manufacturing, which had long been used in defense, automotive, and consumer electronics. What was new was the application of contract manufacturing to a high-profile, mass-market product, where speed and time-to-market mattered more than vertical integration. That shift helped legitimize a production model that would become central to the personal computer and electronics industries.

The Expansion of Contract Manufacturing in Tech

During the 1990s, contract manufacturing of tech products expanded rapidly as personal computers, networking equipment, and telecommunications hardware moved from niche products to mass market staples. Firms such as Flex, Jabil Inc., SCI Systems, and Solectron invested heavily in printed circuit board fabrication, product assembly and testing, and logistics capabilities that individual brand-name manufacturers found difficult to replicate on their own. They brought economies of scale, especially with regard to purchasing components and raw materials, and efficient management of labor. As product cycles shortened and demand became more volatile, outsourcing assembly also enabled branded goods companies to scale production up or down without owning a lot of fixed manufacturing assets on their own books. They just contracted for it as they needed it. What began as a way to gain speed and flexibility increasingly became the most efficient way to produce complex electronics.

A key competitive advantage for contract manufacturers is their ability to pool production volumes across multiple customers, something individual companies could not easily do. By assembling products for multiple firms at once, contract manufacturers can keep factories running at high utilization even when demand for any single firm's product fluctuates. This aggregation supports investment in specialized equipment, process engineering, and quality systems that might not have been economic for smaller, captive plants.

It also gives the contract manufacturers a lot of buying power for the components used in assembly. They are generally able to procure them for substantially less than what a brand could get.

Demand pooling works especially well for standardized modular products. When companies like IBM, Hewlett-Packard, and Digital Equipment Corporation spun off or sold their computer disk drive manufacturing operations to specialists like Hitachi, Quantum Corporation, or Western Digital, those original equipment manufacturers (OEMs) could aggregate sales volumes across customers and the whole industry for that matter.

Combining Internal with External Sales

For a number of years, people believed that an alternate approach was for big vertically integrated companies to also sell their products and services on the open market—that would ensure that they had to be competitive in order to survive. For example, IBM sold its disk drives to its competitors, and it tried to keep semiconductor production in house while simultaneously selling foundry services to outside customers. Manufacturing volume is especially critical to production learning in both of these areas, so that made a lot of sense. When I was at IBM in the early 1990s, I was part of a team that had worked hard to secure Apple as a partner in the PowerPC processor family, which competed with Intel. That partnership brought volume to IBM's fabs, so it was vital.

IBM had some success for a while. When I worked at Silicon Graphics Computer Systems in the mid-1990s, we had one of our key chips manufactured at IBM's fab in Burlington, VT (see Figure 5.1). Cray Research also used IBM to make the chips for their J90 supercomputers, as did Sony for the Cell processor in its PlayStation 3.

FIGURE 5.1 Router chip used in Silicon Graphics Origin 2000 manufactured by IBM. *Source:* Willy Shih.

But IBM eventually ran into incentive problems—prioritizing internal customers over external ones. In the early 2000s, Apple wanted IBM to focus on low power chip technology while IBM's mainframe units wanted high performance even if it meant using more power. This tension was one factor contributing to Apple's eventual decision in 2005 to transition to Intel processors.

Becoming the Dominant Model in Tech

By the late 1990s, the contract manufacturing model had become dominant for tech products, with companies like Cisco Systems exemplifying the shift. Cisco focused on product architecture, software, and customer relationships, while relying pretty much exclusively on contract manufacturers to assemble its networking hardware. This allowed the company to grow rapidly without growing manufacturing assets. Firms like Cisco, HP, and Apple helped cement contract manufacturers as a distinct supplier tier in electronics supply chains, companies that specialized not in design or branding but solely in high-volume, rapidly scalable production for many customers simultaneously. This layer became a dominant feature of supply chains, separating product conception from physical manufacturing and reinforcing the tiered structure that now characterizes much of the tech industry.

Contract manufacturers like Flex, Solectron, and Jabil expanded globally in the 1990s and early 2000s, adding facilities in Mexico and China. Mexico's maquiladora program encouraged U.S. and multinational firms to set up assembly operations just across the border to take advantage of lower labor costs and preferential tariff treatment. Many U.S. and global manufacturers were already operating facilities in Mexico for components and subassemblies that fed into North American supply chains.

Contract manufacturers soon accumulated enough engineering capability, product knowledge, and scale to go beyond mere assembly. They started to take on the responsibility for actually designing products, and some came to be known as original design manufacturers (ODMs). Brand-name firms like Dell and HP, facing shorter product cycles and intense price competition, increasingly chose to simply specify their product requirements and market positioning rather than do the actual detailed designs by themselves, especially for products like notebook computers. Taiwanese ODMs like Compal, Inventec, Pegatron, Wistron, and Foxconn then did complete turnkey product development, often all the way up to shipping the finished product directly to the customer.

In 2016, I took a class to visit a large Taiwanese ODM's "factory city" in the vicinity of Shanghai where they were making notebooks for *everybody*. On a line adjacent to one assembling Dell notebooks was one assembling notebooks for HP. A student pointed out the packaging that they went into, with the prominent banner "The Computer is Personal Again," a tagline that was part of HP's global marketing campaign at the time. "Yeah, right," was all he could say while a wave of chagrin spread across the class.

This means your Dell notebook wasn't manufactured by Dell. The company is commendably open about this and conveniently makes their supplier list public (Dell Technologies 2026). On it we can see the various tiers, with ODMs like Celestica, Compal, Foxconn, Inventec, Luxshare Precision, Pegatron, and Wistron at the "Final Assembly or ODM" tier, and major component suppliers like the following:

- AU Optronics, BOE, CSOT, Innolux, LG Display, Qisda, Samsung, Sharp, and TPV (Displays and display components)
- AMD, Broadcom, Intel, Nvidia (semiconductor chips)
- BYD Lithium Battery (batteries)
- Delta Electronics (power supplies)
- Micron Technology, Samsung, and SK Hynix (memory chips)
- A host of other component suppliers

Since I have visited almost every one of these companies and I know what they do, it's easy for me to organize them into tiers.

If you want to be a successful ODM, you definitely need to be careful *not* to compete with your customers. Acer, the pioneering Taiwanese PC maker, split its PC-branded marketing division from its manufacturing operations in 2000–2001. Acer formed an independent company, Wistron, to give it arms-length independence. Once I visited Acer at their offices in New Taipei City—it was a huge office building, and some floors were Acer, and some were Wistron. As we rode up in the elevator, stopping on some Wistron floors on the way to our Acer floor, I asked my host, "Hmmm, how's the split working?" Noting the co-mingling, he told me that for several years, customers weren't sure if they trusted Wistron. But then during a period when Intel microprocessors were in short supply, people watched to see whether Wistron would allocate their allotment of chips to producing the Acer or the Dell products that it was manufacturing at the time. When it favored Dell, he said the Acer people realized, "Okay, it's over." But from that point on, Dell trusted Wistron.

Similarly with Asustek. Here was a company that was a leader in making motherboards for PC companies that started moving into making PCs under its own brand. They too realized that they would have to split off their manufacturing, so they spun off those activities as Pegatron in 2010. When I visited Asustek at the time, they had a nice building but the engineers and staff weren't as neatly organized by floor as Acer had been. They told me they segregated them into two parts of the same building that shared a ground floor entrance, cafeteria, and other facilities. And they told me they set up a "Chinese Wall" internally though the engineers still ate together. It took a couple years before customers trusted them too.

Not Just Tech: Contract Manufacturing in Athletic Shoes

Contract manufacturing is pervasive in many industries, much more than many people realize. Let's look at athletic shoes. From its inception, sportswear company Nike owned no factories. Its founding premise was to be responsible for understanding customer needs, spotting new trends, and translating those insights into designs that they brought to market, using Asian contract manufacturers to do the work of producing the product. Founders Phil Knight and Bill Bowerman had been importing running shoes from Onitsuka Tiger in Japan and selling them through a company named Blue Ribbon Sports, but they changed the name to Nike in 1971 (Locke 2003). Thanks to outstanding advertising and marketing, it became a dominant athletic wear brand by the early 1980s.

The competitive pressure from Nike drove other athletic shoemakers like the German company adidas to establish their own Asian supply chains. They turned to Asian specialists that operated factories in low-wage countries like China, Vietnam, and Indonesia. The largest athletic footwear specialist, Taichung, Taiwan–based Pou Chen Corporation was founded in 1969 in Taiwan as a canvas and rubber footwear manufacturer. It has produced for multiple brands, including Nike, adidas, Reebok, Asics, Under Armour, New Balance, Puma, Converse, Salomon and Timberland. They also take responsibility for adapting designs to its production systems. Over time it also successfully transformed itself to become an ODM (Pou Chen Group 2026). Overall Pou Chen produces hundreds of millions of pairs of shoes annually and accounts for a significant share of the combined wholesale value of the global branded athletic and casual footwear market even though most people have never heard of it.

Firms like Pou Chen are Tier 1 suppliers and supply branded goods to sellers directly. The Tier 1s are in turn fed by Tier 2 firms, who are predominantly subcontractors for piecework and components. Tier 3 suppliers feed the Tier 2s with raw materials like fabrics and synthetics and are generally located nearby. Manufacturers used standardized processes in their production systems and use large lot sizes to spread fixed costs and drive down unit costs.

As reported in Nike's May 2025 10-K filing, the company was supplied by 97 finished goods footwear factories located in 11 countries, operated by

15 different contract manufacturers. Factories in Vietnam, Indonesia, and China manufactured approximately 51%, 28%, and 17%, respectively, of all Nike-branded footwear (Nike Inc. 2025). In comparison, adidas sourced 39% of its footwear from Vietnam, 32% from Indonesia, and 14% from China, though it sourced 23% of its apparel from Cambodia and 26% of accessories and gear from Turkey (adidas Group 2024; Tabassum 2025). But there's a pretty good chance that a lot of competing branded products ended up coming from the same factories.

This style of outsourcing has been called "abstention-based," when a firm purchases goods or services from another organization even though it has never made or conducted any of those on its own in the past (Gilley and Rasheed 2000). This became all the rage in the 1990s. Andrew Rappaport and Shmuel Halevi heralded the arrival of the "fabless" computer chip design companies like Qualcomm, Broadcom, Nvidia, and MediaTek and built major enterprises focusing solely on the design of semiconductor chips, as we discussed in Chapter 2 (Rappaport and Halevi 1991). Many companies today outsource not only manufacturing but also some of their R&D. Major pharmaceutical companies such as AstraZeneca, Bristol-Myers Squibb, Pfizer, and GlaxoSmithKline often turn to contract research organizations (CROs) like ThermoFisher Scientific, Laboratory Corporation of America, and WuXi AppTec to supplement their own internal development activities.

Contract Manufacturing of Personal Care Products

Contract manufacturing plays a central role in the personal care industry because making creams, shampoos, and sunscreens is far more complex than it appears just from looking at the bottle. Modern products rely on dozens of chemical ingredients such as surfactants, emulsifiers, preservatives, polymers, fragrances, and active ingredients. Each of these must meet strict safety, quality, and regulatory standards. Building and running facilities that can consistently blend, heat, cool, fill, and package these formulations at scale requires large, fixed asset investments and specialized expertise. As a result, many brand owners choose not to manufacture themselves, instead turning to contract manufacturers that specialize in formulation, scale-up, and production.

Over time, this has produced a tiered supply chain. Upstream specialty chemical firms such as BASF, Croda, Evonik, and Lubrizol manufacture key ingredients like surfactants, emollients, rheology modifiers, and active ingredients, often tailoring them to customer specifications. Downstream, personal care contract manufacturers—such as Intercos SpA, Fareva, Kolmar, and Cosmetica Labs—combine these ingredients into finished or semi-finished products on behalf of brands. These firms often support regulatory testing, stability studies, and packaging integration, and they pool volumes across many customers to achieve economies of scale that individual brands could not reach on their own.

This structure has enabled an explosion of product variety and new niche brand entry in personal care. Large incumbents can rapidly launch line extensions without expanding internal manufacturing, while independent and private-label brands can enter the market with minimal capital investment. Manufacturing and formulation capabilities have become increasingly concentrated in a relatively small number of global specialists.

Some years ago I wrote a case on Living Proof shampoo, a brand that is today owned by Unilever (Shih 2014). The case writing had some unique aspects—to interview one of the cofounders, I made an appointment to have him cut my hair. When they told me how much it would cost (he's a high-end celebrity hairdresser), I almost chickened out but my wife assured me it was for a good cause. I interviewed him while he washed and cut my hair (my wife subsequently said it was a really good haircut). Anyway, out of that research came a map of some of the major suppliers and contract manufacturers in personal care products, things like hair care, skin care, and sun care products. While large companies like P&G and Unilever do a lot of their own manufacturing and sometimes outsource niche products, smaller players might outsource more to what this sector calls contract manufacturing organizations or CMOs. It certainly enabled a start-up like Living Proof to get to market much faster with less investment.

The result mirrors patterns seen in electronics and apparel: branding, marketing, and customer relationships remain with the brand owner, while production and much of the technical know-how reside with contract manufacturers that quietly sit behind hundreds of products consumers use every day.

Reducing Minimum Efficient Scale and Making It Easy to Private-Label

Contract manufacturers make it possible for many smaller companies to get started, or for stores to have their own house brands. In the food and beverage industry, they facilitate a proliferation of product varieties.

I once toured a "co-packer," as contract manufacturers in food and beverage are known. As I walked through the factory, they told me they manufactured 800 different products. I saw a major brand cola being bottled in various sized plastic bottles, sports drinks, energy drinks, coffee drinks, aseptic boxed juices, you name it. They probably covered a good percentage of the beverage aisle in a supermarket. Beverages are mostly water, so they are heavy and expensive to ship long distances, which is probably why there are so many beverage plants near major metropolitan areas. The other insight I gained from the visit was that packaging is a significant percentage of the overall cost of the beverage, especially when you are looking at things like sodas and energy drinks. So putting tariffs on aluminum for cans can be a big deal. But more on that in Chapter 10.

There are also significant differences in product manufacturing by sector. I was talking to someone from Haleon last year. Haleon is a company that was formed from the spin-off and merger of the consumer brand businesses of GlaxoSmithKline (GSK) and Pfizer. It produces well-known products like Advil, Panadol, Sensodyne, and Flonase. Of course, I had to ask where their products are made. He told me that their branded products for the U.S. market are primarily manufactured in the United States and Canada. The core ingredient of Advil, ibuprofen, comes from a BASF factory in Bishop, Texas, and I think he told me they formulated it in Pennsylvania. It's the store brands that come from India and China.

In 2012, I brought a class to visit Hyderabad, India. We visited several Indian pharmaceutical companies, who were all located there because of early public-sector investments in pharmaceutical research and development. We also visited Granules India, Ltd., in Jeedimetla, a suburb of Hyderabad. Granules had found a more efficient way to manufacture paracetamol, also known as acetaminophen, the main ingredient in Tylenol. When we visited, they were also making ibuprofen and guaifenesin; the latter is used in a lot of cold medications. As we toured the plant, we learned that they were producing *18 billion* tablets a year, with a lot of them going to U.S. and European markets. The factory was something else; I had never seen so many tablets in my life, streaming through chutes and getting packaged. It was like you were processing truckloads of cranberries, but these were little white tablets. They were primarily destined for store brands and bulk institutional customers. "I thought this stuff came from New Jersey," commented one of the students. Nope.

Supply Chain Service Organizations

Over the past three decades, contract manufacturers have evolved from simple providers of excess production capacity into coordinators of complex global supply networks. In industries such as electronics, apparel, and consumer goods, branded goods firms increasingly separated the design and marketing of products, and outsourced the production to contract manufacturers.

As Gereffi et al. explain in their global value chains framework, when product specifications can be clearly articulated and transmitted, governance shifts toward "modular" relationships in which specialized suppliers take on substantial responsibility for production and supply coordination (Gereffi et al. 2005). In electronics, firms such as Flex, Jabil, and Foxconn have moved beyond assembly into procurement, supplier management, logistics, and even design-for-manufacturability, effectively integrating multiple tiers of suppliers on behalf of their customers—the brands (Sturgeon 2002). This transformation marked a shift from manufacturing as a task to manufacturing as a system-level coordination function.

Leading contract manufacturers are no longer merely factories-for-hire. They operate as supply chain service organizations that coordinate procurement, production, quality, and logistics across geographically dispersed networks.

CHAPTER 6

Why So Much Labor-Intensive Assembly Work Is Done in China

What do Henry Ford and the Chinese Communist Party have to do with assembling iPhones in China? If you were actually *able* to disassemble an iPhone or for that matter any complicated piece of modern electronics, you would probably marvel at how so much stuff could be packed tightly in a tiny device with such beautiful fit and finish. Even the packaging is beautiful, with stickers neatly placed in precisely the right places on the box. Yet it probably came from a factory in China, and it was assembled by workers who had only a few days of training. How is this even possible?

One of the phenomena that helped China become the "workshop of the world" in the late 1990s and early 2000s was a uniquely efficient manufacturing system that was built around self-enclosed "factory cities" that incorporated not only factory buildings and the warehouses but also dormitories for the workers and better housing for the managers. There were also canteens to feed everybody, convenience stores, and medical clinics. They were a supremely efficient way to put anywhere from a few thousand to as many as several hundred thousand workers close to work without causing huge stress on the local housing market or unbearable traffic at commute time. This model enabled factory owners in coastal provinces like Guangdong, Jiangsu, and Zhejiang to recruit countless workers from rural inland provinces, young people who had minimal skills, to come assemble phones, kitchen appliances, computers, furniture, and a wide variety of other wares in factories that sprang up on the eastern seaboard.

To understand how this Chinese manufacturing model developed, we need to look at two questions.

- First, how do you design complex assembly processes so that regular people without special skills can perform the work?
- Second, how do you recruit, organize, and provide for the housing and living needs of those workers, when you might need tens or hundreds of thousands of them?

Designing the Assembly Process

Modern mass production relies on several key principles. Two of the most important are making parts to precise standards so that they can be used interchangeably, and the division of labor that comes with breaking down complex task sequences into a wide range of simpler but repeatable operations that lots of different workers can specialize in. You need interchangeable parts so that those workers won't have to do any custom fitting—the craft work that skilled artisans would otherwise perform. And you need the underlying precision to enable that interchangeability. The thinking on ensuring the underlying precision dates back to the time of the Revolutionary War in the United States.

Getting Away from Craft Assembly

As is often the case, great inventions arise from the needs of the military. French general Jean-Baptiste de Gribeauval is thought to have originated "le système Gribeauval" to make more precise artillery. Historically artillery had been used only to conduct long sieges because the cannon barrels were extremely heavy and hard to transport. The barrels of the cannons were cast out of molten metal in a mold with a core to form the bore that was removed after cooling. This produced a weapon that hurled a chunk of metal filled with explosives. Messy and definitely brute force, but it was effective. The cannons weren't very precise because the insides of the barrels had rough surfaces, but they worked because you were just trying to hurl a cannonball approximately in one direction.

Gribeauval came up with the idea of boring out the barrel after it was cast. This created a precise, straight, and smooth bore, which was then used with cannonballs that were standardized and perfectly spherical. The resulting lighter weight cannons were not only more accurate, but they also were mobile, enabling the French armies of Napoleonic times to dominate the military stage as they trod over European battlefields. This system of weapons using standardized parts became a huge advantage, at least until others copied it (Berkowitz et al. 2016).

French military thinking had great influence on the U.S. War Department during and after the American Revolution. Through the efforts of Frenchman Honoré Blanc, Americans learned of the benefits of uniformity of musket parts. Thomas Jefferson, who would later become the third American President in 1801, wrote to Henry Knox, the first American Secretary of War from Paris in 1789 about what Blanc showed him (Jefferson and Boyd 2018):

> *In a letter which I had the honour of writing to the Secretary for foreign affairs some three or four years ago, I informed him that a workman here had undertaken, by the help of moulds and other means to make all the parts of the musket so exactly alike as that, mixed together promiscuously, any one part should serve equally for every musket. He had then succeeded as to the lock both of the officer's fusil and the souldier's musket. From a promiscuous collection of parts, I put together myself half a dozen locks, taking the first peices which came to hand. He has now compleated the barrel, stock and mounting of the officers fusil, and is proceeding on those of the souldier's musket. This method of forming the firearm appears to me so advantageous, when repairs become necessary, that I have thought it my duty not only to mention to you the progress of this artist, but to purchase and send you half a dozen of his officers fusils. They are packed in a box marked TI.*

Though Knox did not reply to Jefferson, le système Gribeauval and the desire for uniformity and interchangeability of parts became ingrained thinking in the War Department (Hounshell 1984).

The American System of Manufactures: Interchangeable Parts and Division of Labor

Jefferson's lobbying set the stage for the Armory Bill of 1794, which established two sites "for the erecting and repairing of Arsenals and Magazines," one in Springfield, Massachusetts, and a second in Harpers Ferry, Virginia (Harpers Ferry National Historical Park n.d.).

At the armories, a desire for a more consistent way to produce weapons led to the introduction of several production innovations. Henry Morgan, who took charge of Springfield in 1802, introduced a division of labor to the process for making muskets. Rather than craftsmen who made the complete musket, he divided the work among barrelmakers and forgemen, filers, stockers and assemblers, and grinders and polishers. Combined with a move to eliminate the traditional apprenticeship system, this led to a decrease in output, leading to Morgan's dismissal in 1805. His successor tried to increase production by paying piece-rates to the workers, but that wasn't effective either (Hounshell 1984).

Nonetheless, as the War Department pushed to increase production of muskets, Springfield increased the division of labor from 20 different occupations in 1810 to 55 in 1816, and 100 by 1825. This was accompanied by the introduction of special machines for jobs like grinding and cutting that allowed "even boys and common hands" to produce parts without compromising accuracy (Smith 1973).

In concert with this increasing specialization, they introduced tools and equipment that made interchangeability possible. These included precision machine tools, gauging systems for enabling accurate and repeatable measurements, uniformly accepted standards of measurement, and advanced techniques for producing mechanical drawings. All of these were aimed at making parts that were perfectly reproducible across multiple units, but it took until 1844 before they could produce a conventional musket entirely from interchangeable parts (Ford 2005).

Armory practice and interchangeable parts spilled out of the armories into local industries, particularly across the Connecticut River Valley. The design and manufacture of sewing machines, the McCormick reaper, bicycles, and numerous other mechanical products benefited from the knowledge carried by the mechanics who worked at the armories. This system of manufacturing was described by an editor in the *Civil Engineer and Architect's Journal* in England as an "American system of manufactures" in 1851 (Hounshell 1984).

Historian Donald Hoke offers an alternative view suggesting that government funding wasn't quite as important in developing this American system. Looking at four industries—wooden clock movements, axes, typewriters, and watches—he argues that individual mechanics invented ingenious machinery and redesigned products so that they could be mass produced (Hoke 1990). But it took Frederick W. Taylor to codify and Henry Ford and his mechanics and engineers to pull it all together into what we now recognize as the modern system.

Frederick W. Taylor, Scientific Management, and the Division of Labor

Frederick Winslow Taylor was an American engineer and one of the first management consultants. He is best known as the father of scientific management, a systematic approach to improving industrial efficiency by studying work processes and optimizing them through measurement, analysis, and standardization.

In his 1911 book *The Principles of Scientific Management*, Taylor argued that productivity could be greatly increased by breaking down complex tasks into smaller, simpler motions, measuring the time it took workers to complete steps, and training them to perform each motion in the most efficient way possible (Taylor 1911). He believed management, not workers, should design and control work methods, replacing traditional "rule-of-thumb" approaches with science-based systems. His ideas shaped early modern management practices (Wrege and Greenwood 1991; Kanigel 1997), especially the thinking of people like Henry Ford.

Henry Ford's Simplification of Assembly Steps

When Henry Ford established the Ford Motor Company in 1903, it was his third try at building a successful car company. Ford believed he could sell a lot more cars if only he could offer them at a lower price. Writing to the editor of *Automobile*, he said, "[The] greatest need today is a light, low priced car with an up-to-date engine of ample horsepower, and built of the very best material . . . It must be powerful enough for American roads and capable of carrying its passengers anywhere that a horse-drawn vehicle will go without the driver being afraid of ruining his car" (Henry Ford to the Editor, Automobile 1906).

Ford introduced the Model N in 1906, and this was when he became convinced he had to use interchangeable parts. According to Max Wollering, who was the production superintendent of the Ford Manufacturing Company in 1906, "One of Mr. Fords strong points was interchangeability of parts . . . He realized as well as any manufacturer realized that in order to create great quantity of production, your interchange-ability must be fine and unique in order to accomplish the rapid assembly of units . . . There can't be much handwork or fitting if you are going to accomplish great things" (Ford Motor Company Archives 1955).

Ford's engineers were also inspired by the slaughterhouses they visited in Cincinnati and Chicago, who were running *disassembly lines* in which carcasses of cows hanging on meat hooks could be pushed from one worker to the next. Each worker was assigned to slice off a particular cut of meat, in a process that was much faster than having an individual butcher do all of the work (Chakrabarti 2013).

Ford engineers tried to do something similar with car production. This meant taking complex machining or assembly tasks and breaking them down into short sequences of simple steps that did not require special skills to perform. As they did in the armories decades prior, Wollering had his mechanics build fixtures, jigs, and measurement gauges, which he called "farmer tools" because he wanted young farm boys that they hired to be able to turn out work as good as a top tier mechanic. This was the real genius of Ford's manufacturing approach—the conversion of the majority of the jobs in the factory into routine tasks (Hounshell 1984).

Ford introduced the first moving assembly line at its Highland Park, Michigan, factory in 1913, a sliding line to assemble fly-wheel magnetos. Production engineers saw a large reduction in labor cost, so they began working on a moving assembly line for putting together the vehicle chassis. Four months later they began experimenting with a 600-foot-long moving assembly line made with rope and a windlass. Six assemblers traveled with the chassis as it was pulled past stationary component-supply stations. Assembly labor time was reduced from 12 hours and 28 minutes to 5 hours and 50 minutes, a greater than 50% savings. Continual refinement ultimately led to a labor reduction to 2 hours and 40 minutes, which meant lower costs that could be passed on to consumers in the form of lower prices (Abernathy and Wayne 1974).

The Model T was an enormous success, capturing 55% of the American market by 1921 and giving the company huge economies of scale. Ford's elimination of the need for skilled labor in production of complex products sparked a revolution.

The Next Big Innovation: Toyota and Lean Manufacturing

Toyota, the Japanese car maker, was behind the next big innovation in mass production. For them, it arose out of necessity in post-World War II Japan. Japanese automakers at the time had to produce small quantities of many varieties of models for a market that had low demand. How could they hope to compete with American manufacturers like Ford and General Motors?

Some of the core ideas of the Toyota Production System (TPS) came from a visit by Kiichiro Toyoda, the company's founder, to an American supermarket, where customers took the desired amount of items off the shelf and went to the cashier and purchased them. Taiichi Ohno, the inventor of TPS, translated this into the factory setting, where parts would be held at a "store shelf" and would be "pulled" or withdrawn by a production process in the quantity needed only when it was about to be used. The store shelf would be restocked by the work center that made it, matching precisely what was consumed. This came to be called the "just-in time" system (Ohno 1988).

Each link in a production chain is connected and synchronized, and the system uses a kanban (sign board) to indicate the amount needed.

The *takt time* is the required duration of these synchronized steps for the process to meet the pace of customer demand. One of the powerful aspects of just-in-time systems is that disruptions to the flow of materials become visible immediately.

While TPS was conceived and its implementation began in the post-war years, it didn't attract that much attention within Japanese industry until the 1973 Arab oil embargo when many firms were forced to cut their production. This led to a collapse in profits for many Japanese companies, but profits held up much better at Toyota, which put the company in the limelight, in Japan at least.

American car makers, and manufacturers more broadly, didn't really pay attention, or for that matter they really didn't understand TPS until much later. Meanwhile during the 1970s and early 1980s, imports of low-priced Japanese made cars took the United States by storm. From 1976 to 1980, the market share of Japanese cars in the United States went from 9.3% to 21.1%, as GM, Ford, and Chrysler each lost $1.5 billion before taxes and domestic dealers and parts plants closed in droves. Partly this was driven by the surge in oil prices that followed the revolution in Iran and the shift to smaller cars that had far better fuel economy (Secrest 1981). Partly, the Detroit automakers were in denial, hiding behind import quotas and not really changing much of how they operated.

Broad understanding of TPS came out of the International Motor Vehicle Program, a ground-breaking study launched by the Massachusetts Institute of Technology (MIT) in 1979. *The Machine That Changed The World*, a book that documented the study's findings, was really the first major English-language explanation of TPS as a coherent system that the authors framed as "lean production." It explained the technical ideas behind TPS in language that Western managers could understand, and it sparked a lean manufacturing revolution across multiple manufacturing sectors (Womack et al. 1990).

While it took more than a decade, by the early 2000s many manufacturers globally adopted at least some elements of lean production. While embracing all of the elements of TPS was still not that common in the United States, many of the tools and techniques were widely practiced, especially in China by the early 2000s.

The American System of Manufactures, Henry Ford and mass production, and the Toyota Production System established the modern practices for complex assembly processes that regular people without special skills could perform. That leads to the next big issue: how to efficiently mobilize large numbers of workers.

Recruiting and Organizing the Workforce

How the modern Chinese factory city organizes its workforce combines some of the features of the company towns that arose during the first industrial revolution in England, some features of the mill town of Lowell, Massachusetts, and the danwei (單位) work units of post-Communist Revolutionary China. The common thread was satisfying the demand for labor by bringing in people from the countryside and locating them close to work, providing housing where there might otherwise not be an adequate supply, and providing for their basic living needs while minimizing labor unrest. When you are making millions of devices like iPhones, that can mean *a lot* of people.

Factory Towns for English Textile Mills

At the start of the industrial revolution, textile work in England like the spinning of yarn and thread or the weaving of cloth had been done through a system of farming the work out to people who did it in their homes. Mechanization meant building factories for the big new machines because they would no longer fit in people's living spaces.

Some of the first factory towns were built adjacent to English textile mills, and by the middle of the eighteenth century, entrepreneurs building factories frequently also built adjacent villages. Sir Titus Salt, a textile manufacturer built the town of Saltaire, constructing 800 dwelling units with gardens located on wide streets with spacious squares and recreational grounds. Salt also built churches, a hospital, a community center, schools, and a park.

Other British companies like Cadbury built their "factory in a Garden" on the outskirts of Birmingham, and the Lever Brothers (a predecessor to the company Unilever) built their model industrial colony Port Sunlight in Cheshire with 720 old-English-style homes with gardens (de Gier 2016).

The "Mill Girls" of Lowell

The United States also had its share of factory towns. The first time I visited the Lowell National Historical Park to look at some of the first big textile mills just north of Boston, my reaction was, "Wow, this shares so many features with the modern Chinese factory city." The signage in the museum tells some of the stories about these "mill girls" who came in from the countryside, and how they saved money and gained a measure of economic independence. Just like China.

In 1814, Francis Cabot Lowell and two partners established the Boston Manufacturing Company and built their first textile mill in Waltham, Massachusetts alongside the Charles River. They used plans from Samuel Slater, an English textile worker, for water-powered looms to weave cloth. As the business prospered, they opened a second factory in what was then East Chelmsford on the banks of the Merrimack River, a town today known as Lowell (McCabe 2001).

The sparse population in the area led the mill owners to New England farms to recruit the daughters of farmers. Farming was a difficult life, and in addition to outdoor chores, women did the cooking, cleaning, and sewing of clothing. Factory jobs offered the promise of income that might not have been possible otherwise, along with a bit of freedom from the daily labors on the farms (Pershey 1990). By the early 1800s many farm families faced severe economic challenges, so the decision to leave for the factory was often born of necessity (The Mill Girls of Lowell—Lowell National Historical Park [U.S. National Park Service] n.d.).

Many of the young women were 13–22 years old, and initially hundreds and eventually thousands of workers needed housing, supplies, churches, banks, and all kinds of other services. The company built rows of boarding houses, which were leased out to older women who managed them, providing meals and laundry services. The companies assured the reluctant parents that the boarding houses would be carefully supervised with strict rules and carefully cultivated self-governance through social peer pressure (Pershey 1990).

Workdays in the mills started with bells ringing at 4:30 a.m., and after a quick breakfast workers were expected to be at their position in front of the power looms and spinning machines by 6:30 a.m. The work was repetitive and tedious and generally ran until 6:30 p.m. with a half hour off for lunch. Most young women came for a few years and then moved on (Pershey 1990). But this "company town" model got repeated across New England.

While the pictures and stories made me feel like Lowell must have contributed to the Chinese factory city model, there were big differences, at least initially between how the labor market was structured in the United States versus in China after the Communist revolution.

- In the United States, employment has generally been a voluntary contract between workers and employers, terminated at will by either side albeit with some protections for employees against things like discrimination on account of age, race, sex, etc.
- The Chinese system after the revolution had a much broader context of employment bundled with social services like healthcare, welfare, and the provision of housing along with political control (Naughton 1997).

But perhaps the history of places like Lowell helped Americans accept the Chinese model as they moved manufacturing offshore to China.

China's Danwei Model

After the Chinese Communist Party founded the People's Republic of China (PRC) in 1949, it nationalized private housing and organized most factories, schools, and government offices into work units all under a central planning system, with the *danwei* work unit as the basic building block (Schurmann 1966; Lü and Perry 1997; Man et al. 2011). It was a socialist factory town in miniature that combined factories and residences within one or several walled compounds. These provided guaranteed lifetime employment, housing, schools, healthcare, and welfare services, often referred to as the "iron rice bowl," all within close proximity.

Was the idea of this factory town in miniature inspired by those in England and the United States at the start of the industrial revolution? It's hard to say party leaders read up on the history of the industrial revolution, but the model was well known at the time, and it's easy to see them following the same logic of putting people close to the buildings that house the machines and the work.

Along with these benefits, the danwei also provided the party with political control, with a party branch monitoring both the work and the personal activities of residents. The party branch could make sure that the danwei was going in the right direction, aligned with its overall policy goals and directions. The party branch also ensured social cohesion and provided welfare benefits to employees. It organized holiday celebrations, arranged visits with sick employees, and provided assistance to families in need, building a sense of community tied to the party. The party offices also had a variety of rewards and sanctions that they could mete out to encourage or discourage acceptable behavior, which contributed to a high level of urban social order (Lü and Perry 1997).

Just inside the main gate of a typical *danwei* past a small courtyard would typically be the *zhulou* (主樓) or principal building that housed administrative offices for *danwei* officials. Other centrally placed buildings would house factories and workshops. Housing was usually in low-rise apartment blocks containing family housing units with shared toilets and kitchens, and there were more widely shared laundry units, canteens, medical clinics, schools, and recreational spaces (Al 2012). Residents paid heavily subsidized rents, which typically didn't cover maintenance costs let alone the cost of construction, so housing quality generally suffered from underinvestment (Man et al. 2011).

The danwei was a building block for urban China from the mid-1950s until the mid-1970s. It functioned not only as a workplace but also the principal organizing institution for most urban residents in China during this period, with nearly 95% of urban workers belonging to one kind or another by 1978 (Schurmann 1966).

Changes to the Danwei System with China's Opening and Industrial Reforms

Economic reforms beginning in 1978 brought a lot of changes. It also coincided with intense pressure on employment with large numbers of young people entering the job market. Older workers were encouraged to retire, which meant sharply increased spending on pension and other special provisions. The government allowed the danwei to retain more of the profits they generated, and this led to a boom in housing construction. More danwei set up stores within their grounds to provide employment for workers' children (Naughton 1997). Beginning in 1988 the Chinese government started privatizing urban public housing, and between 1993 and 1997 it encouraged the private sector to get into housing development.

By the 1990s, urban young people's aversion to careers in some sectors and the availability of peasants from the countryside pushed many danwei to recruit more rural young people from inland provinces to fill factory positions. This apparently was also influenced by the demand for workers from foreign firms establishing factories in China. But rather than treat these new crops of workers according to the socialist model as permanent labor, they would be more "disposable" and pliable (Solinger 1997), with companies flexing their workforces up and down as the demand for work fluctuated. The permanent jobs evolved to a contracted labor model, and social functions like hospitals and schools were divested.

Did Hong Kong and Taiwanese companies who moved into China's special economic zones as the country opened up in the 1990s follow the danwei model when they stood up their factories? It's hard to argue that they were trying to copy the *whole* thing, but it sure looks like they copied major pieces—like the residential units tightly packed around factory and warehouse buildings, the perimeter walls, medical clinics, and on campus dining. It was an efficient way to marshal a lot of workers who didn't have much of a commute to work—they could walk. Also, if you were going to hire young men and women from the countryside, it was an efficient way to make sure they got housed, and it would keep them out of the hair of the local populace. It certainly would not stress the local housing market, which was a big plus for local governments who were trying to grow their economies as quickly as possible.

Companies like Foxconn of Taiwan (whose official name is Hon Hai Precision Industries Company) built factory cities like its mega campus in the Longhua subdistrict of Shenzhen, where as many as 450,000 workers lived and worked within the boundaries. If you wanted to control that many people, the danwei model provided a lot of useful ideas, if not at least a template. As David Bray said in his book *Social Space and Governance in Urban*

China, "Forms and practices from the past are constantly redeployed and reinvented in the present" (Bray 2005). And the term *danwei* is still widely used today to refer to the work unit people are connected to, so there seems to be a pretty strong connection or heritage even though nobody talks about it this way.

The Modern Chinese Factory City

In the early 2000s if you wanted to have electronics or consumer products manufactured in China, an array of contract manufacturers around Shenzhen and Dongguan made it easy (Kroeber 2002). Many of these companies had come over from Taiwan, and they had all built their own danwei-like factory cities. They were always eager to sell their capabilities to western companies, so they made visiting their factories easy. Usually they would send a cross-border car to pick you up at your hotel in Hong Kong, and you would drive up to the China border, get out and go through border control while your driver took the car around to meet you on the other side. Or maybe they would pick you up at the ferry terminal in Shenzhen, which you could get to in an hour from Kowloon by high-speed passenger ferry. Then you would be whisked away, usually in a shiny black Mercedes, along the new expressways into one of the factory districts.

In those years, most of Dongguan was new or under construction factory districts, walled complexes several city blocks on a side, with an entrance gate and guard station. Driving in to the front-office building you might be greeted by banners welcoming you and your company by name, especially if you were considering buying something or signing any kind of partnership agreement.

I once flew into Hongqiao airport on the west side of Shanghai to visit a state-owned enterprise, and they gave me a police escort. That was a little embarrassing as they closed the taxiways and we shot across the tarmac in a minibus led by police motorcycles with sirens blaring and officers yelling on the public address system to get out of the way. As we turned onto the main roadways in the city, street cleaners dived into the bushes as we sped toward the factory. As we entered the gate, my name (in Chinese characters) emblazoned the welcome banners.

Buildings for Work and Home While these factory cities all looked different, they had the same general layout. Usually there was a cluster of buildings where the actual production took place, warehouses and truck docks for incoming materials and outgoing finished products, dormitories, and canteens. Many manufacturers prided themselves on offering separate factory floors, which they offered to dedicate to your production, screened from prying eyes to protect confidentiality of the brand who they manufactured for.

But the reality was they were pretty transparent about who they were making things for. After all, it was a badge of honor to manufacture for well-known premium Japanese and American brands, with the not-so-subtle implication that if it was good enough for those companies, it should be good enough for you. Visiting a lot of factories in those days, which was common when you were shopping for a supplier, was a great way to find out who was making what for who. Although if you were manufacturing for Apple, widely referred to as "the fruit company" (or 苹果—Píngguǒ) and rarely if ever by its real name, these manufacturers were very protective, and this got worse over time as occasional leaks occurred. They wouldn't show you anything because they faced severe sanctions—huge fines or termination of contracts—if Apple ever found out. But they would let you know by how much they couldn't tell you, with a nod and a wink.

There were dormitories for the workers, usually multistory concrete structures, where standard accommodations in a room might include four triple-bunk beds, a shared bathroom or a community one down the hall, and a balcony where the residents could hang their laundry. In the early 2000s 12 workers per room was quite common, and the rooms did not provide much space for much beyond changing clothes and sleeping. I sometimes got to see what were then considered to be "better" dormitories. I recall one older woman holding a key ring with perhaps 500 room keys, offering to show me any room of my choice. She had multiple key rings, well actually let's call them hoops.

Managers also had dormitories in separate buildings. These might have fewer stories, or they might have more of the feel of clustered residences. In those days, managers also left their families at home, whether it was Taiwan, Japan, Hong Kong, or the West. When the workers went home over the traditional Lunar New Year break, the managers did as well. I remember countless managers telling me they only went home to their families in Taiwan or Japan once a year. Some even had "second families" in China, though people didn't talk about that practice very much.

Workers took their meals at canteens. Depending on the company, the food on offer ranged from pretty basic to better but still standardized fare. Usually they had soup and a stir-fried meat dish, vegetables, and of course rice. Canteens were generally centralized and closer to the factory buildings than the dormitories so that they were convenient for lunch. Meals were subsidized, so workers often used a meal card to facilitate payment. Better campuses would let you see their kitchens, and I walked through quite a lot of them. Others never offered.

Typically some kind of sports or recreational facilities like a soccer field or basketball court might also be available, along with a medical clinic, a post office, and a bank or ATM machines. There might also be restaurants on site, but generally these were right outside the walls or just off campus.

Size, Safety, and Shifts A typical factory city might have 15,000 people working and living within its walls though it was not uncommon to see 50,000 or more at a single site. Foxconn tended to operate megasites like Longhu Science & Technology Park in Shenzhen, or what became known as "iPhone City" in Zhengzhou, Henan Province. The former had a peak employment of more than 400,000 workers. I have visited many with a size around 50,000–100,000 workers; 15,000 workers is about the size you need to assemble 100,000 smartphones a day.

The factories themselves that I saw in those days spanned a range from clean and bright high-tech assembly to dark and scary—from the point of view of someone who had been trained to Western safety standards. In one factory I remember a young worker wearing flip-flops working on top of a hot aluminum die casting machine pulling cast metal trees of helical scan videocassette recorder heads out, flipping them to young women who quickly chucked them into lathes to turn them down to final dimensions. On the same trip we saw office laser printers for a major American brand moving down a clean, air-conditioned, and well-lit assembly line.

Security was tight at many factories, especially ones who made phones, computers, and high-value products or ones that had expensive components. Workers had dressing rooms equipped with lockers where they had to leave jewelry and personal phones locked up as they changed into anti-static uniforms. They usually had to walk through a metal detector or be screened by a guard with a wand.

Electronics assembly factory floors were generally organized with production in the center and engineering support around the periphery, along with stockrooms for components, and a shipping department at one end. Taiwanese and Chinese run factories tended to have workers sitting (see Figure 6.1) while Japanese-run factories tended to have workers stand (see Figure 6.2). Restrooms were on the side, and sometimes guards were posted outside the restrooms if the factories used a lot of valuable components. Early on, there was a lot of theft out of factories and these components often made their way onto the black market; I'm not sure how they got out. Expensive components like microprocessors or memory modules were often under lock and key and were issued from locked cages as they were used in assembly steps.

FIGURE 6.1 Taiwanese-run factory in Dongguan, China, circa 2000. *Source:* Willy Shih.

FIGURE 6.2 Japanese-run factory in Dongguan, China, circa 2000. *Source:* Willy Shih.

FIGURE 6.3 Western-run factory in Guangdong Province, China circa 2008.
Source: Willy Shih.

Many factories worked two shifts. The day shift at one that we spent a lot of time at started around 7:30 a.m. and ran until close to 5 p.m., and the evening shift started around 7 p.m. and ran until the early morning hours. Day shifts tended to be more intense with a lot of engineers setting up machines for new product introductions or running around fixing things. Night shifts had a very different vibe; much more relaxed. Workers were often rotated between the shifts, switching every few weeks. Some campuses run by Western firms were quite pleasant (see Figure 6.3).

Workforce Recruitment, Scheduling, and Living Conditions

Workers were recruited from inland provinces, places like Shaanxi, Sichuan, Hubei, Anhui, and Jiangxi among others. Sometimes companies relied on contract employment agencies who would travel to those provinces and visit high schools, looking for graduates. In the late 1990s and early 2000s, this was followed by long bus trips to the coastal factories. Factories also held job fairs to poach workers from other local companies, or if another factory had a temporary surplus of labor or was laying workers off.

I remember visiting a job fair where floor managers from the factory sat behind tables under tents and quizzed prospective workers lined up in front of them (see Figure 6.4). I knew just enough Chinese to understand what was going on during the questioning. I didn't get too close because if I seemed to pay too close attention, the rejection rate of candidates went up. Maybe they thought I was an auditor of some sort.

FIGURE 6.4 Job fair interviews, Guangdong Province, China, circa 2008.
Source: Willy Shih.

One of the significant advantages of this danwei-like workforce organization is if you needed to contend with a sudden surge of product demand, it was relatively easy. Apple famously needs millions of extra products on hand when they do iPhone launches. The way a factory manages this is by scheduling overtime. Or sometimes if you have a manufacturing problem and you need to do re-work (a nice name for collecting all the units that fail quality control inspection and repairing them), you can schedule overtime as well. People who rush to buy new iPhones the first weekend they are available probably don't appreciate the effects all the way back at the factory where excessive overtime and more night shifts become the norm (The Straits Times 2025).

As China's workforce has aged and there is less interest in working in factories, living conditions at the factories have generally improved. I brought a class to visit a furniture factory in Shenzhen just days before the COVID-19 pandemic hit. The company made leather recliners, and the scale of production was breathtaking. It was a microcosm of globalization.

In their inbound materials warehouse, we saw a half million cowhides imported from the United States and Italy, lumber imported from Argentina, and urethane monomer for making polyurethane foam imported from the Netherlands (see Figures 6.5 and 6.6). They stuffed finished products into 40-foot containers, 150 or more containers a day, and sent them off to the nearby Yantian (Shenzhen) port. The dormitory buildings looked

FIGURE 6.5 In-bound materials warehouse at furniture factory, Guangdong Province, China, circa 2020. *Source:* Willy Shih.

FIGURE 6.6 Assembling leather recliners, Guangdong Province, China, circa 2020. *Source:* Willy Shih.

nice, with only four workers per room, and managers had their own private apartments. There was also a beautiful showroom where customers from all over the world could look at the variety of offerings available for sale. The company had become one of the dominant suppliers of this style of furniture globally.

Chinese Communist Party Offices One of the interesting features of many Chinese factories is that they sometimes have an office of the Chinese Communist Party inside. I first saw these when visiting state-owned enterprises (SOEs), and that seemed entirely logical. In an SOE, the branch secretary is often a key figure who in principle can influence major decisions on hiring, promotions, budgets, and strategic direction. But over the years I saw more and more of them in private companies as well.

Western observers tend to associate all of this with "a new model of corporate governance" implying that the party gets a voice in corporate decision-making (Livingston 2025), although I'm not so sure. It's easy to misunderstand because comparisons between China and the West aren't always straightforward. For example, while there are labor unions in China, their role is oriented toward providing welfare for employees and organizing leisure activities to enrich workers' lives, compared to a collective action role focused on negotiating wages, benefits, and working conditions in the United States. So in China the party office might be viewed quite differently than from the U.S. vantage point. It could be just a throwback to the danwei model. As Barry Naughton has argued, the pace of dismantling the danwei system was hindered by ambivalence about giving up political control, revealing Chinese leaders' anxiety about a more open and fluid society (Naughton 1997).

Unique Advantages of the Chinese Factory City Model

The modern Chinese factory city model has given manufacturers who use it a significant competitive advantage. It's a great way to mobilize a large workforce when you need to build a surge of products for the next iPhone launch or for the holiday season. It has also been described as a system that provides continuous access to fresh labor reserves from the countryside and one that inhibits any kind of collective action like unionization among workers because of its very transitory nature (Smith and Pun 2006).

Sometimes called the "dormitory labor regime" by academic researchers, some say the Chinese model is far more competitive than systems found in other countries because labor costs are low, worker productivity is high, and there is no long-term build-up of labor institutions that would lead to pressure for better working conditions or labor solidarity (Ngai and Smith 2007). It's not a model that transplants easily to countries like India or Vietnam where there is more dependence on local rental markets to provide housing (Pham and Nguyen 2023).

Maybe that's why many people who have built or used factories in China will tell you that the country will remain a manufacturing powerhouse for the foreseeable future regardless of the geopolitical forces buffeting it today. And that's why so many smartphones, computers, clothing, home appliances, toys, car parts, industrial parts, and for that matter so many of the products that you find in a Walmart or Home Depot still come from China.

CHAPTER 7

How Industrial Clusters Can Play a Big Role in Global Supply Chains

Somewhere in your refrigerator or pantry right now, there is probably something that can trace its roots to Denmark. Not a product with a Danish flag on the label, but rather an ingredient so fundamental to what you're eating that nobody bothered to mention it. The cultures in your yogurt. The enzyme that set your cheese. The yeast that made your beer. Or maybe the insulin in your medicine cabinet or the active ingredient in that Ozempic pen. Even the enzymes in your laundry detergent that get rid of those food stains have a good chance of tracing their origins to a cluster of companies operating within a few hours' radius of Copenhagen.

How does a country of six million people, less than the New York metro area, come to quietly dominate so many unrelated industries at once? The answer is that they aren't unrelated at all. They are connected by a single underlying technology: fermentation, a technology that uses microorganisms to make useful products. And the story of how that technology took root in Denmark, and kept branching into new industries decade after decade, is one of the most instructive examples of how industrial clusters actually form. Not through top-down planning, but through an accumulation of knowledge, talent, and happy accidents that compound over time.

Industrial clusters are one of the most powerful and least understood forces in economic geography. Once a critical mass of related expertise concentrates in one place, it tends to stay and grow. Skilled workers attract companies, companies attract more workers, and knowledge leaks across organizational boundaries in ways that formal research and development budgets can't replicate. A breakthrough at one company becomes common knowledge at another when an engineer changes jobs; a production problem solved at a brewery quietly shapes how a pharmaceutical plant is designed a century later. This compounding of know-how is why certain places—Silicon Valley for software, northern Italy for luxury goods, China for battery manufacturing—can convey powerful advantages to companies located there. Denmark's fermentation cluster is a masterclass in how it happens. And to understand where it started, you have to go back a very long time.

13,000 Years in the Making

Thirteen thousand years ago, in a cave near Mount Carmel in present-day Israel, a group of people called the Natufians were making beer. Archaeologists believe that humans' thirst for beer and other early products that resulted from fermentation provided the impetus to domesticate cereal crops (Braidwood et al. 1953). Between 2004 and 2011, archaeologist Li Liu led a team that collected plant residues from a well-preserved bowl-like stone mortar, presumably used to grind grains or food materials in the Raqefet Cave near Mount Carmel. They concluded that the Natufians who lived there collected locally available plants, stored malted seeds, and made beer as a part of their mortuary rituals (Liu et al. 2018). That was 13,000 years ago.

The ancient process for making beer started with malting—soaking grains like barley, wheat, or millet until they began to germinate. The malted grains were then crushed, which released natural enzymes that broke down the starch into fermentable sugars, ones that microorganisms could break down into smaller molecules like alcohol. In the next step, the malted grain was mixed with water to form a porridge-like mash that was heated by hot stones or sun-warmed vessels. This released sugars into the liquid, after which natural or wild yeasts from the air or on the grain itself converted the sugars into alcohol and carbon dioxide.

For thousands of years, beer brewers relied on spontaneous fermentation, harnessing naturally occurring yeasts that floated around in the air. But simply relying on nature often produced mixed results because slight changes in the number and types of microbes in the air could have dramatic effects on both the efficiency of brewing and, more problematically, could change the product quality and taste. Brewers eventually realized that if they inoculated a new batch they were just starting with a small portion of a successful batch that they had just finished, they could produce a faster and more reliable product (Whittington et al. 2019). This process, which became known as "backslopping," is the same thing we do when we use a starter culture to make sourdough bread, sauerkraut, or kefir (Kim et al. 2018).

Though more than 2,000 different species of yeasts have been described, it is estimated that we know only about 1% of them. They are found in the soil, in plants, and in the air. Yeasts belonging to the genus of fungi *Saccharomyces* tend to naturally take over the later stages of beer fermentation because they are good at both producing alcohol and tolerating higher concentrations of it as they make it. They also produce desirable flavors (Steensels and Verstrepen 2014). Constant backslopping and reduced exposure to wild yeasts led to a *de facto* domestication of brewers' yeasts, which meant less variety of species ultimately used in the brewing process. This narrowing was also encouraged by a shift that occurred in the Middle Ages in Europe when taverns and monasteries became the favored sites for brewing. The German "Reinheitsgebot" or purity laws from the fifteenth and sixteenth centuries limited the ingredients that could be used in making beer, which further reduced which species were used (Hanisch 2023; Eble and de Vries 2018).

Unknowingly at the time, brewers who made beer during the winter months ended up harnessing a different species, *Saccharomyces pastorianus*, which likes cooler temperatures and ferments at the bottom of a vat. This yielded beers with a cleaner, crisper taste, and these beers became known as lagers. Batches fermented in warmer months employed top-fermenting yeast strains like *Saccharomyces cerevisiae*, producing a wider range of flavors in what became known as ales (Anderson 2012; Unger 2004). But the brewers didn't really understand at the time that they were harnessing different strains. That had to wait until the nineteenth century.

Understanding the scientific basis of brewing took a big step forward when Louis Pasteur, the French chemist and microbiologist, began studying fermentation when one of his students, a local winemaker, sought his advice. Pasteur demonstrated that the conversion of malt sugar into alcohol and carbonic acid was due to the activity of a microbe, which was the yeast that was being used by brewers (Pasteur 1857). Over time, Pasteur's work had a broad impact on many food production processes, especially beer.

Better Beer Through Science

J.C. Jacobsen founded the Carlsberg brewery in 1847 in Copenhagen, Denmark. His father, Chresten Jacobsen, was a brewer as well, and an admirer of the great Danish chemist and physicist Hans Christian Ørsted, who was famous for discovering that electric currents create magnetic fields. Ørsted was the founder of the Polytechnical College, which became the Technical University of Denmark, whose purpose was to create scientific and technical competence outside of the traditional university system (Kragh 2015). Ørsted was well-known in Danish society at the time, and he constantly talked about the importance of the natural sciences to the progress and development of industry.

Chresten Jacobsen, J.C.'s father, wanted his son to pursue the natural sciences (Tamm 2020). J.C. recognized that Danish beer was a poor-quality comparison to imported German beer, and he began to experiment with methods used in Bavaria at the time. After a visit to the Zum Spaten brewery in Munich in 1845, he began making Bavarian-style lagers back in Copenhagen using bottom-fermenting yeast (Tamm 2020). Later when he founded the Carlsberg brewery, he copied Bavarian methods and styles. He also secretly attended lectures by Ørsted, where he began to realize that while brewing better beer was considered an art, it had to be based on scientific principles (Home of Carlsberg 2025).

Giving Away the Secrets of Great Beer

In 1875, J.C. converted a storage building at the brewery into the first Carlsberg Laboratory, and in 1876, he established the Carlsberg Foundation as a gift to Danish science and heir to his brewery (see Figure 7.1). The foundation's charter articulated two purposes—to continue and expand the work of the Carlsberg Laboratory in subjects important to beer production and to support basic research in the natural sciences, mathematics, and the humanities.

FIGURE 7.1 The Carlsberg Research Laboratory with a statue of its founder J.C. Jacobsen in the foreground, August 2005. *Source*: user:Stork / Wikimedia Commons / Public Domain / **https://commons.wikimedia.org/wiki/File:Carlsberg_Laboratory.jpg**

Developing as complete a scientific basis as possible for malting, brewing, and fermentation was a top priority. Importantly, the foundation's charter stipulated that all of the lab's activities should be shared publicly and that no result that was of theoretical or practical importance should be kept secret. Initially the lab had two sections, devoted respectively to chemical and physiological problems associated with the brewing process (Walsh 1972).

Meanwhile in Paris in 1876, Louis Pasteur published his study of beer production, *Études sur la Bière*. In it he claimed to have solved the problem of how to produce beer consistently, regardless of season or location, without the expensive cooling methods that brewers of the time depended on. Pasteur identified numerous impurities in the production yeasts used to make beer, including bacteria, molds, and wild yeasts, and developed a simple heat treatment to eliminate them (Pasteur 1879). This process became known as pasteurization and brought about a revolution in food production because it destroyed or deactivated microorganisms and enzymes that contributed to spoilage, extending the shelf life of processed foods.

Emil Christian Hansen became one of the first directors of the Carlsberg Research Lab in 1877. Building on the work of Pasteur, he hypothesized that not only did production yeasts contain impurities, but also that there were many different yeast strains in the mix, with only a few actually contributing to the results brewers wanted. He took a sample from the Carlsberg production line, and by counting how many cells were in a milliliter (one cubic centimeter of volume), he could calculate how many times he would have to dilute it to get down to one yeast cell in a milliliter. He then inoculated these diluted suspensions into sterile test tubes containing beer wort (the liquid extracted from the mashing process) or onto gelatin plates (Hansen 1902). He believed correctly that with enough dilutions he eventually could get to yeast colonies that sprang from a single cell (Riis 2012).

Hansen propagated these individual strains into larger pure cultures. He was then able to show that certain species of yeasts caused beer ropiness (becoming thick and viscous) and others produced off flavors. He then produced a pure culture of bottom-fermenting yeast and named it Carlsberg Yeast No. 1. This strain was duly named *Saccharomyces carlsbergensis* (today known as *Saccharomyces uvarum*). Carlsberg introduced it into production in late 1882, and by 1884 all of Carlsberg's production used this pure strain (Casey 2020).

J.C. Jacobsen chose not to patent Carlsberg Yeast No. 1. Instead, he distributed pure cultures freely to brewers around the world. All they had to do was ask, and the lab would send them along with detailed instructions on how to use them. Carlsberg's introduction of single-strain cultures, yeast propagation methods, and rigorous fermentation protocols triggered a revolution in brewing, with much more consistent fermentations and greatly reduced spoilage and off-flavors. Within five years, most European breweries had adopted Carlsberg Yeast No. 1, and American brewers Pabst, Schlitz, and Anheuser-Busch soon all switched over to using pure yeast strains (Ebling 2025).

Hansen and people at the brewery also designed and produced equipment for propagating yeast strains under controlled conditions. This equipment was used in industry for the next century and paved the way for large-scale beer production globally (Høiby 2024). Carlsberg Group is among the top five global brewers today, but even if your beer wasn't brewed by them, there is a good chance it was made with a yeast descended from one first isolated at the Carlsberg Lab in Denmark, or at a minimum used the methods for brewing first developed there.

The Carlsberg Lab Worked on More than Beer

While J.C. Jacobsen assumed his scientists would work primarily on beer, he also allowed them to work on a "second direction," which encouraged them to broaden their research. S. P. R. Sørensen, who took over the chemical section in 1901, gained international renown for establishing the first really accurate way of measuring pH, a measure of the acidity or alkalinity of a substance. He moved the lab into the study of protein chemistry, which attracted an increasing flow of visiting scientists. A wide variety of methods and discoveries came out of the lab, as it became a global center for the study of protein chemistry (Walsh 1972). Predictably, the Carlsberg Lab trained scientists went on to work at other Danish companies, bringing with them know-how and skills.

The Carlsberg Lab helped set foundational practices in industrial microbiology and fermentation methods for sectors beyond brewing. Such capabilities would come to play an important role in the growth of other firms in the Copenhagen area in areas like food ingredients, industrial enzymes, and pharmaceuticals.

Standardizing Cheesemaking

Cheese is another food that is made using fermentation, and like beer, it has been made for a long time. It is basically concentrated milk proteins and fats along with other nutrients and substances that give it flavor and aroma.

An Ancient Accident

Evidence of dairy products made from cow and sheep milk was found in the tomb of Ptahmes, the mayor of Memphis under Pharaohs Sethi I and Ramses II (1290–1213 BCE), and was discovered in 1885. Archaeologists working on the other side of the Mediterranean in Croatia found dairy residues in distinctive pottery from as early as 5700 BCE that tested for fermented milk fats such as cheese. These researchers speculated that turning milk into cheese made it a better food for child nutrition, reducing the lactose content to which many people were intolerant and making the vital nutrient calcium available to infants during an important stage of growth (Gross 2018).

Some historians believe that cheesemaking was discovered by accident. They speculate that nomads traveling on hot days carried milk in bags made from the stomachs of ruminant animals, most likely camels. Ruminants graze on grasses and other plants and extract their nutrients from them by fermenting what they eat in specialized stomachs. The milk in the bags probably clotted because of rising acidity thanks to microbes that ferment some of the milk sugars (lactose) as well to a clotting enzyme, chymosin, that originated from the stomachs from which the bags were made (Harboe et al. 2010). The name for this enzyme came from the Greek word for gastric liquid "chyme" from the fourth stomach (the abomasum) of the calf. A soft coagulum formed in the bag, and some of the liquid phase (the whey) was probably absorbed into the skin or seeped out through the walls of the bag and was lost by evaporation (Tamime 1993).

Curd, Whey, and Everything in Between

Cheese is essentially concentrated milk protein. Milk contains two kinds: caseins, which digest slowly and clump together under acidic conditions, and whey proteins, which digest quickly and stay liquid. Cheese is what you get when you coax the caseins into a gel, trap fat inside it for richness, and squeeze out most of the water (Fox et al. 2015). The firmer the cheese, the more water has been removed. Cheddar's dense, linked proteins hold very little moisture, while brie retains more water and fat, which is what makes it soft and creamy.

Getting there requires two basic steps: first clotting the milk to form a gel and then cutting and draining it to form a curd. How the curd is handled after that—salted, pressed, molded, aged—determines what kind of cheese you end up with. For most cheeses, clotting is triggered by enzymes originally derived from calf stomachs. For softer fresh cheeses like cottage cheese, adding acid does the job instead (Guinee and O'Brien 2010).

For centuries, cheesemakers used a mix of enzymes derived from calf stomachs that was called rennet. The stomachs were dried and cut into pieces, bringing with them dirt and contaminating microorganism leading to widely varying quality, similar to what happened with early beer. On top of that, traditional cheesemaking also suffered from poor-quality milk.

The Pharmacist Who Standardized Cheese

In 1870, the Danish pharmacist Christian D.A. Hansen (not related to Carlsberg's Emil Christian Hansen) developed a method for extracting pure and standardized rennet enzymes from calf stomachs. In 1874, the company he established, Chr. Hansen, set up its first rennet production plant in Copenhagen. The products were an overnight success, with first shipments to Sweden, Switzerland, and Germany that same year, and exports to England starting in 1875 and the United States as early as 1876. The company set up production on West 16th Street in New York City in 1878. Years later in 1929 it expanded to Milwaukee (New York State Cheese Manufacturers Association 2020). Chr. Hansen's rennet was the first enzyme to be industrially produced anywhere in the world (Harboe et al. 2010).

Chr. Hansen's standardized rennet cultures gave cheese makers much better control of their production. When dairies started to pasteurize their milk, this caused a major challenge because it killed the naturally occurring microorganisms that fermented the milk sugars. So Chr. Hansen expanded into producing standardized lactic acid bacteria cultures for cheesemaking as well. Cheese producers could then purchase vials of cheese starter and grow them to the volumes they needed. This gave them much more consistent production, and they could even start producing cheeses on a regular schedule (Johnson 2017).

As meat producers allowed more calves to grow to maturity, increasing shortages of calf-derived rennet caused the company to develop microbial coagulants that could act as substitutes. *Rhizomucor miehei* is a fungus that produces mucorpepsin, a milk-clotting enzyme, and again this meant the enzyme could be produced via fermentation. The company started introducing microbial coagulants for cheesemaking in the 1960s, which allowed makers to label their products as organic, vegetarian, halal, and kosher. These alternatives to calf rennet produced lower yields, but over the years the company kept improving them (USDA Agricultural Marketing Service 2021).

Chr. Hansen expanded into other food ingredients, starting with natural colorings for butter and cheese. They also moved into yogurt, another milk product that had been produced since ancient times.

Ferment and Live Longer

Yogurt is the product of the symbiotic growth of naturally occurring *Streptococcus thermophilus* and *Lactobacillus bulgaricus*, two bacteria that ferment the lactose in milk. The *S. thermophilus* grows faster, and some of the chemicals it releases encourage the *L. bulgaricus* to grow (Weerathilake et al. 2014).

Pasteurization of milk had the same impact on yogurt-making that it did on cheese; it eliminated these species along with other contaminant bacteria. Recognizing the same need as in cheesemaking, Chr. Hansen launched its first yogurt cultures in 1893.

While yogurt is one of the most popular fermented milk products in the world today, when companies first started making it industrially, it had limited popularity in Europe and North America, probably because of its acidic taste. Then in 1907, Élie Metchnikoff at the Pasteur Institute published a book, *The Prolongation of Life*, in which he attributed the longevity of hill tribesmen of Bulgaria to their lifelong consumption of yogurt and the beneficial effects of lactic acid fermentation in their digestive tracts. This inspired widespread interest in yogurt's nutritional benefits, which continues to this day with the links to the gut microbiome and its impact on human health (Metchnikoff 2004). Yogurt producers also started adding sugar and fruit flavorings, which (no surprise here) dramatically expanded sales (Bintsis and Papademas 2022).

For decades, manufacturers of yogurts bought starter cultures from sources like Chr. Hansen. They couldn't inoculate them directly into their batch production because the resulting culture concentration would be too low to grow efficiently. Instead, they had to scale up by first propagating the initial culture into a "bulk starter" at their own facilities. This involved inoculating the starter into a series of progressively larger growth vessels and mediums. Then they took the large starter culture and mixed it into the production batch.

In 1978, Chr. Hansen patented a process for producing highly concentrated and purified lactic acid-producing bacteria that could be directly inoculated into batches of yogurt without having to go through these bulk starter culture steps (Porubcan and Sellers 1978). Its Direct-Vat-Set (DVS) culture system, in which it supplied freeze-dried, blended, and concentrated strains of lactic acid bacteria, made the company one of the dominant suppliers globally of yogurt cultures and a huge part of the company's business.

A few years ago, I visited Chr. Hansen's cold storage distribution center outside Copenhagen. Imagine a gigantic warehouse operating at −70°C, with boxes and pallets stacked on shelves to the ceiling. Workers were wearing polar suits that were more in keeping with Antarctica in the winter, with thick boots and special protective gear. I saw somewhere that the warehouse is so cold that they have to heat the floor so that you don't develop permafrost underneath it. The company operates others like it in New Berlin, in Wisconsin, and at its other main production sites in Germany and France.

What is amazing is that between microbial products like probiotic cultures, nutraceuticals, and cheeses, the company claims to be an ingredient in foods consumed by more than a billion and a half people globally every day. And those ingredients all pass through production and distribution centers like these.

Enzymes, Insulin, and Laundry Detergent

In 1922, August Krogh, a University of Copenhagen professor who had just won the Nobel Prize in physiology, traveled to the United States with his wife, Marie, for a lecture tour. Marie was a physician with type 2 diabetes, and while they were there, the couple heard about a remarkable new treatment: insulin, just extracted and patented by two Canadian researchers the year before. The Kroghs obtained permission to produce it in Scandinavia, and in 1923, together with a local pharmacist, they founded Nordisk Insulinlaboratorium in Copenhagen (Blake 2013).

Nordisk extracted insulin from the pancreases of slaughtered cattle and pigs. The bovine (cow) pancreatic insulin differed from the human form by three amino acids in its chain, and the porcine (pig) version only differed by one amino acid, so it was less likely to provoke an immune response and was therefore preferable (Alberts et al. 2022).

To build out the production process, the company hired an engineer named Harald Petersen and his brother Thorvald to handle the chemistry. The brothers were good at their jobs—perhaps too good. They soon developed an improved liquid insulin process of their own, which they offered to Nordisk. When the company passed, the brothers went off and founded a competitor, Novo Therapeutisk Laboratorium, in 1925 (Blake 2013). The two companies would spend the next six decades competing fiercely before finally merging in 1989 to form Novo Nordisk.

But here is where the story takes its first unexpected turn. Extracting insulin from pig pancreases left behind a useful byproduct: the enzyme trypsin, which cuts protein molecules into smaller chains. Rather than discard it, Novo found a buyer—leather manufacturers, who discovered that trypsin softened hides without damaging the underlying collagen (Sorenson 1999). The company also started recovering amylase from the same process and selling it to textile makers for removing starch from fabrics. So here we have a pharmaceutical company that stumbled into the industrial enzyme business through its waste stream.

Then the war intervened. When Germany occupied Denmark in 1940, animal feed grew scarce, and with it the supply of pig pancreases. Novo couldn't make enough trypsin or amylase the old way. A fermentation specialist at the company named Bruno Steinhardt proposed an alternative: what if bacteria could be engineered to produce enzymes directly, without any animals involved? By the late 1940s he had succeeded, and in 1952 Novo put its first fermentation-produced amylase on the market (Laursen 1996). The wartime constraint had forced a technological leap that would define the company for the next half century.

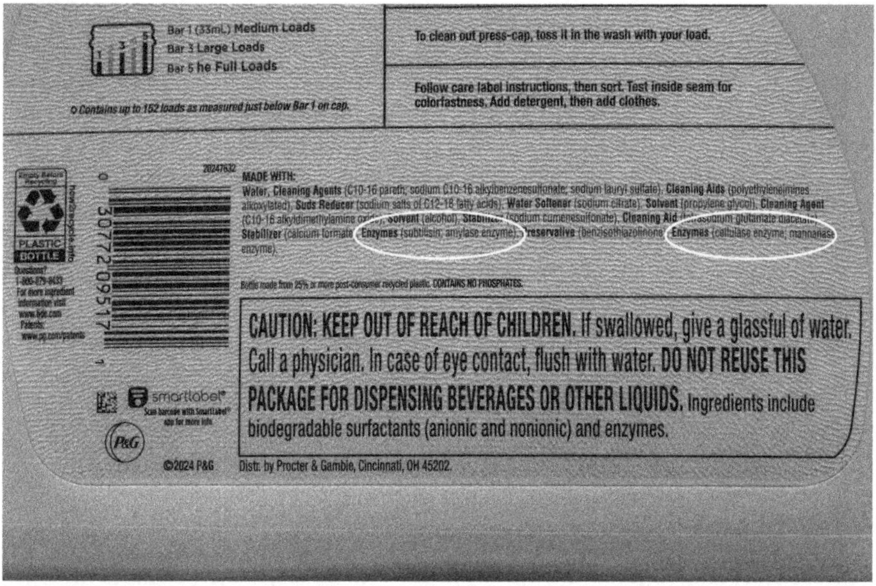

FIGURE 7.2 Ingredient label on a package of ultraconcentrated Tide Free & Gentle laundry detergent. Note the four different enzymes! *Source*: Willy Shih.

The market for industrial enzymes really took off with Novo's introduction of Alcalase, produced by the bacterium *Bacillus licheniformis*. With this it pioneered the use of enzymes in laundry detergent to attack protein stains and boost washing performance. Procter and Gamble, Unilever, Colgate-Palmolive, and Henkel all started looking at incorporating enzymes into their laundry products in 1965 (Laursen 1996). This is one of the major reasons laundry detergents have gotten more compact with better washing performance using colder waters. There's actually less detergent and more enzymes (see Figure 7.2)! In subsequent years, Novo introduced a succession of enzymes for applications like the stone-washing of denim, for bleaching dyes, for preparing cotton fabrics for dying, and for other kinds of stain removal.

When I visited Novozymes' development labs—the enzyme business was spun out from Novo Nordisk in 2000—researchers were working on enzymes capable of breaking down corn cobs and stalks into ethanol for fuel (Shih and Chai 2013). The descendants of a Copenhagen brewery's research lab were now engineering molecules that don't exist in nature. In 2023, Novozymes merged with Chr. Hansen, the cheese and yogurt culture company from earlier in this chapter, to form Novonesis, bringing two of the cluster's oldest branches back under one roof.

Novo wasn't the only Danish company building a fermentation-based empire. Danisco had grown from a Danish sugar company into one of the world's largest food ingredient businesses through a series of mergers, eventually acquiring Genencor, a pioneer in industrial biotechnology, in 2005. At that point, Danisco and Novozymes together controlled 63% of the global market for industrial enzymes, meaning that nearly two-thirds of the world's enzyme supply was flowing out of a small country best known for Vikings and LEGO bricks. DuPont acquired Danisco in 2011, folding it into its nutrition and biosciences operations (Reisch 2011). Ongoing research led to (among other things) its introduction of enzymes that reduced stickiness in pasta after cooking, preventing overcooking and improving its shape (Food Ingredients Online 2019).

Recombinant DNA Comes to Fermentation

In 1973 Stanley Cohen at Stanford University and Herbert Boyer at the University of California – San Francisco launched the revolution in genetic engineering by demonstrating that they could insert recombinant plasmids (small circular double-stranded DNA molecules) into *Escherichia coli* bacteria. This meant that foreign genes inserted into a species could then replicate and express those genes (Cohen et al. 1973). This opened the door to enabling microbes to produce all kinds of proteins and laid the foundation for genetic engineering and the entire biotech industry. Those microbes, of course, were propagated via fermentation.

Insulin

In 1976, Boyer and venture capitalist Robert Swanson founded the company Genentech with the goal of commercializing recombinant DNA technology to produce therapeutic proteins. In 1978, the company produced the first recombinant DNA human insulin using modified *E. coli* grown by fermentation, which it licensed to Eli Lilly. Lilly introduced it as Humulin® to the market in 1982 (Quianzon and Cheikh 2012).

Interestingly, Genentech first offered to license the recombinant insulin to Novo, but Novo declined because at the time there was wariness in Denmark about the production or use of recombinant DNA products. So Genentech went to Lilly. When Novo changed course and had to catch up, it heavily recruited scientists from the University of Copenhagen and other businesses in the region. It also found some of the world's leading gene technologists and yeast physiologists at the Carlsberg Lab, and it acquired a small company that had expertise in therapeutic and recombinant proteins

(Shih and Chai 2015). Unlike Genentech and Lilly who used *E. coli*, Novo turned to modified *Saccharomyces cerevisiae*, the familiar top-fermenting yeast for making ales. It introduced its first recombinant product in 1991, and by 2015 it was producing half the world's supply of insulin at its massive fermentation facility in Kalundborg, Denmark (Landgraf and Sandow 2016).

The Kalundborg site is quite remarkable on a number of counts. Since the Novo plant is producing a drug, it's done inside a giant cleanroom where you have to suit up, wear shoe covers, and scrub your hands and put on gloves before entering. The scale is gigantic, with enormous multistory high stainless-steel bioreactors that are cleaned and sterilized before each use. What is even more impressive is the purification process, often referred to as the "downstream processing," which starts with the recovery of the insulin from the fermentation broth and then the isolation and removal of impurities.

They use high-performance liquid chromatography (HPLC) in a key purification step, which passes the material through a column packed with tiny resin particles. I'm used to seeing such columns in the laboratory, and the columns are typically less than 5 mm in diameter. Not in this factory, where the HPLC columns must have been a meter or more in diameter or larger. When you consider that the key to making HPLC work is spreading the material extremely uniformly at the business end of the column, using a column that big is kind of staggering, to me at least. When I asked if they were nervous about making half the world's supply in a single factory site and that millions of people around the world depended on them, they assured me that they had a safety stock of five years supply in the freezer. Must be another one of those gigantic freezers!

The other thing that was remarkable about the factory was that it was part of the Kalundborg Symbiosis, a partnership among firms operating there that was established in 1972. Seventeen firms collaborate today in a circular approach to production, where the residuals from one company's production serve as the input to another. This is most visible on the water and energy side. I brought a class of Harvard Business School students to visit the wastewater treatment plant several years ago. Of course, I wanted to be able to say I took rising young MBA students to see a wastewater treatment plant; that was right before we went to one of the world's most advanced municipal waste incinerators in Copenhagen the next day. Sewage and trash—an educationally enriching experience.

They had cooling water from a nearby oil refinery used as feeder water for the boilers producing steam and electricity and also as input water for a desulfurization process at the refinery. The desulfurization process produced industrial gypsum for a local wallboard factory, and the cogeneration power plant also produced heat for the town of Kalundborg and steam for the Novo facility and the oil refinery (Jacobsen 2006). Chr. Hansen and Novozymes were also located nearby. Talk about taking advantage of being in a cluster!

Cheesemaking Gets an Upgrade

Meanwhile in the United States, Pfizer developed a process for extracting the RNA coding for chymosin from the abomasum of calves and inserting it into *E. coli*. The *E. coli* were then grown via fermentation. After growing a batch, the *E. coli* cells were killed and broken open, and the chymosin extracted from the fermentation broth (Eck 2013). In 1990, the FDA approved fermentation produced chymosin in food, the first time a bioengineered product was permitted (Tolchin 1990).

Chr. Hansen started using recombinant technology to make chymosin via fermentation as well. Its first-generation product used a calf chymosin gene that had been inserted into *Aspergillus niger*, a fungus that had long been used industrially to produce citric acid via fermentation and therefore was "generally recognized as safe" (GRAS) by the U.S. Food and Drug Administration. Over the ensuing years it refined its offering so that its coagulants could do more precise cutting of the casein proteins to yield a stronger network in the cheese that preserved more of the fat and proteins (CheeseScience 2008). Its second-generation recombinant chymosin took a gene from *Camelus dromedarius*, the dromedary camel found in the Middle East and North Africa, which had better milk-clotting properties. By 2021 the company claimed that 55% of all cheese produced globally used fermentation-produced chymosin (USDA Agricultural Marketing Service 2021).

Weight-Loss Drugs

Using recombinant DNA in microorganisms like yeast to produce specific chemicals or ingredients has come to be known as precision fermentation. One such product is a key building block for Ozempic, a pioneering drug that has shown remarkable effectiveness in helping people to lose weight. It came about because Novo Nordisk was trying to make better treatments for diabetes and was experimenting with new approaches. Once again, there is a long history that led to these discoveries.

Some History Complex things happen in the body after we eat food, and scientists have long sought to understand these events better. In 1902, William Bayliss and Ernest Starling discovered that a chemical was released by the duodenum (the first part of the small intestine connecting to the stomach) in response to acid, and this caused the pancreas to release bicarbonate to neutralize it. Since they had cut the nerves to the organs under study, they concluded that it must be a chemical that did the signaling, and they named it "secretin" for the hypothetical messenger. They hypothesized that this chemical was secreted by the inner lining in the intestine (the mucosa) and traveled via the bloodstream to the pancreas (Modlin and Kidd 2001). This idea became the foundation for the modern field of endocrinology.

In 1906, another group of researchers found that an extract from the intestine could lower blood glucose and they named it "incretine." Then in 1922, two scientists at the University of Rochester, C.P. Kimball and John Murlin, prepared an extract from pancreases and found that when they injected it into rabbits and dogs it would increase the animals' level of blood glucose briefly until the insulin kicked in and lowered it again (Robertson 2023). They concluded that this must be some hormone that did the opposite of insulin, so they called it "the glucose agonist," or more succinctly "glucagon" (Müller et al. 2017). These puzzle pieces would sit for several decades as people turned their attention more toward insulin, whose increasing availability made it a very direct way of treating diabetes (Friedman 2024).

Interest picked up again in the 1960s when three groups discovered that glucose taken orally increased insulin concentration in the bloodstream and lowered blood glucose levels more than if the glucose was given intravenously. That was an unexpected result because usually the bloodstream is the most direct route to everything in the body, as the digestive tract tends to break down everything in the process of absorbing food. This suggested that the gut made some hormones that regulated insulin levels in the blood, and that their release might be triggered by carbohydrates that a person had eaten. So the search for incretins began (Friedman 2024).

Joel Habener and Svetlana Mojsov, working at the Massachusetts General Hospital, identified the first glucagon like peptide in 1986. This was a chain of 37 amino acids, and they called it GLP-1(1-37). It didn't appear to have any effect on the production of insulin, but when they "cleaved" or cut it between positions 6 and 7, which they referred to as GLP-1(7-37), the remaining chain from amino acids 7–37 pushed up the secretion of insulin by six-fold (Mojsov et al. 1986). They called the GLP-1(1-37) long chain peptide a prohormone, as it was a precursor to the active hormone. Something in the body seemed to cut the prohormone in order to activate the hormone.

In 1992–1993, researchers at the Royal Postgraduate School at Hammersmith Hospital in London tested the GLP-1(7-37) on both healthy volunteers and a subgroup who had type 2 diabetes. A 30-minute intravenous drip of a solution containing GLP-1(7-37) led to a threefold increase in insulin secretion in the diabetic patients and a significant reduction in blood glucose for both groups, but there was no such effect in the absence of glucose (Kreymann et al. 1987). Thus it seemed that the GLP-1(7-37) would be a powerful tool for treating diabetes, except for one little problem. When it entered the bloodstream, it lasted for only one to two minutes, which meant a patient would have to be connected to a continuous infusion for it to do its work.

Novo Nordisk's Work This is when Lotte Knudsen, a scientist at Novo Nordisk, came into the picture. In the early 1990s, Novo Nordisk had formed an innovation team to explore new approaches to treating diabetes, and she led a team that was trying to develop GLP-1(7–37) into a drug. But she started to believe that it could be more than just a treatment for diabetes; it could potentially treat obesity. Her team tried to make the molecule more stable by attaching other groups to it, trying to extend its half-life from 1–2 minutes to 10 hours or more. Their first success was liraglutide, which had a fatty acid attached at position 26 and the amino acid lysine at position 34 substituted for arginine. This molecule had a half-life of 13 hours, and Novo soon launched clinical studies with it. Unfortunately several patients reported nausea, which led them to reduce the dose, but then it became much less effective (Friedman 2024).

With competition emerging from companies like Amylin Pharmaceuticals and Merck, the Novo team pressed onward, using a phased increase of dosage. Interestingly, the treatment caused a 5% or greater weight loss in 54% of patients. With considerable further experimentation, they managed to develop semaglutide (the first formulation was named Ozempic®), which was stable enough to last seven days when administered as a shot. Ozempic treatment also came with a surprise: diabetics showed a dose-dependent weight loss that averaged six kilograms for a 2 mg dose, with 40% of patients losing more than 10% of their weight (Tschöp and Friedman 2023). The company followed with clinical trials at higher doses, in which treated patients lost an average 12.4% of their initial weight. Diabetic patients also saw a 26% reduction in the incidence of cardiovascular events. More recent studies suggest benefits for patients with heart and kidney failure (Friedman 2024).

Ozempic® received its FDA approval in December 2017, and it also received a positive opinion from the EU Committee for Medicinal Products for Human Use (CHMP) for the treatment of type 2 diabetes (Dhillon 2018). In 2019, Novo received FDA approval for Rybelsus, the first oral GLP-1 tablet, and Ozempic was approved in the United States for cardiovascular risk reduction in people with type 2 diabetes and established cardiovascular disease (Novo Nordisk 2020). Ozempic reached blockbuster status in only 18 months as sales took off. By 2024 Novo Nordisk's sales exceeded $40 billion on a 56% rise in obesity treatments (Kuchler 2025).

Novo Nordisk introduced three distinct formulations for its semaglutides.

- Ozempic was administered via a shot and was targeted at controlling blood sugar in patients with type 2 diabetes.
- Wegovy was also given as a shot and was specifically approved for weight management.
- Rybelsus was a tablet taken orally and was meant for type 2 diabetes treatment; it was formulated with an absorption enhancer that shielded it from degradation by the acids in the stomach (Lewis et al. 2022).

The apparent benefits of the drugs kept expanding, with Wegovy receiving FDA approval to treat a serious form of liver disease in August 2025 (Kresge and Cortze 2025).

Manufacturing all three drugs relies on a hybrid approach. The company starts with recombinant DNA technology to insert a gene that expresses a semaglutide precursor into (you guessed it) *Saccharomyces cerevisiae*, the now familiar yeast strain used to ferment beer and make insulin. The semaglutide precursor is secreted into the fermentation broth, from where it is recovered and purified. Then it is chemically modified through multiple steps, followed by purification using a technology called reverse-phase high-performance liquid chromatography (RP-HPLC). This is followed by another chromatography step (ion exchange) and freeze-drying to provide the drug long-term stability (Parisis et al. 2025).

Once these drugs hit the popular consciousness, Novo Nordisk's biggest challenge became keeping up with demand. As it raced to expand manufacturing capacity, Eli Lilly entered the market with Mounjaro and Zepbound. Nonetheless, Novo's success propelled the company to the top market cap in Europe, briefly surpassing luxury goods maker LVMH (Raitano and Masoni 2023).

Industrial Clusters and the Economics of Agglomeration

So why Denmark? The answer is partly brilliance, partly accident, and partly the way knowledge behaves when it concentrates in one place. The economist Paul Krugman spent much of his career trying to explain why industries cluster geographically at all. Why, in a world where goods and information travel freely, does location still matter so much? His answer was that proximity lets knowledge flow in ways that markets can't fully capture or replicate. Workers carry their knowledge and expertise from firm to firm, competitors learn from each other, and techniques developed for one purpose quietly migrate to another (Krugman 1992). Denmark is a near-perfect illustration of his thesis.

J.C. Jacobsen didn't set out to build a fermentation empire. Emil Christian Hansen wasn't trying to seed a pharmaceutical industry. The Petersen brothers just wanted to sell insulin. But each of them added something to a growing pool of expertise: scientific experiments, trained workers, production techniques, a culture of rigorous experimentation that the next generation could draw upon. The result, 150 years later, is that a small Nordic country quietly plays a major role in industries spread across your refrigerator, your medicine cabinet, and your laundry room. That's what a cluster does. It turns local knowledge into a global advantage, one breakthrough at a time.

CHAPTER 8

Supply Chain Design and Management

For a book about where things come from, it might seem strange that we've waited this long to talk explicitly about supply chain management. But before we could examine how supply chains operate, we needed to understand why they look the way they do. As you ideally discovered in previous chapters, wages differ across countries. Some inputs travel easily across borders; others don't. Some activities demand specialized expertise or expensive equipment. Geography, regulation, and risk all shape what's actually possible. Now that we've laid out those forces and constraints, we can look at how firms knit them together and try to manage them as a whole.

Supply chain management is the discipline of designing and coordinating the networks that get products to consumers. Entire careers are built around mastering it, and business schools devote full courses to it. We'll be more selective in this book. The goal here isn't to catalog every tool or technique but to pull out a few ideas that illuminate how the way supply chains are structured shapes the geography of production and why they sometimes fall apart in ways that might have been unexpected.

At its core, a supply chain is the network of organizations, people, resources, and information that connects raw materials to finished products. When a company decides how to organize that web, it faces a set of interconnected choices: what to make itself and what to source from others, where to locate each stage of production, how much inventory to hold at each stage, and what's the best way to connect each stage. These are strategic decisions, and they reflect everything we've explored: comparative advantage, tradability, specialization, the costs associated with distance. In practice, all of these forces converge in the design of the chain.

The basic goal of supply chain management is simple: match supply to demand, reliably and as cost effectively as possible. Every firm in the network depends on the others, and in principle, everyone benefits when the whole system runs well. In practice, each participant has its own objectives, its own incentives, and its own often incomplete picture of what's happening elsewhere. What looks rational from inside one firm can create chaos for the system around it. The result is a sometimes-uneasy balance between coordination and conflict.

This chapter focuses on three themes that go a long way toward explaining where things ultimately come from: how supply chains are designed to serve different kinds of demand, how supply chains can be organized around the timing of demand, and how coordination across multiple firms and multiple stages is essential across complex global networks.

Supply Chain Design

If I want to match supply with demand, what do I do if I don't know for sure what the demand is? Economists like to explain this problem using a simple scenario of a person who sells newspapers on the street; the setting reflects a time when these types of jobs still existed (Morse and Kimball 1962).

This is called the "news vendor problem." A seller has to buy some quantity of newspapers in the morning with the intention of selling them at a newsstand throughout the day. The news vendor might have a rough idea of how many they could sell but doesn't know for sure. Running short means lost opportunities to make more money selling additional copies, but buying too many means having to eat the cost of excess inventory that will be tossed out and recycled rather than generate revenue. This is a proxy for the broader question of how much of a perishable good should a merchant stock. How many croissants should a bakery bake overnight to sell in the morning, or how many flu vaccines should a pharmacy order knowing that unused ones will expire?

The heart of the dilemma is that the news vendor has to commit to buy their entire daily supply before knowing the demand for that day's newspapers. For most businesses, this amounts to a *make-to-stock* production policy: I'm going to produce or procure some amount before I know how much I can sell in total. This is what many retailers do, especially with things like seasonal buys for back-to-school or holiday clothing and soft goods. This is a hard problem, and many of them often don't get it quite right all of the time. One estimate for U.S. nongrocery retailers found that 60% of their merchandise could be sold at full price, and the rest had to be marked down to clear it out. Close to 30% of the problem merchandise was from buying too much, and around 17% was from buying the wrong stuff (Weinswig 2019).

It's also why a lot of the merchandise that ends up as unsold winds up in the hands of resellers like TJX (which operates chains like TJ Maxx and Marshalls). TJX describes it this way: "We take advantage of opportunities to acquire merchandise at substantial discounts that regularly arise from the production and flow of inventory in the apparel and home fashions marketplace. These opportunities include, among others, closeouts from brands, manufacturers and other retailers; special production direct from brands and factories; order cancellations and manufacturer overruns" (**TJX.com** 2025). In other words, when a retailer bought too much or picked too many of the wrong styles, they sell it at pennies on the dollar to TJX. The company is pretty closed-mouthed about how they know what to buy; I think that is their secret sauce. I once asked someone at the company how they managed their inventory when they bought truckloads of stuff that other retailers had been forced to unload. When I heard the answer, I decided I really had to go buy some of the company's stock. That was a bet that retailers would continue to make mistakes, which turned out to be a great investment. It's one of the few retailers whose stock I would want to own!

Optimizing for Demand Type: Efficient vs. Responsive Supply Chains

Another way of thinking about supply chain design comes from Marshall Fisher, who begins with a simple question: what kind of product are we dealing with (Fisher 1997)?

- Some products are staples with predictable demand and long lifecycles. Fisher calls these "functional" products—items like milk, bread, or toilet paper. They meet basic needs that do not change much over time. Because they tend to face intense competition and thin margins, success depends on having a highly efficient, low-cost supply chain.
- Other products are "innovative." They incorporate frequent design changes, have shorter product life cycles, and face more uncertain demand, but they often carry higher margins. Think of the latest fashion trend or a newly released smartphone. In such cases, efficiency alone is not enough. What matters is responsiveness. If you produce too much, you are forced eventually to take markdowns. If you produce too little, you lose sales and frustrate customers. You need a supply chain that can deliver product quickly and adjust to product style and mix changes. The right supply chain depends on which problem you are trying to solve.

A legendary example of aligning supply chain design with product characteristics comes from the Spanish firm Inditex, the company behind fast fashion brands Zara, Zara Home, Bershka, Massimo Dutti, Oysho, Stradivarius, Pull & Bear, and Uterqüe, all of which sell trendy and decently made but inexpensive products in attractive, upscale stores. Company founder Amancio Ortega Gaona early on decided that he needed to control what happened to his products right up to the point a customer buys them (Ferdows et al. 2004). The flagship Zara brand treats much of its assortment as "innovative" products with short life cycles, uncertain demand, and with high markdown risk.

Rather than chasing the lowest possible labor cost, a substantial portion of Zara's fashion-sensitive production takes place close to company headquarters, around La Coruña and across Spain, but also Portugal, Morocco, and Turkey. By keeping cutting, sewing, and finishing geographically close to its design teams and its core European markets, the company dramatically shortens lead times. The company's designers, planners, and manufacturers operate in tight coordination, enabling new styles to move from concept to store in a matter of weeks (New York Times 2012).

Basic products like simple T-shirts, knitwear that doesn't change much, and other long-lifecycle items are produced in lower-cost locations, like Bangladesh and other parts of Asia (see Figure 8.1). For these "functional" products, the risk of going out of style is lower, and longer shipping times are acceptable. This dual structure offers proximity for uncertainty and distance for stability. The result is a hybrid supply chain that combines regional responsiveness that also takes advantage of global cost arbitrage (Ferdows et al. 2004).

Zara's distribution model reinforces this design. All finished garments, whether produced nearby or overseas, pass through Zaragoza. European stores are replenished primarily by truck, while more distant markets receive weekly shipments by air freight. The company prioritizes rapid replenishment and frequent assortment refreshes over minimizing transportation cost per unit. Speed reduces the impact of forecast errors and allows the company to respond quickly to emerging trends.

FIGURE 8.1 Garment on Zara rack in Boston, made in Bangladesh. *Source:* Willy Shih.

Equally important is how Zara manages store inventory. It offers a wide range of dresses, shirts, jackets, and other garments but only puts a small range of sizes and quantities for each style on the racks at any one time. This fosters a "treasure hunt" mentality among shoppers who know if they see something they like, they better buy it right away as it likely won't be there when they come back. Store managers keep limited additional stock in a back room and can order more product if there's demand. They also collect customer feedback and send it to the headquarters in La Coruña, Spain.

At headquarters, production decisions are adjusted in near real time. Successful styles are replenished quickly, and weak performers are discontinued before excess inventory builds up. By designing its supply chain around rapid information feedback and constrained inventory, Zara minimizes markdown exposure while maintaining constant novelty.

The geography of Zara's production reflects a strategic decision to trade some labor-cost advantage for speed, coordination, and control. The company's supply chain is not simply efficient or responsive; it is segmented. And that segmentation determines where its clothing ultimately comes from.

Optimizing for Timing: Make-to-Order vs. Make-to-Stock

Another way to reduce the risks of supply/demand mismatch is to delay producing your product until more accurate demand information becomes available. *Make-to-order* is such an approach, in which a manufacturer postpones production until an order is in hand. Dell Computer was famous for this when their main business was assembling desktop computers, which they did only after you told them on the phone how you wanted them to configure it *and* you paid for it.

If you visited their factory (which was around the corner from my office) in Austin, Texas, in the early 1990s, their assembly process consisted of pulling computer memory boards, disk drives, the latest graphics cards, and other components from bins stocked by their suppliers (called line-side stocking), plugging them into motherboards installed in the computer case of your choice, packing it, and shipping it to you via UPS or FedEx. One of the brilliant features of their system was that when they took your order, they also charged your credit card and they would be paid by the credit card company usually within 24 hours. But they paid the vendors that maintained their line-side stocks only as they pulled the materials from the bins and used them, and for that they usually had payment terms that would allow them to delay paying for a month or two. Dell thus generated negative cash flow in the process: as they sold more product, they generated more cash that they could invest and earn a return on until they eventually had to pay for the parts. Meanwhile, your computer came from Texas even though many of the parts came from Asia.

When consumer demand shifted to notebook computers, that was a little more challenging for Dell's business model, as consumers often wanted to get the feel of the product in a retail store rather than purchase online. Competitors leveraged the original design manufacturers (ODMs) in Asia that we talked about in Chapter 5 and used their retail channels to balance inventory with immediate availability, something Dell's highly customized order fulfillment system struggled to match at large scale with their notebooks.

Dell eventually shifted to a *make-to-stock* model for consumer notebooks and stayed closer to the build-to-order model for their enterprise customers. Instead of building everything only after an order, Dell pre-assembled common configurations, and postponed final configuration on others until they knew what they needed, holding some finished goods in inventory. They segmented their supply chains according to how much uncertainty there was (Lee 2002).

Supply Chain Coordination

Regardless of the design, managing a supply chain across multiple entities is inherently a complex undertaking. Each party operates with its own goals, forecasting methods, and inventory policies while typically having only limited visibility into what the others are doing. Thus, rather than functioning as a single coordinated system, a typical supply chain is more like a loose confederation of independent decision-makers, each responding to the signals they observe and each trying to optimize their own operations or protect themselves from disruption. This creates myriad opportunities for miscommunication, misaligned incentives, and mistakes that can ripple across the entire network.

Who Ordered All That Beer? The Bullwhip Effect

One of the most significant sources of dysfunction in a multi-firm supply chain is the presence of delays and time lags at different stages of the process. When a retailer places an order, that demand signal must travel upstream to the next link in the chain, which may take days or weeks to process and fulfill it before passing their own order for inputs along to the next upstream party, and so on. Each handoff introduces further delay (lead time), and during that time, conditions on the ground can change.

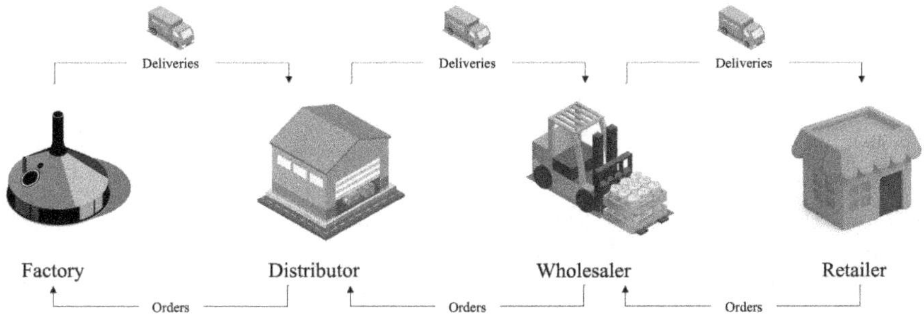

FIGURE 8.2 Structure of supply chain for the "Beer Game." *Source:* Willy Shih.

One of the ways we teach about supply chain coordination is with "The Beer Game," a classroom simulation developed at MIT in the 1960s that has since become a staple of business school education (Hieber and Hartel 2003). It is a replica of a production and distribution system for a single brand of beer. Players are divided into sets of four teams, each team representing a different stage of the supply chain: a retailer, a wholesaler, a distributor, and a brewery. They are not allowed to talk to each other; the only way they can communicate is through the placement of orders. The retailer sells beer to customers and orders from the wholesaler, the wholesaler orders from the distributor, the distributor orders from the factory, and the factory produces beer (see Figure 8.2).

In the main version of our simulation, no one can see what's happening at the other stages. Each order takes two weeks to reach the next stage, and product also flows back along the chain with two-week delivery delays. Each team only knows their own inventory level and the volume of orders arriving on their desk. There is a delay between placing an order and receiving it, just as in real supply chains. The goal is simple: keep your customers supplied without running up huge inventory costs. Running out means lost business and incurs a stock out charge.

We tell students that demand has been flat, running at six kegs a week, but summer is coming. Then when the simulation begins, we increase demand to 12 kegs, a small one-time bump, but nothing dramatic. We then keep demand flat at 12 kegs per week for the remainder of the simulation. Within a few rounds, players are almost always sitting on enormous piles of inventory or screaming for inventory they can't get. I've often seen wholesalers place orders for 100 kegs for a week, and they would have ordered more if we let them. Costs spiral. The factory is producing at full capacity while retailers are drowning in beer, or vice versa. The chaos feels like it must have an external cause—a demand shock, a supply disruption, or simply bad luck. But there is no external cause, the instability comes entirely from inside the system from the way each player's reasonable, self-interested decisions interact with everyone else's.

What makes the game so effective as a teaching tool is how little it takes to send the whole system into crisis. The typical order pattern looks like a sinusoid that is growing in amplitude, which is what led to the name "bullwhip effect"; it looks like a bullwhip being cracked by a cowboy (see Figure 8.3). There is *delay* and *amplification* as the impact moves up the chain. The causes were explained really well by my friend Hau Lee at Stanford University (Lee et al. 1997). As each entity in the chain adjusts its orders based on incomplete information and protective instincts, small fluctuations in end consumer demand become progressively amplified the further upstream you look. A modest uptick in retail sales can prompt a retailer to significantly increase its order to a wholesaler, who in turn overreacts by placing an even larger order with the distributor, who then overwhelms the factory with demand that bears little resemblance to what consumers actually were buying. The result is a cycle of periods of excess inventory followed by costly shortages that wastes resources, strains supplier relationships, and undermines the efficiency that a well-functioning supply chain is supposed to deliver.

The bullwhip effect has several root causes and understanding them helps explain why it persists even among experienced managers who've seen it before.

Poor Demand Signaling The most fundamental cause is poor demand signaling. Each firm in the chain forecasts based on what its immediate downstream customer is ordering, not on what consumers are actually buying at the end of the chain. That's already one step removed from reality, and every firm adds its own judgment on top—safety stock based on past shortages, optimism about a sales trend, or maybe caution because of long lead times. A brief spike in orders that was just random noise can get interpreted as a new uptrend, and everyone amplifies it on the way up the chain. "Hey, our product is a hot seller!" Product managers love to believe that this time is different.

Japanese whisky producers offer a vivid example of the opposite problem: when they were making production decisions in the early 2000s, sales had been declining for years, so they planned conservatively. By 2018, as the *Financial Times* reported, the most popular lines had been drunk nearly to depletion. Demand had surged in ways no one anticipated when those batches were being distilled and barreled, and the long lag times on delivery exacerbated the problem (Lewis 2018).

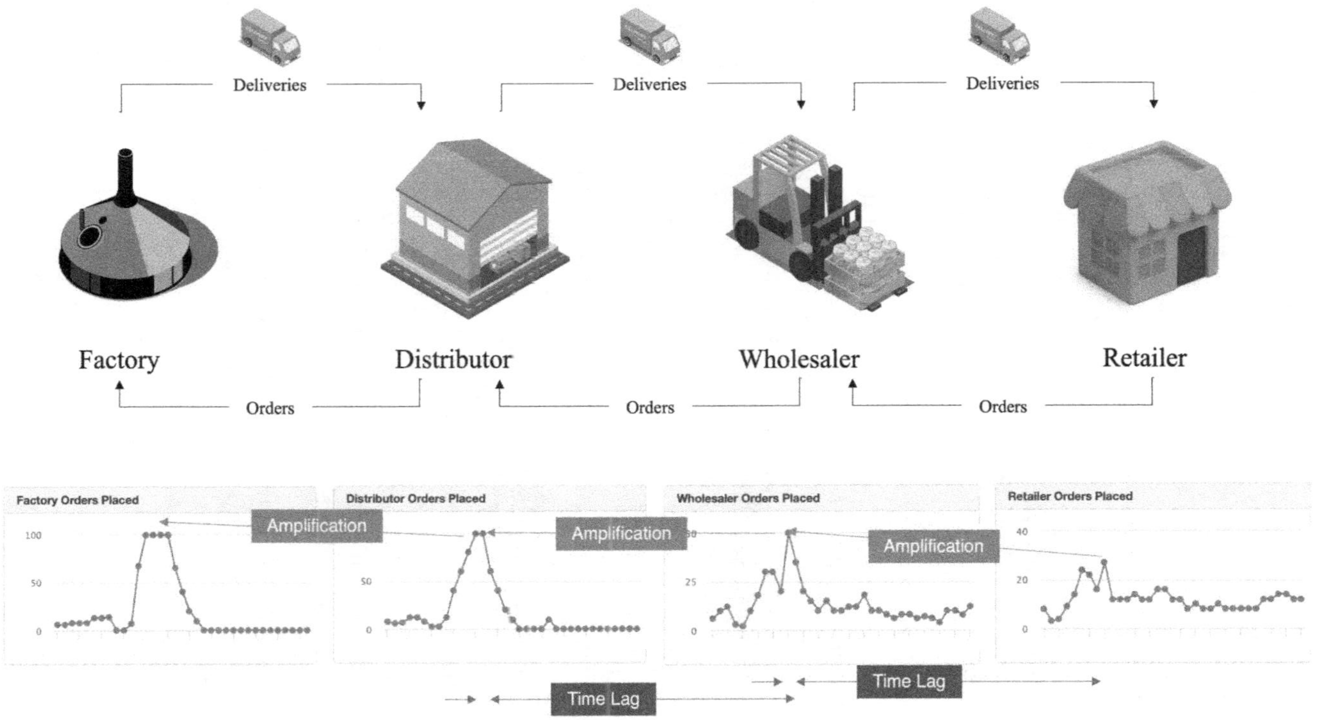

FIGURE 8.3 Ordering pattern in a typical "Beer Game." *Source:* Willy Shih.

Ordering Policies Ordering policies can add another layer of distortion. There are real economies of scale to placing orders in batches. Shipping costs and administrative overhead can be spread over more volume, so buyers can save money by bunching orders periodically rather than ordering more frequently in smaller quantities. From the supplier's perspective, this can look like swings in demand even when underlying consumption is steady. The effect is compounded when many customers happen to order at the same time, such as at the end of the month or the start of a week. That unintentional synchronization can create artificial peaks and valleys that can again have nothing to do with what consumers actually want.

If you look at Google search trends for commodities like toilet paper during the COVID-19 pandemic, you can probably imagine what was going through the minds of product managers who were scrambling to meet demand (see Figure 8.4).

Trade promotions, incentives by a manufacturer to boost sales, can make things worse. An example is when a manufacturer offers a time-limited discount: order a certain quantity by some date and get this discount! Retailers respond rationally by stocking up while the price is lower, buying more than they currently need. Suppliers often see this as a feature rather than a bug, since loading up the sales channel encourages retailers to push the product harder. Some cynics (including myself) call this "channel stuffing." But that floods the supply chain with inventory that distorts everyone's read on true demand.

Retailers do the same thing to consumers through their own promotional sales, encouraging shoppers to buy right away rather than waiting until they run out. Some people (including myself) call that "pantry loading." Either way, it shifts consumption forward in time. People stock up now and stop buying later, which eventually shows up as a demand trough.

During the toilet paper panic of 2020, shoppers panicked and loaded up on inventory. Eventually they ran out of space to store it and stopped buying, causing demand to fall off a cliff (Terlep 2021). That was completely predictable, but it happened anyway.

Shortage Gaming Finally, there is shortage gaming. When a popular product is scarce and suppliers start allocating based on order history, retailers have every incentive to inflate their orders, such as by asking for more than they need in order to secure a larger allocation. Some powerful retailers negotiate terms so that they can return unsold inventory with few penalties, so there's almost no downside to over-ordering. The result is a wave of inflated orders that makes the shortage look worse than it is, triggering even more production upstream and setting up the inevitable glut when the panic subsides.

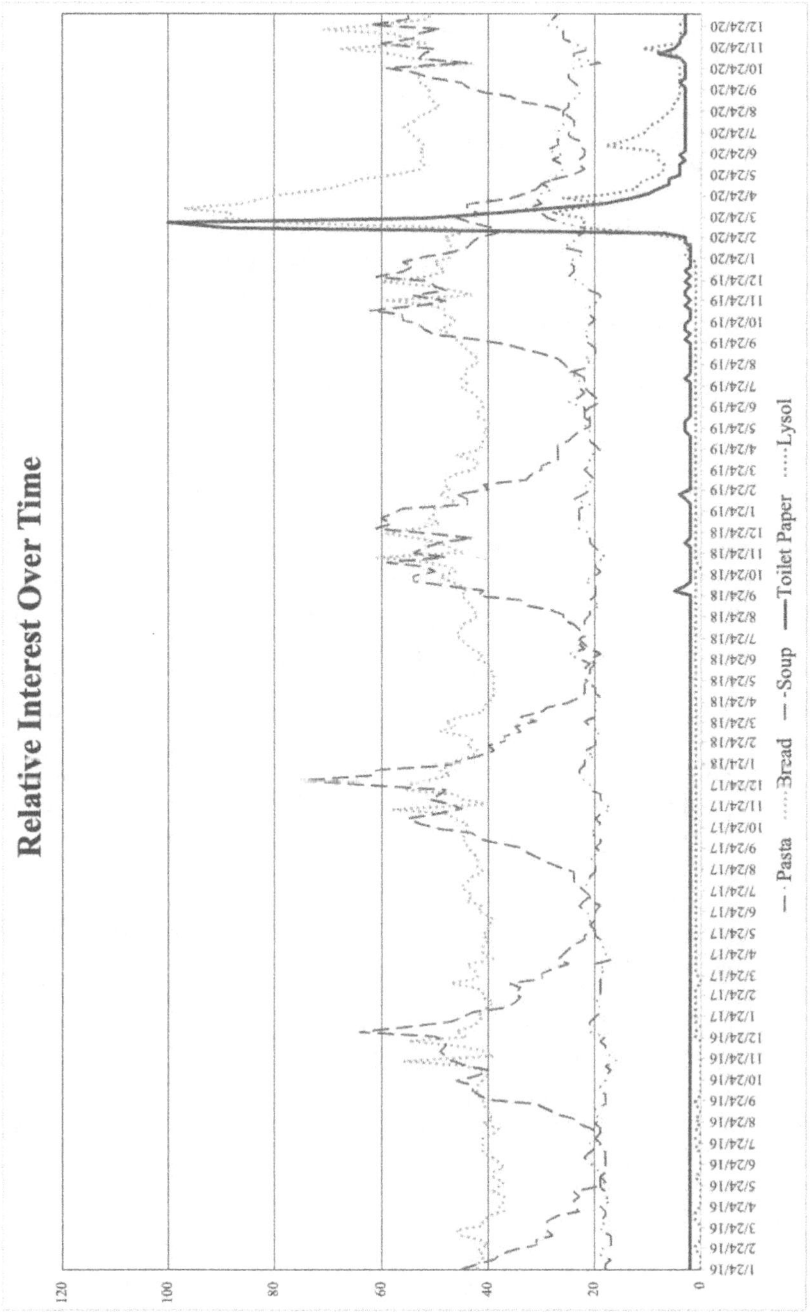

FIGURE 8.4 Google Search interest in different products during the COVID-19 pandemic. *Source:* Willy Shih.

Lessons to Learn from the Bullwhip Effect

There are several key takeaways from the Beer Game exercise. First, longer delays make the effect worse simply because it takes longer for any link in the chain to see and feel the impact of their actions (orders). We often divide the class and give some groups of students a one-week delay instead of two. The bullwhip invariably still happens but usually has a lesser magnitude, i.e., less overstocks and shortages.

The second is that visibility to true demand should help, because that should help circumvent the gaming. In classes we usually give some teams point-of-sale (POS) visibility—which means everybody in the chain can see the actual retail demand. You would think that would help because then everyone shares a single source of truth, but more often than not it doesn't. In the debrief this usually leads to a lot of screaming and charges of mental instability directed at other supply chain members.

In the real world, manufacturers that sell components into long supply chains will often buy retail POS data to try to understand how much product they should really be producing. For example, microprocessor suppliers for consumer PCs like Intel and AMD buy retail POS data on consumer PCs because they want to know the true level of demand (in addition to how much market share they are winning against each other). This allows them to allocate their production fairly.

During the COVID-19 pandemic, demand for notebook computers skyrocketed. I heard from one of the big ODM manufacturers of notebook computers that two of the big brands were each trying to corner the market on critical components for PCs, like microprocessors, storage, etc. They bought high dollar value components directly from suppliers and then consigned the parts to the ODMs. If one brand could secure more than they needed when others were short, that would allow them to grab market share. But apparently, they each grabbed disproportionate shares of different components but were then short on others. Taken as a whole, there was plenty to go around, but each brand on its own didn't have enough.

Both of these brands probably learned this maneuver from Steve Jobs. When Apple introduced its original hard disk-based iPod music player, one of my friends at Apple told me they purchased the entire world's supply of 1.8″ hard drives from Toshiba. Nobody else could get any, so it was hard to compete with Apple. When Apple switched over to flash memory, it bought a substantial share of Samsung's flash memory production, again to its great advantage. This type of behavior just encourages more people to engage in this kind of shortage gaming.

If you happened to have studied control systems engineering (which I did out of necessity during graduate school), you will recognize that the bullwhip effect is really a control systems problem. It's a loop oscillation caused by delay and too much gain (amplification). And if you were a control systems engineer, you would know the solution is to reduce the gain or reduce the delay. This is actually the same problem as the bullwhip effect, but I usually get blank stares when I explain this to businesspeople.

When I was experiencing a bullwhip effect in one of our products at Eastman Kodak, I told my supply chain lead, "Every time the sales guys tell you to increase your orders, increase it by half what they say, and every time they tell you to cut orders, cut it by half what they say." That was the equivalent of reducing the gain in the control loop. Sure enough, the oscillation damped down, just as control theory would predict.

Managing Inventory to Reduce Bullwhips

Several inventory management models have emerged that address these problems by restructuring who owns what and when. In retail, for example, the buyer usually takes full responsibility for issuing purchase orders and managing its inventory. It also takes responsibility for inventory carrying costs and risks such as price changes, markdowns, and obsolescence. If it has sufficient purchasing power like Walmart, it can negotiate contract terms with suppliers that provide for allowances and return privileges, market development funds taken as a discount off the invoice price, fees for the prominent display of products (known as slotting fees), or other concessions.

But there are other models that have worked well in some sectors. With vendor-managed inventory (VMI), a *supplier* decides when and how much inventory to order. The retailer and supplier jointly agree on the objectives to guide replenishment decisions, such as the minimum percentage they want to guarantee as in-stock. The retailer shares demand data (usually POS), and this is used to generate automatic replenishment. VMI usually goes hand-in-hand with the elimination of trade promotions, and the supplier usually agrees to lower prices as a way of sharing the savings. Procter & Gamble and Walmart were among the first companies to identify the gains that were possible by implementing VMI. This was one key enabler of Walmart's "everyday low prices." A risk is that the buyer gives up control while maintaining most of the same inventory cost and risk associated with the VMI model.

Another model is consigned or vendor owned inventory. In this hybrid, the manufacturer controls the order flow, but the actual transfer of ownership of the goods does not happen until the product is used. One form of this is rack jobbing in which a manufacturer agrees to display products in a retail store, and the retailer pays for them only when a consumer purchases them at the check-out. The retailer splits the profits with the manufacturer. The manufacturer (or its distributor, who may act as an independent operator) is responsible for arranging in-store displays and keeping them full. The rack jobber owns the inventory and assumes all of the associated costs. Soft drinks, potato chips and other snack foods, and many of the products found in convenience stores are typically offered through rack jobbers.

Consigned/vendor managed inventory is used in many high-tech manufacturing operations, as well. Parts suppliers, for example, a disk drive manufacturer, maintain stocks of components inside the assembly plant (or contracted assembly plant) of a computer producer as we discussed earlier with Dell, and when the part is pulled from the stock for use in assembling a product, a bar code scan initiates a transaction that transfers ownership from supplier to manufacturer. This triggers an invoice for payment to the supplier.

These techniques share the responsibility for managing inventory across a supply chain, and that forces a lot of communication that helps mitigate bullwhip effects.

Long Logistics Chains Can Produce Similar Effects

As we saw earlier in this chapter, the bullwhip effect is fundamentally a problem of delay. When it takes time for information and inventory to move through a supply chain, small disturbances at one end get amplified by the time they reach the other end. The longer the delay, the worse the problem becomes because there is more room for misjudgments to compound and accumulate.

Ocean shipping from China introduces exactly this kind of delay, at a scale that dwarfs the lags in the Beer Game. A retailer in the United States ordering from a factory in Guangdong is looking at perhaps four to six weeks of transit time alone, before accounting for production lead times, port congestion, or customs clearance. By the time a shipment arrives, the demand signal that triggered the order is ancient history. If consumer demand shifted in the intervening weeks, as it did dramatically during the COVID pandemic when Americans stopped buying clothes and started buying home office furniture, it is usually too late to course-correct. Orders that looked sensible when placed arrive into a market that has already moved on. And because every importer along the chain is making the same bets simultaneously, the overshoots and shortfalls tend to hit all at once. Hello TJX! This is exactly the kind of inventory mismatch that fills their store racks.

One partial remedy is having better visibility, knowing at any given moment exactly what is in the pipeline headed your way. A retailer who can see that six container loads of furniture left Shenzhen two weeks ago and are due in Long Beach on Thursday is in a fundamentally different position than one that placed an order and is simply waiting for a truck to show up. With that visibility, the retailer can monitor how demand is evolving while the goods are still at sea, adjust plans for receiving and distribution, and avoid placing redundant orders out of anxiety about whether the first ones will arrive. In the Beer Game, much of the chaos stems from players ordering more because they aren't sure when their previous orders are coming, a panic that good pipeline visibility would largely eliminate. Modern tracking systems, electronic data interchange between supply chain partners, and the digitization of shipping documentation have all made this kind of visibility more achievable than it once was. It doesn't shorten the pipeline, but it makes the wait far less dangerous.

What Supply Chain Design Tells Us About Where Things Come From

The frameworks in this chapter—the news vendor problem, Fisher's efficient versus responsive supply chains, make-to-order versus make-to-stock, the bullwhip effect—might seem like management theory, but they have direct consequences for where in the world things get made. A retailer who needs to respond quickly to uncertain demand has a strong motivation to source nearby, even at substantially higher labor cost. A retailer selling stable products with more predictable demand can afford to reach farther away geographically to get the lowest cost, accepting longer lead times because the forecast risk is lower. The geography of production is not just a function of labor costs; it is a function of time, uncertainty, and the cost of getting it wrong.

The bullwhip effect adds another layer to that story. Long supply chains are not just expensive to run; they are structurally prone to the kind of amplified demand swings that leave factories overwhelmed one moment and idle the next and that fill the racks of close-out merchandisers with someone else's ordering mistakes. Every additional week of transit time between a factory and a consumer is another week during which demand can shift and orders can pile up in ways nobody intended. The remedies, like better visibility, vendor-managed inventory, tighter information sharing, reducing the gain in the ordering loop, are all ways of shrinking the effective distance between supply and demand, even when the physical distance remains large. Understanding these dynamics doesn't just explain how supply chains are managed. It helps explain why the production of so many products is arranged the way it is and what it would take to arrange it differently.

CHAPTER 9

Where Prices Are Made: Concentrated Nodes and the Geography of Value

Why does a country that sits on top of vast mineral wealth so often fail to capture the economic value of processing that wealth? Australia exports iron ore to China, which turns it into steel, which Australia then buys back. Sierra Leone digs up diamonds that end up being cut in India. Resource-rich nations have long been advised to "move up the value chain" and process what they dig up rather than ship it raw. Yet the processing stubbornly ends up somewhere else. The conventional explanation invokes labor costs or capital availability, as we saw with cacao bean and cashew nut processing in Chapters 2 and 4, but these explanations are incomplete.

A more fundamental answer lies in the distinction between what is fixed and what is mobile in a supply chain. The resource is anchored by geology or the climate and ecology where things grow. On the other hand, the processing is footloose and can, in principle, locate anywhere. Where it actually lands is determined by where the capabilities are: the accumulated skills, trust networks, supplier relationships, and craft knowledge that make complex processing possible.

Paul Krugman's economic geography framework explains why processing, once it clusters somewhere, tends to stay there. Scale economies and thick labor markets create self-reinforcing agglomeration that is hard to dislodge (Krugman 1991). Ricardo Hausmann and César Hidalgo's economic complexity framework explains why it is so hard to build processing capability from scratch. They argue that a country can only move into industries whose capability requirements are close to what it already produces, and raw material extraction sits in a sparse, poorly connected corner of what they call the "product space," far from the complex manufacturing activities that generate sustained prosperity (Hidalgo and Hausmann 2009).

There is another dimension to supply chain geography that standard trade theory largely ignores: the power to set prices. Most economists argue that commodity prices are determined in competitive world markets where all participants are price takers. This fits in a world where there are many buyers and many sellers trading the same or similar goods. But in the world we live in, processing capacity and consumption are often geographically concentrated in ways that give the concentrated node a decisive influence over what the commodity is worth.

Michal Kalecki observed in the 1940s that prices in industrial markets are not set by anonymous competition but by firms with market power, applying a markup over costs that reflects their structural position (Kalecki 1944). He was writing about manufacturing firms, but his insight generalizes to any node in a supply chain that is sufficiently concentrated, whether it processes the majority of a commodity, consumes the majority of it, or controls the infrastructure through which its value is certified. This means firms in that node can exercise pricing power over less concentrated nodes upstream and downstream. This is the supply chain analog of monopsony: not a single buyer of a good or service but a dominant node in a global value chain that sets the terms on which others participate. Such nodes often are part of a cluster like what we described in Chapter 7, but they don't have to be. More often they are tied to where there are large markets.

In this chapter we're going to look at three examples that I find particularly interesting: sapphire and ruby processing in Bangkok, Thailand, Australian iron ore mining, and what has happened to the market for American hardwoods.

Colored Gemstones in Thailand

I have been to many Southeast Asian countries over the last decade, and I find them fascinating because they are so different. Thailand is an export powerhouse beyond seafood (we discussed this in Chapter 1). It is also big in electronics and machinery, and it historically has been an automotive manufacturing hub for the region. Toyota's first overseas location outside Japan was Thailand.

Imagine my surprise when I learned that gemstones like rubies and sapphires along with precious metals were among the top five exports, even though a large proportion of the colored stones today come from Madagascar, Sri Lanka, and other countries (Lawson 2019). Rubies and blue sapphires were mined in Chantaburi, Trad, and Kanchanaburi provinces, but the story of why the processing cluster ended up in Bangkok has more to do with the tortured history of its neighbor Myanmar (Rouay 2019).

Mining Gemstones in Burma

Mogok is a city in northern Myanmar, about 50 miles west of the Irrawaddy River with many Buddhist shrines and gold-leaf covered pagodas. The region is best known for its gemstones, including rubies, sapphires, spinel, peridot, and moonstone. For centuries it has been one of the world's premier sources of high-quality rubies, especially the highly prized "pigeon's blood" stones, a term that was first used in 1829 to describe the finest stones from the Mogok mines (AMNH 2014). They have a vivid red color with a slight blue hue, exceptional clarity and brilliance along with a fluorescent internal glow (Sotheby's 2025). The mines here have produced some of the largest pigeon's blood rubies in the world, and the stones can sell for more than $300,000 per carat. Sotheby's says the top stones have sold for more than $30 million.

Under British colonial administration, Burmese rubies were integrated into imperial trade networks, but even then much of the cutting and polishing occurred outside the mining region. As gemologist Richard W. Hughes documents, Mogok produced exceptional stones but Burma (which is a former official name for Myanmar) did not historically develop into the world's dominant cutting and trading center. That role increasingly shifted elsewhere as global markets evolved (Hughes 1997).

British rule ended in 1948, but economic development of the former British colony was hobbled by a complex history of military rule, ethnic conflicts, and international sanctions. The turning point came after Burma's 1962 military coup, when General Ne Win's government nationalized major industries including gemstone mining and imposed tight state control over exports. This put the country into an economic dark age, chasing away trade and foreign investment. The military junta renamed the country Myanmar in 1989.

Years of economic mismanagement and poverty led to protests that culminated in an uprising and general strike on August 8, 1988 ("8/8/88"). Activists organized citizens to step in and perform basic government tasks as the administration collapsed, but that ended five weeks later when a new military ruler imposed martial law and crushed the rebellion. The military promised elections, and in 1990 the National League for Democracy (NLD), the party of Aung San Suu Kyi, won 80% of the seats, but the junta didn't cede power until 2010. In 2012, the NLD won a parliamentary by-election, and this marked the beginning of an opening up as both the European Union and the United States suspended sanctions.

I visited Myanmar twice in 2019, scouting sites to bring a class to visit the following January, which at the time seemed to be quite safe and making significant headway on its economic development. After the class arrived in Yangon in early January 2020, I took it to visit a Chinese company that was installing the optical fiber backbone (to provide Internet services) for the country. When we were assembled in a conference room in their offices, I asked the CEO, Dana, what it was like to install infrastructure in conflict zones toward the Chinese border. An executive sitting next to her commented, "Yeah, you know with all the guys carrying all the guns!"

"Oh, it's not a problem," Dana retorted.

"She went to the warlord's wedding," commented the executive.

"Well, I wanted to talk to him, and I knew he would be there," Dana replied. "Once they understand what you are doing, they send out soldiers to show you where the landmines are and to protect you."

It turns out that all the people fighting with each other use Google Maps and WhatsApp, so they appreciate good infrastructure. That's when I realized doing business in Myanmar was still a little rugged, and it no doubt got worse after the coup in 2021. I've told students we're not going back there for a while.

Escaping Burma for Thailand

After the 1962 coup, Burmese gem merchants and miners were cut off from their livelihoods so many crossed over into Thailand, bringing with them the knowledge and trading relationships that had made Mogok famous. Meanwhile, the Myanmar Gems Enterprise came to dominate official sales, often through controlled auctions, while private trading was heavily restricted. These policies pushed much of the gemstone trade underground; i.e., stones were routinely smuggled across the Thai border, where they could be sold to processors.

Thailand already had domestic sources for the stones, but the influx of Burmese expertise coincided with a homegrown technical breakthrough that would prove transformative. In 1968, a craftsman in Chanthaburi discovered a new heat-treating process that could dramatically improve the color of sapphires. Heating the stones to 1,000–1,700 °C improved their color, enhanced clarity, and could sometimes remove hazy inclusions. This was particularly valuable for upgrading lower quality stones, and the technique was subsequently extended to rubies. The heat-treatment process became a closely held body of tacit knowledge that was passed between generations of Thai artisans, which gave Thailand a competitive advantage that was entirely independent of its geology.

FIGURE 9.1 Sorting sapphires in Bangkok, circa 2017. *Source:* Willy Shih.

The cluster that built up around the Burmese expertise and the Thai heat-treatment knowledge attracted rough stones from progressively further afield. Thai gem merchants traveled to Sri Lanka, Australia, Madagascar, Mozambique, and East Africa, buying rough material and bringing it back to Thailand for treatment and cutting. As gemstone volumes grew, so did the supporting infrastructure: grading laboratories, certification services, gem schools, and the trading markets of Bangkok's Silom district and the provincial center of Chanthaburi, where stones from around the world change hands in open-air markets every weekend. Today Bangkok is the go-to spot for gem cutting and enhancement techniques (Sikri 2024). Major mining com panies including Gemfields and Fura Gems have relocated their rough-stone auctions to Bangkok, drawn by the concentration of buyers and the depth of trade infrastructure. When I visited some of the processing houses in 2017, I was amazed at the sheer quantities of sapphires and rubies being graded and sorted in small workshops (see Figures 9.1–9.3).

From Mass Market to High End

The depth of Thailand's jewelry manufacturing base is perhaps best illustrated by Pandora, the Danish company that is the world's largest jewelry brand by volume. Pandora makes virtually all of its jewelry, more than 100 million pieces a year, at two large factories in Thailand, one in Bangkok and one in the northern city of Lamphun, together employing tens of thousands of craftspeople (Chen 2018; Graff 2022). The concentration of skilled labor, supplier relationships, gem-testing laboratories, and logistics infrastructure that had built up around Bangkok's colored gemstone trade created the conditions a high-volume fine jewelry manufacturer needed. Thailand's

FIGURE 9.2 Assembling necklaces in Bangkok, circa 2017. *Source:* Willy Shih.

FIGURE 9.3 Sorted gemstones in Bangkok, circa 2017. *Source:* Willy Shih.

Board of Investment reinforced this with targeted incentives for the sector, including tax holidays, duty-free machinery imports, and provisions for full foreign ownership, that made Thailand not merely attractive but the obvious choice (Asia News Monitor 2015).

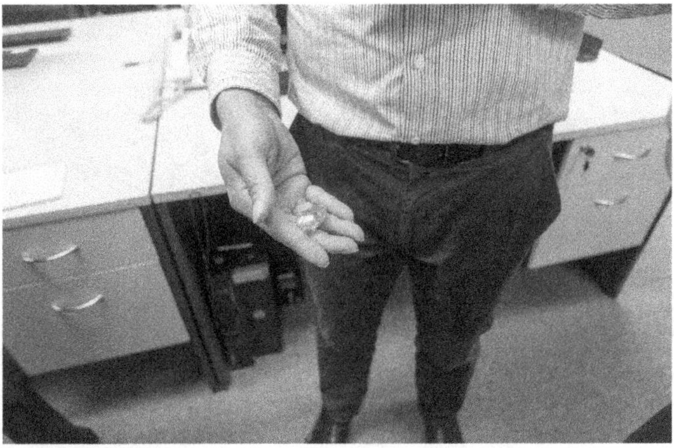

FIGURE 9.4 That's me holding a 111 carat fancy vivid yellow diamond worth $15 million, circa 2017. *Source:* Willy Shih.

When I brought a faculty group to visit them in 2017, we saw an army of craftspeople making charm bracelets for the Danish company to sell in shopping malls from Copenhagen to Chicago. They make them in Thailand because that is where the capabilities are and where the government made sure they would stay.

It gets more interesting! I also visited a diamond cutter that was quite extraordinary. Bangkok's deep infrastructure around colored gemstones meant there were trading relationships, grading expertise, export logistics, gem-testing laboratories, and a concentration of buyers who traveled to Bangkok, which seemed to have spilled over into diamond processing. The facility I visited was just upstairs from a major security firm, and when they brought out the stones for me to examine, I could see why. That's me holding a 111 carat fancy vivid yellow diamond worth $15 million (see Figure 9.4). The shop was filled with craftspeople using the latest computer-driven tools to analyze and perfect cutting strategies (see Figure 9.5).

Diamond cutting began in Venice around 1330, and as Europe's economic center shifted north, it migrated to Paris, Bruges, and Antwerp where Flemish craftsmen first developed the techniques for faceting stones (Mobley 2025). New York later became a significant center, and Israel built a substantial industry after World War II.

It turns out that the center shifted to India early in the twentieth century but accelerated dramatically after Indian independence, when the government liberalized the import and export of rough diamonds. The city of Surat, in the state of Gujarat on India's west coast, became an unlikely cluster. Cutting had begun around 1900, but before the Second World War much of the actual cutting work was concentrated in Rangoon

FIGURE 9.5 Diamond processing in Bangkok, circa 2017. *Source:* Willy Shih.

(today Yangon), Burma, where a skilled community had developed. When Japan invaded Burma in 1942, those diamond artisans fled home to Surat-Navsari in Gujarat. The merchants who had been sending rough stones to Rangoon followed their cutters and redirected shipments to Surat instead (Sikri 2024).

Iron Ore in Australia

Australia is one of the world's leading producers of bauxite (the primary ore for extracting aluminum), iron ore, lithium, gold, lead, diamonds, rare earth elements, uranium, and zinc (Geoscience Australia 2025). Yet, as the head of Science Strategy at the Australian scientific research agency CSIRO once told me, "We didn't necessarily want to always be just a large quarry where people dug ore up and shipped it out."

A Complicated History of Ore Exports

Iron ore was first identified in Australia by the explorer Edward John Eyre, who passed through the Middleback Ranges of South Australia in 1839 and noted the area's substantial ironstone deposits (Iron Knob n.d.). Today more than 90% of identified reserves can be found in Western Australia, with almost 80% of that in the Hamersley Range in the Pilbara region.

Prior to the mid-1930s, almost all iron ore mining fed domestic steel mills, principally BHP's works at Newcastle, which opened in 1915, and Port Kembla (National Museum Australia 2026). Small quantities had been exported to the Netherlands and the United States from the 1920s onward and to Japan from the early 1930s—close to 300,000 tons in 1935–1936 alone. In 1936, the British firm H.A. Brassert reached an agreement with the Nippon Mining Company to establish a mine on Koolan Island in Yampi Sound, Western Australia, with plans to ship one million tons of ore per year to Japan. But Japan's full-scale invasion of China in 1937 instilled fears of a wider Pacific war. After a government-commissioned survey concluded that Australia's accessible reserves amounted to only around 264 million tons and that they were not abundant and should be deemed a strategic resource for future national security, the government announced a ban on all iron ore exports in May 1938 (National Museum Australia 2026).

The ban survived until 1960, when a large trade deficit prompted the government to search for exports that could help close the shortfall. Technological improvements in railways and ocean shipping had made the movement of large quantities of ore far more economical (more tradable; see Chapter 1), but the government remained cautious. It ultimately agreed to lift the ban only partially. Exports from the three largest known high-grade deposits would remain prohibited, but exports from smaller or newly discovered deposits would be permitted up to one million tons per year.

The following year, in 1961, Lang Hancock, a pastoralist and amateur geologist who owned the Ashburton and Mulga Downs stations in the Pilbara, informed Conzinc Rio Tinto of vast deposits of high-quality ore he had spotted from the air in the Turner River area in the early 1950s. The estimated reserves nearly quadrupled Australia's known iron ore resources overnight (Lee 2013). That discovery set off a race among companies to secure leases and sign long-term contracts with Japanese steel mills, and by May 1966 the government had rescinded all remaining export restrictions.

From Tokyo to Beijing: Changing Destinations for Pilbara Iron Ore

The iron ore industry that emerged from the Pilbara in the late 1960s was centered around Japan. The Japanese market was the primary target, and to Japanese buyers, the Australian suppliers were the main source (alongside smaller volumes from India and Brazil) with its proximity easily the most important factor (Sukagawa 2010; Drysdale 1970). The Australian miners signed long-term contracts with the Japanese steel industry, which permitted them to obtain the capital needed to finance infrastructure for mines located hundreds of kilometers from the coast. Those contracts funded development of the railways, ports, and towns that made the Pilbara operational. By the end of 1967, Japan had overtaken Great Britain to become Australia's largest export partner, with iron ore exports climbing steeply. By 1972 Australia had become Japan's primary supplier of iron ore.

Iron ore contracts were pegged through annually negotiated benchmark pricing between Australian mining companies and Japanese steel firms. The two sides were organized into informal cartels, with a representative firm from each side, typically Nippon Steel and Rio Tinto, acting as a "champion" that would negotiate prices on behalf of their respective groups, who would then adopt the same prices. Nippon Steel's strategy was to constantly encourage iron ore producers to expand production. That was a strategy that worked in part because Japanese mills had the cost structure to sell large volumes of steel at margins that Australian mills operating at a fraction of the scale could not sustain. Encouraging the Australian miners to expand production kept the price of iron ore relatively flat in nominal terms for much of the 1980s and 1990s.

Japanese contracts were structured to foster security of supply, stable prices, mutual cooperation, and long-term relationships, in contrast to European buyers, who preferred market-linked "evergreen" contracts revised annually (Sukagawa 2010). Korea joined as a significant buyer during the 1970s and 1980s as its own steel industry developed, and the development of Taiwan and South Korea in those decades drove total Pilbara exports beyond 200 million tons per annum by the early 2000s though Japan remained the anchor buyer throughout.

The emergence of China changed everything. For most of the twentieth century, China had been considered a sleeping dragon in the iron ore market. But the combination of market liberalization, urbanization on an unprecedented scale which created demand for enormous quantities of steel, and the strategic focus on steelmaking in successive five-year plans made China the world's dominant steel producer. China became Australia's largest iron ore buyer in 2004 and has held that position ever since. Between 2001 and 2011, the value of Australian iron ore exports to China increased at an average of 46% per annum, while volumes grew at 24% annually (Department of Foreign Affairs and Trade 2012). The growth of the China market initiated the Pilbara's major twenty-first century mining boom, increasing Australian exports to more than 800 million tons per annum by 2016; Australian producers overtook Brazil as the world's largest iron ore exporter in 2007 (Australian Mining Review 2025; Hurst 2015).

When I had an opportunity to visit the Pilbara region, it was in the midst of a major capacity expansion to feed what at the time was insatiable demand. After stepping off a three-hour company charter flight from Perth, I entered a land where everything was covered by red iron ore dust. The mine used a highly efficient surface grinding approach, and the ore was crushed in a processing plant that had been built on-site (see Figure 9.6). It was then loaded on to 220 car long trains pulled by two and pushed by two 4,000 horsepower diesel

FIGURE 9.6 Iron ore mine, Pilbara region, Western Australia. *Source:* Willy Shih.

FIGURE 9.7 220-car-long iron ore mine train. *Source:* Willy Shih.

electric locomotives (see Figure 9.7). I rode the train to Port Hedland, which is on the northwest coast and sits on the Indian Ocean. There the train cars passed through an automatic dumper, where the ore was unloaded into massive stacks before being loaded on bulk carriers destined for China (see Figure 9.8).

FIGURE 9.8 I'm standing on a ship loader at Port Hedland, Western Australia. *Source:* Willy Shih.

China Becomes the Dominant Purchaser of Australian Iron Ore

The shift in destination for where most Australian ore was sold was accompanied by changes in how prices were set. The cozy bilateral arrangement between a few Australian miners and a few Japanese mills had rested on the fact that both sides were small enough in number to coordinate. China's steel industry was different. It was fragmented among hundreds of mills, growing too fast for annual contracts to track, and served by a spot market that increasingly diverged from the benchmark. Japan's three largest steelmakers had accounted for roughly 70% of national steel production, while Baosteel, China's largest steelmaker and ore buyer, was responsible for only 6% of Chinese production. There were 7,300 companies producing steel in China at the time, and the top two accounted for only 10% of ore imports. Baosteel and later the China Iron and Steel Association struggled as smaller steel companies struck deals with ore producers based on spot market prices (Massot 2025).

What replaced long-term contracts was a more volatile spot market that was more responsive to Chinese construction cycles and in which the center of gravity for price discovery shifted inexorably toward China. China now absorbs more than 80% of Australia's iron ore exports by volume, a concentration that makes the Pilbara's fortunes almost entirely hostage to decisions made in Beijing about infrastructure spending, property development, and the fate of large Chinese consumers, like its automobile industry, which is now the largest in the world.

The question of where, exactly, iron ore prices are now set does not have a tidy answer, but increasingly it is in China and on China's terms. The nominal benchmark since 2010 has been a daily index, the Platts 62% Fe fines assessment or its equivalents, which tracks seaborne spot transactions and is reflected in futures contracts traded on the Singapore Exchange and, more importantly, on the Dalian Commodity Exchange (DCE), the world's largest iron ore derivatives market. Dalian futures prices frequently lead physical market negotiations, with spot deals referencing DCE settlements as benchmarks, and price movements in Dalian routinely precede similar movements in other markets (Zadeh 2025).

Beijing has not been content to let this happen passively. In 2022, the Chinese government established the China Mineral Resources Group (CMRG), a state-owned enterprise with a mandate to centralize iron ore purchasing and convert China's dominant share of global demand into real market power. By 2025, CMRG had become the single largest iron ore trader in the world, representing more than half of China's steelmakers in negotiations with Rio Tinto, BHP, and Vale. It also started using stockpiles of ore as a kind of strategic reserve, built up when prices are low, released when domestic steel margins are under pressure (**Mining.com** 2025). In early 2026, under pressure from CMRG, both Rio Tinto and Fortescue suspended the use of the Platts index for Chinese shipments entirely, shifting to alternative pricing mechanisms more closely aligned with Chinese market conditions (Cang and Gemmell 2025). The Japan-Australia bilateral monopoly that governed iron ore pricing for 40 years was replaced by a state-directed power in Beijing.

Consolidating China's Buying Power

The strategic logic behind China's push to reorganize iron ore pricing did not stop at financial instruments and state trading companies. In November 2025, the first shipments left Guinea from Simandou, Africa's largest greenfield mining project and one of the most consequential investments in the history of the iron ore trade. The deposit, located in the remote southern highlands of Guinea, holds an estimated 2.4 billion tons of ore averaging around 65% iron content—significantly higher grade than the Pilbara's current average of roughly 61%, which has itself been declining as the richest deposits are exhausted. The project, capitalized at more than $20 billion and built on 622 km of new trans-Guinean railway, is a joint venture involving Rio Tinto, Chinese state steelmaker Baowu, aluminum giant Chinalco, and a Singapore-based shipping consortium. Chinese entities control roughly three-quarters of the overall investment.

At full capacity, Simandou is projected to export up to 120 million tons annually, enough to supply around 13% of China's current iron ore imports from a source that China itself largely controls (Hirtenstein and Cang 2025). Industry analysts have taken to calling it the "Pilbara killer," though the more precise description is a structural hedge: China is using its financial power to develop an alternative supply node, giving it leverage over Australian producers that no amount of futures trading or state purchasing bodies could fully replicate (S&P Global Commodity Insights 2026). The resource, in this case, is no longer entirely fixed.

American Hardwoods

The eastern United States contains one of the great temperate hardwood forests on earth. A prominent New Hampshire-based hardwood supplier told me that there is substantially more wood in the forests than 60–70 years ago, because much of it hasn't been harvested. He said the finest cherry mostly comes out of Pennsylvania, the best walnut comes from western New York, Pennsylvania, Indiana, and Missouri, and New England is mainly a source for red oak and maples. The best quality trees are around 80–100 years old, and these forests produce timber of a quality and variety that no other region can match at scale.

For most of the twentieth century, the price of that timber was set in America, specifically by the decisions of a relatively small number of large domestic furniture manufacturers. Wood household furniture makers, concentrated in North Carolina and Virginia, were the single largest buyers of graded hardwood lumber from the 1960s through the 1990s, and their willingness to pay determined what sawmills charged, which in turn determined what loggers received and ultimately set the value of standing timber across millions of acres of private forest. The construction and remodeling industry reinforced this, as demand for hardwood flooring, kitchen cabinets, and millwork kept prices elevated even as the furniture industry began to weaken (Luppold et al. 2014).

The relocation of furniture manufacturing to China and Southeast Asia changed all of this. The collapse of domestic furniture manufacturing was part of a broader phenomenon that economists David Autor, David Dorn, and Gordon Hanson documented in a widely cited study: rising Chinese import competition, which accelerated sharply after China joined the World Trade Organization in 2001, explained roughly a quarter of the aggregate decline in U.S. manufacturing employment between 1990 and 2007

(Autor, Dorn, and Hanson 2013). Furniture was among the hardest-hit sectors. North Carolina, historically the center of American furniture making, lost more than half of its furniture factory jobs in just ten years, between 1999 and 2009 (Lacy 2020).

Between 2000 and 2006, increased furniture imports from China and other Southeast Asian sources caused the value of domestic shipments of wood household furniture to decline rapidly, and hardwood lumber consumption by the combined furniture industries fell by nearly 90% between 2000 and 2009. The construction market, which had partly compensated, collapsed in the same period. Consumption of graded hardwood lumber by construction and remodeling product manufacturers fell 64% between 2005 and 2009, tracking a 74% decline in single-family housing starts. The domestic industry that had priced American hardwoods for a century contracted so severely that by 2012, exports accounted for nearly half of all graded hardwood lumber consumed, a figure that had been 18% just eight years earlier (Luppold et al. 2014). Sawmill output dropped 22% between 2004 and 2008 alone (Buehlmann et al. 2010).

China came to dominate demand for American hardwoods, accounting for roughly half of all U.S. hardwood exports by 2016. As the executive director of the American Hardwood Export Council observed at the industry's European convention that year, if it were not for Chinese demand, total U.S. exports would have been lower than they had been a decade earlier (Spencer 2016). Europe, long the prestige market for American cherry and walnut, had been overtaken. Hardwood lumber prices, which had historically tracked domestic housing starts, were now driven by overseas demand rather than domestic construction (Spencer 2016).

This is a different form of concentration from the processing bottleneck that we saw earlier in this chapter with colored gemstones. China does not cut, dry, or grade American hardwoods. It buys the raw or semi-processed lumber and transforms it into furniture and flooring domestically, often for re-export: Vietnam plays a related role as a processing intermediary, receiving American lumber and exporting it back to the United States as finished furniture. The concentration is on the demand side, a monopsony of consumption rather than of transformation. Yet the pricing consequence is identical in structure to the processing bottleneck cases: a dispersed set of producers (American sawmills and the woodland owners behind them) faces a concentrated node of buyers, and the concentrated node sets prices.

When Chinese government policy shifts incentives within the furniture sector or when the bilateral tariff environment changes, the reverberations run upstream through the entire American hardwood value chain, reaching the price of standing timber in Maine or New Hampshire woodlots owned by families who have never done business with anyone in China and may not know that anyone in China has ever heard of their trees (Luppold et al. 2014).

What makes this case theoretically interesting is that the concentration was not planned and is not stable. No single Chinese firm or agency coordinated the purchase of American hardwood market share. The concentration emerged from the aggregated decisions of thousands of Chinese furniture manufacturers responding to their own cost structures, labor markets, and government policies. The industry surveys of Chinese and European importers of American hardwood confirm what the aggregate trade data show: Chinese buyers evaluate American suppliers primarily on price, color consistency, and species availability, and they have sufficient alternatives—tropical hardwoods, European species, domestic Chinese timber—to exercise genuine choice (Arias et al. 2020).

The American industry's response has been to move toward certification, customization, and new end-use markets like construction, where hardwood cross-laminated timber panels offer a premium niche less exposed to Chinese price competition (Spencer 2016). These are reasonable strategies. But the harsh reality is that the pricing power for the bulk of the American hardwood resources has settled in a market the producers cannot enter, serving customers they cannot directly negotiate with, in response to conditions they cannot observe in real time.

Where Is the Real Power in the Supply Chain?

The three examples examined in this chapter involve different commodities, different geographies, and different histories. But in each case, the resource—rough gemstones, iron ore, hardwood lumber—is fixed by geology or ecology. It can be found only where nature placed it, and it cannot be moved to a more convenient location.

The processing, by contrast, is footloose. Gem cutting, steelmaking, and hardwood sawing can in principle occur anywhere with the necessary labor, capital, and expertise. Yet in each case, processing has concentrated in a dominant location, and that concentration has given the processing node the power to determine what the unprocessed resource is worth to everyone else. These concentrations were shaped by political events, historical accidents, and deliberate policy choices that conventional trade theory struggles to accommodate.

- Burma's gem processing cluster was displaced by Ne Win's 1962 coup and reconstituted in Thailand by a diaspora that carried its knowledge and relationships across the border.

- China's steel was built by a state with the industrial ambition and financial capacity to sustain overcapacity through decades of below-cost production, crowding out competitors in Australia, Europe, and North America.
- American hardwood exports to China reflect Chinese furniture manufacturers' appetite for species unavailable domestically, combined with a trading infrastructure that emerged from decades of bilateral commercial relationship-building.

In each case, the current geography of processing is the product of a specific history, and a different history could plausibly have produced a different geography.

The implication for resource-rich countries is uncomfortable. Standard development advice urges them to capture more value by processing their resources domestically—to build steel mills, cut their own diamonds, mill their own timber. This advice is not wrong, but it understates the difficulty. The obstacle is not merely the cost of building processing facilities; it is the need to displace an existing concentrated node that has accumulated the capabilities, the infrastructure, and the pricing power that make the concentration self-reinforcing.

Botswana has made more progress than most in this regard, using its control over rough diamond supply to compel De Beers to shift sorting and sales operations to Gaborone—essentially leveraging the stationary nature of the resource against the mobility of the processing. But Botswana's leverage depended on a degree of supply concentration that few resource producers enjoy. Australia cannot dictate to China's steel industry. Madagascar cannot dictate to Bangkok's gem traders. The resource is fixed, but the power flows to wherever the processing concentrates.

Economists have documented the price leadership of concentrated nodes in individual markets. What is less recognized is that this is a structural feature of supply chains wherever processing or consumption is geographically concentrated, regardless of industry. The concentrated node, whether it consumes or transforms, becomes the market. This principle has implications beyond commodity economics. It shapes the strategic logic of industrial policy, the leverage available to resource-exporting nations, and the vulnerability of supply chains to political disruption. A country that understands where prices are actually made as opposed to where they are formally quoted is better positioned to decide where along the value chain its own investments will generate the most durable returns. In Chapter 11, we'll turn to the question of what governments have actually done when they have tried to shift that geography deliberately and what the evidence suggests about when such efforts succeed.

CHAPTER 10

Tariff and Nontariff Barriers

In earlier chapters, we discussed the forces that shape modern supply chains. Their global and interconnected character emerged most strongly from the 1990s onward, as large economies such as China and India opened to international trade. More broadly, starting in the post–World War II period and accelerating after the 1980s, there was a sustained decline in many of the barriers to cross-border trade—a liberalizing tide that reshaped where goods were made, who made them, and on what terms.

In recent years, however, that tide has turned. Tariffs and other barriers to trade that were negotiated down over decades have been reimposed in recent months; regulatory and technical barriers have proliferated alongside them. The result is a world in which the question of where things come from is increasingly shaped not by comparative advantage or logistics costs but by government policy. This chapter examines how tariff and nontariff barriers work, why they are used, and why their effects on where products come from can be more dramatic and more durable than they first appear.

A Quick Primer on Tariffs

Tariffs are taxes levied by governments on goods when they enter a country. They are calculated either as a percentage of the value of the good (an *ad valorem* tariff) or as a fixed charge per unit. Although often described as taxes on foreign producers, the legal obligation to pay the tariff arises at the border when an importer declares a shipment to customs authorities. Thus, they are the responsibility of the "importer of record" and ultimately are the responsibility of domestic firms that import them. The economic burden of the tariff may be shared among importers, foreign exporters, and domestic consumers, depending on market conditions such as competition, substitutability, and price sensitivity. In practice, tariffs frequently raise costs for downstream firms and prices for final consumers, even when policymakers frame them as penalties imposed on foreign countries.

Tariffs Have a Long History

Tariffs have been around a long time. In the Bronze Age (third–second millennium BCE), merchant records from the Assyrian trading colony at Kanesh (in Anatolia) showed that local officials imposed levies on caravans trading metals and textiles (Hoffman 2025). Governments have long used tariffs as a source of revenue. Before the rise of modern income and consumption taxes, tariffs were among the easiest ways for states to finance themselves. Goods crossed borders at a limited number of ports, trade was visible, and duties were relatively simple to collect. In the United States, tariffs accounted for the majority of federal revenue throughout the nineteenth century, funding everything from infrastructure to the government bureaucracy. While tariffs today play a much smaller fiscal role in advanced economies, they remain an important revenue source in many low- and middle-income countries where tax collection capacity is more limited (Irwin 2017; Baunsgaard and Keen 2010).

Governments frequently use tariffs to protect domestic producers and jobs from foreign competition. By raising the price of imported goods (making them less tradable), tariffs give domestic firms the ability to charge higher prices when competing with lower-cost or more efficient foreign rivals. This is often framed as a way to protect strategic industries, preserve employment, or prevent sudden shocks from import surges. The benefits of protection tend to be concentrated and accrue to specific firms, workers, or regions of the country, while the costs are spread broadly across consumers and downstream industries, making tariffs an especially durable policy choice despite their economy-wide inefficiencies (Grossman and Helpman 1994).

Tariffs are often justified as a way to encourage domestic industrial development, improve national security, or, especially in the second Trump administration, provide bargaining leverage. The "infant industry" argument holds that new industrial sectors may need temporary protection to achieve scale, increase learning by doing, or attain technological maturity. More recently, governments have invoked tariffs to reduce dependence on foreign suppliers in defense-related or critical industries or to gain leverage in trade negotiations by threatening or imposing economic costs. In practice, these objectives blur into one another: tariffs meant to strengthen domestic capability also reshape global supply chains and alter negotiating positions, sometimes in ways that persist long after the original rationale has faded.

What Do Trucks Imported into the United States Have to Do with Chickens?

A famous *ad valorem* tariff example is the so-called "chicken tax" imposed by the United States: a 25% tariff on the value of imported light trucks, including pickup trucks and cargo vans. This tariff was introduced in 1964 and was originally intended as retaliation over countries blocking the import of American-raised chickens into Europe. The tariff was calculated as a percentage of a vehicle's declared customs value, and it sharply increased the cost of importing pickup trucks into the United States. This effectively excluded most foreign-made trucks from the U.S. market. And because the tariff was in response to blocking American chickens, it's been called the chicken tax ever since.

Historically, the "light truck" category included pickup trucks, cargo vans, and utility vehicles designed primarily for carrying goods rather than passengers. Early SUVs that were derived from truck platforms and marketed as utility vehicles often fell into this category and were treated as light trucks for tariff and regulatory purposes. This helped make light trucks the most profitable segment for the Detroit automakers because they were protected from import competition.

One of the more perverse outcomes of the chicken tax was Ford's import strategy for its Transit Connect cargo vans, which were designed and manufactured by its subsidiary in Turkey. To reduce the duty, between 2009 and 2013 Ford imported the vehicles as passenger vans. Because under U.S. customs rules passenger vehicles were subject to a much lower duty rate (around 2.5%), the company equipped the vans with temporary rear seats, seat belts, and other passenger features before they reached U.S. customs. Once they cleared customs, Ford removed the rear seats, seat belts, and other equipment (if purchasers didn't want them) and converted the vehicles back to their intended cargo configuration (Krizan 2009).

U.S. Customs ultimately ruled in 2013 that this practice was a misclassification aimed at evading the chicken tax, not a legitimate use of the passenger classification. The U.S. Department of Justice sued the company, accusing it of tax fraud (the court agreed that tariffs are a tax!) by disguising imported cargo vans as passenger vehicles. This ended up going all the way to the Supreme Court, which declined to hear the case in 2020. In 2024 Ford agreed to a $365 million settlement (Dennis 2024).

Chinese Tariffs on Auto Parts and Australian Barley

Cars seem to come up a lot in fights over tariffs and trade, probably because they are usually a major source of manufacturing employment. In 2006, China instituted measures that effectively placed a 25% tariff (the same rate applied to fully assembled vehicles) on imported auto parts if they were used to assemble cars in China above certain foreign content thresholds. The United States asserted that to circumvent the principle that tariffs are collected at the border, China assessed them as "customs duties" charged to domestic Chinese auto manufacturers for using foreign parts, but this had the same effect as tariffs and thus circumvented provisions of an agreement it accepted as part of joining the World Trade Organization (WTO) (United States Trade Representative 2007). It amounted to a local content rule.

This is interesting in retrospect because at the time the China auto market totaled around seven million vehicles per year while the United States was around 16 million. This was when internal combustion engines still reigned supreme and China was behind in technology. The big sellers were foreign brands like Buick (from GM), Volkswagen, Hyundai, and Toyota, all of whom worked with Chinese joint venture partners. Thus, China was probably thinking of infant industry protection. This was before the Chinese market surpassed the United States in size around 2009 and before the transition to electric vehicles, which China has led.

The United States, the European Union, and Canada challenged the policy at the World Trade Organization, and in 2008, the WTO ruled against China, finding that the measures violated its WTO commitments because they discriminated against imported parts relative to domestic ones (World Trade Organization 2008). China subsequently removed the policy in 2009.

Australian barley is another interesting story. Before May 2020, China bought most of its barley from Australia to the tune of 5–6 million tons per year. But then it imposed tariffs of more than 80% on Australian barley imports, ostensibly as an anti-dumping and anti-subsidy measure but widely seen as retaliation for Australia's call for an independent inquiry into the origins of COVID-19. This forced a huge reshuffling of global grain flows, as Australian growers redirected their barley to Saudi Arabia, Southeast Asia, and others while China turned to alternative suppliers like France, Canada, Argentina, and Ukraine to fill the gap. This "trade diversion" forced buyers and sellers who had built efficient, long-standing relationships to pivot, raising costs and logistics complexity for everyone. The disruption also affected freight markets, since shipping routes had to be reorganized, and it put pressure on global feed grain prices because the reallocation was imperfect. China paid more for barley than it had before, and Australian farmers got lower prices in their new markets (Kastner and Simes 2021).

China dropped the tariffs in August 2023 as relations with Australia thawed, and trade largely resumed. Politically motivated tariffs can create years of unnecessary supply chain disruption.

U.S. E-Commerce and the "De Minimis" Rule

The Tariff Act of 1930, also known as the Smoot-Hawley Tariff Act, was intended to protect American farmers and manufacturers from foreign competition. Enacted during the Great Depression, it imposed increased duties on more than 20,000 items. In 1938, Congress enacted Section 321 (a)(2)(C), which authorized the Secretary of the Treasury to waive or reduce certain duties "in order to avoid expense and inconvenience to the Government disproportionate to the amount of revenue that would otherwise be collected" on certain imported goods with a fair retail value in the country of shipment of $1 or less (Casey 2025). That became known as the *de minimis exemption*.

The threshold was raised to $5 in 1978 and then $200 as part of the legislation implementing the North American Free Trade Agreement (NAFTA) in 1993. The threshold rose to $800 in 2016 (one of the highest in the world) when President Barack Obama signed the bipartisan Trade Facilitation and Trade Enforcement Act (NPR 2025). That helped make the United States one of the most permissive markets for low-value cross-border parcels in the world. The practical consequence was that virtually any individual consumer purchase from China could now clear customs duty-free and with minimal paperwork. *De minimis* package volume increased to 685.1 million packages in FY 2022, with the vast majority coming from China. Customs data indicated that more than 10% of Chinese imports by value were coming in under *de minimis*, up from 1% a decade earlier (Kaufman 2023).

What lawmakers intended as a convenience for ordinary travelers returning home from abroad became the foundation for an entirely new category of global e-commerce. This rule made it economically viable for Chinese e-commerce platforms such as Shein and Temu to send individual packages directly to customers in the United States without paying duties. By creating shopping apps for smartphones, they could operate under the branding of a single company while shipping products from a vast network of different warehouses and sellers across China (Chow 2024). The scale was staggering: in 2022, Shein represented 50% of the U.S. fast-fashion retail market, larger than Zara and H&M combined, and by January 2024, Temu and Shein had 51 million and 26 million active users, respectively, compared to Amazon's 67 million (Fajgelbaum et al. 2024).

By 2024, more than 1.36 billion *de minimis* shipments arrived in the United States, more than 3.7 million per day. Companies even set up bonded warehouses in places like Canada and Mexico, where things could be imported in bulk and duties could be deferred prior to exporting items to the United States one at a time, duty free (Fonrouge et al. 2025). Shein and Temu together accounted for more than 30% of daily *de minimis* flows into the United States, and a dominant share of U.S.-bound air freight from China. The Trump administration ended the *de minimis* exemption for Chinese imports in May 2025 and for the rest of the world on August 29, 2025.

Beyond Tariffs: Nontariff Barriers

Nontariff trade barriers (NTBs) are policies and practices other than tariffs that restrict or distort international trade by raising costs, delaying entry, or limiting access to markets. Common examples include quotas, licensing requirements, product standards, sanitary and phytosanitary (SPS) measures, customs procedures, and government procurement preferences. Unlike tariffs, NTBs are often embedded in regulatory or administrative systems, which makes them less transparent and harder to measure. While many are justified on public-interest grounds such as health, safety, or environmental protection, they can also be used strategically to shield domestic producers from foreign competition.

NTBs appear across virtually every sector of the economy. For example:

- Agricultural trade is frequently affected by SPS measures such as limits on pesticide residues or disease-related import bans that can block imports even when tariffs are low.
- Manufactured goods face technical barriers to trade, including product certification, labeling requirements, or national standards that vary across countries and impose costly compliance burdens.
- Services trades are typically constrained by licensing rules, local-presence requirements, and limits on foreign ownership.

As tariffs have fallen globally since World War II, empirical research shows that NTBs have become the dominant form of trade protection, shaping who can trade, what can be traded, and at what cost (Kuenzel 2024; Leonardi and Meschi 2024).

Cabotage, the Jones Act, and Why a Lot of East Coast Gasoline Doesn't Come from Texas

One of the more underappreciated barriers arises from the concept of *cabotage*: the right to operate transportation services within a country, which is usually limited to domestically owned and operated carriers. According to the Seafarers International Union, 105 countries around the world (states) have such rules, but it's a big deal mostly for countries who have long coastlines like the United States. Such rules can have interesting consequences.

FIGURE 10.1 Aerial view of the Bayway Refinery in Linden, New Jersey, an oil refinery operated by Phillips 66. *Source:* Quintin Soloviev / CC-BY-SA-4.0 / **https://commons.wikimedia.org/wiki/File:Bayway_Refinery,_New_Jersey.jpg**

If you have ever driven along the New Jersey Turnpike between New York City and Philadelphia, there's a good chance you noticed the Bayway Refinery (see Figure 10.1). It's that huge refinery just south of Newark Airport between Exits 12 and 13. The Turnpike and U.S. Route 1 pass through the middle of the site, so it's hard to miss if you are paying attention. The main refinery and processing area are on the west side, and on the east side is a waterfront on the Arthur Kill where tankers bring crude oil in. I once paid a visit to refinery operations at the site, but that was a long time ago.

The 1,300-acre facility located in the cities of Linden and Elizabeth has been in continuous operation since 1909 and was owned by ExxonMobil until it sold it to Tosco Refining in 1994. Phillips Petroleum bought Tosco in 2001, merged with Conoco, Inc., in 2002, and then split again, so now it is operated by Phillips 66. It is the northernmost refinery on the U.S. East Coast and converts 258,000 barrels of crude oil per day into gasoline, diesel, jet fuel, heating oil, propane, and petrochemical feedstocks to supply the Northeast corridor (Zhang et al. 2023).

You would think that with the revolution in the production of shale oil with the United States being the largest producer of crude oil in the world, Bayway would buy domestic crude. Nope. Much of its crude comes from countries around the Atlantic basin, and a lot of this represents a balance between the types of crude the refinery is geared to process, the cost of shipping it, and the price of crude at various export terminals. That means sometimes it comes from places like Algeria (Renshaw 2016).

Meanwhile, we export crude from Texas to places like China, Italy, Canada, Singapore, and the United Kingdom. At the Port of Corpus Christi, which is the largest oil export terminal in the United States, exports make up anywhere from 93–97% of total volumes in 2025 (Port of Corpus Christi 2026). How can all this make sense?

Coastal Shipping Restrictions in the 1700s and 1800s Shipping oil domestically is expensive. The most efficient way to do it is in very large crude carriers (VLCCs) or supertankers, but using one of those on a domestic route is tricky. Restrictions on coastal shipping go back to 1789 when the third act of the First Congress (enacted July 20, 1789) permitted foreign ships engaged in domestic trade to operate but imposed high tariffs to encourage the use of American vessels (U.S. Govt Printing Office 1789). This is also known as a *cabotage* restriction, limitations on the rights to transport goods or passengers between two places in the same country. In 1817, Congress extended this by disallowing any vessel wholly or partially foreign owned from transporting domestic cargo between U.S. ports. This prohibition was extended to vessels transporting passengers domestically in 1886 (Frittelli 2019).

For the first half of the nineteenth century, American shipbuilding was a major industry and had a comparative advantage because of ample supplies of large timber. But it was slow to transition to iron steamships, and it lost its competitive advantage as global shipping became centered in the more industrialized economies of Western Europe. Britain's repeal of the Navigation Act, which protected lumber from the country's colonial empire, allowed shipowners to buy ships from wherever they wanted. This forced British shipbuilders to become more competitive and invest in steam propulsion and the design of faster ships (Whitehurst 1986). U.S.-built ships cost significantly more than those built in Canada and Britain, and vessels purchased from domestic shipyards became steadily less attractive.

Even in the nineteenth century, this made domestic shipping in coastal waters more expensive. In a book published in 1886 and subsequently included in the Congressional Record in 1892, economist Henry George said (George et al. 1892):

> *Though our Navigation Laws, which forbid the carrying of a pound of freight or a single passenger from American port to American port on any other than an American-built vessel, obscure the effects of protection in our coasting trade, they are just as truly felt as in our ocean trade. The increased cost of building and running vessels has, especially as to steamers, operated to stunt the growth of our coasting trade, and to check by higher freights the development of other industries.*

The Effects of the Jones Act That wasn't enough. In 1920, Congress passed the United States Merchant Marine Act, more commonly known as the Jones Act, a law that was intended to support the U.S. commercial shipping fleet. The act requires that vessels transporting cargo between two U.S. points be built in the United States, as well as crewed and at least 75% owned by U.S. citizens. It does not apply to international waterborne trade. The domestic build requirement for tanker ships contributes to higher costs in moving domestic crude oil along the coasts. Domestically built tankers are about four times the price of foreign-built tankers, and there is limited capacity in U.S. shipyards to build them, especially large ones.

In 2014, the Congressional Research Service reported that five times more Texas crude oil was being shipped in foreign-flag tankers to refineries in eastern Canada than to refineries in the northeastern United States. Shipments from Texas to Canada cost approximately $2 per barrel, compared with $5 to $6 per barrel for shipments from Texas to the East Coast (Frittelli et al. 2014). Also around that time, Bayway started bringing in crude oil from the Bakken Shale in North Dakota by rail. That oil traveled by train to Albany, New York, and then was transferred to a barge to sail down the Hudson River to Arthur Kill, at a cost that was estimated to be between $13 and $15 per barrel (Shauk 2013).

At the time there wasn't enough capacity to move Bakken Shale to market, so it sold at a discount to make it price competitive when the transport cost was factored in. The price spread between inland U.S. crude (often referred to as the "West Texas Intermediate" or "WTI" price) and the international Brent price (the price for light sweet crude from the Brent field in the North Sea off the coast of Britain) narrowed as pipeline capacity out of the Bakken improved and crude markets balanced, eroding the advantage that once justified the high cost of rail transport. Additionally, new pipelines including the Dakota Access Pipeline, which began operations in 2017, provided far cheaper capacity to mid-continent and Gulf Coast markets. As a result, rail shipments to the East Coast plummeted (Fielden 2016).

Foreign crude oil landed in New Jersey shipped on a non-U.S. flagged tanker is cheaper than U.S. crude shipped a much shorter distance on a Jones Act compliant tanker. That's why a lot of East Coast gasoline might have come from the other side of the Atlantic rather than Texas. In a similar vein, the United States is the world's largest exporter of liquefied natural gas (LNG), yet New England relies on imported LNG because there are no Jones Act-compliant LNG tankers. Constellation Energy brings LNG into the Everett Marine Terminal near Boston from Trinidad and Tobago and Jamaica. Natural gas pipelines to bring gas to New York and New England have faced environmental opposition and been denied state permits, so there aren't any alternatives.

The Jones Act has other perverse consequences. Last year the Sea Challenger, an offshore wind turbine installation vessel, was operating off the coast of Massachusetts, installing wind turbines. I had brought students on board that ship a couple of years ago when it was operating out of Port Esbjerg in Jutland in the west of Denmark (see Figure 10.2). It's an amazing ship that loads four towers, four turbine nacelles, and 12 blades in port; then sails out to the designated location; and lowers its jack-up legs to the seabed. It can install one tower, nacelle, and attach the three blades every 24 hours.

I called up my friend Jesper Bank, the chief commercial officer at the port, and told him, "Hey, the Sea Challenger is operating off Massachusetts!" He told me that thanks to the Jones Act, the ship had to stay at sea, and an American built barge ferries the nacelle, tower, and blades out to the middle of the ocean where it is transloaded to the Sea Challenger. That inflates the cost of each installation by a factor of two. The ship also has to sail to Canada for provisioning.

While this all sounds terrible, the Jones Act and cabotage rules are not completely insane. The effects we see are directly a consequence of opening U.S. borders to trade. Using less expensive foreign crews to serve domestic coastal shipping would just be another form of labor arbitrage. And domestically built ships made from domestically produced steel are far more expensive than foreign built. So the Jones Act is completely consistent with U.S. trade policy.

FIGURE 10.2 I'm standing on the deck of the Sea Challenger, next to a 900-tonne heavy lift crane used to install offshore wind turbines. *Source:* Willy Shih.

Cabotage Rules and Hong Kong's Development

China, like many maritime nations, has long maintained cabotage restrictions. Under its Maritime Code (1992) and related transport regulations, foreign vessels are generally prohibited from engaging in coastal trade between mainland ports unless specifically authorized. These rules were not dismantled during China's broader trade liberalization in the 1980s and after WTO accession in 2001. Foreign container lines calling at Chinese ports could unload import cargo or load exports, but they could not transport cargo along the coast.

Hong Kong, both before and after the handover back to China in 1997, operated (and still operates) under a separate customs and legal regime from mainland China. During the 1980s and 1990s, as export-oriented manufacturing boomed throughout the Pearl River Delta region and especially Shenzhen and Dongguan, Hong Kong was the principal gateway for southern China's international trade. International cargo lines could call at Hong Kong without mainland cabotage constraints, and cargo could then be transshipped via feeder services into Pearl River Delta ports. That was also a time when mainland port infrastructure and logistics services were still developing, so they couldn't handle the larger ships anyway. But Hong Kong's open port status, deep-water facilities, and well-established legal and financial institutions made it an efficient consolidation and transshipment hub for China-bound and China-origin cargo (Wang and Slack 2000).

Hong Kong also didn't levy any tariffs or duties on things crossing its borders. That made it a good place to set up supply chain operations during a time when China still imported many components from the West. I remember talking to a plant manager in a factory in Dongguan who would order hundreds of thousands of "kits" of components—for example, all the components you would need to assemble some electronic device. They would come in from Hong Kong on a small, powered barge that carried a few containers, the factory did their part of the value-add, and then it shipped the assembled subassemblies back to Hong Kong where they would go on to the next step. Even in recent years, you could see these barges plying Hong Kong harbor, moving boxes up into some estuary in the Pearl River Delta (see Figure 10.3).

Over time, as mainland ports such as Shenzhen, Guangzhou, Ningbo, and Shanghai expanded capacity and improved efficiency, a growing share of China's trade shifted to direct calls, reducing Hong Kong's dominance (see Figure 10.4). But for several critical decades, the combination of mainland cabotage rules, regulatory segmentation, and infrastructure gaps helped channel container traffic through Hong Kong rather than directly into coastal Chinese ports.

FIGURE 10.3 Barges serve small ports in the Pearl River Delta and bring containers to Hong Kong for transshipment. *Source:* Willy Shih.

FIGURE 10.4 The Yantian International Container Terminal in Shenzhen is the third largest in the world. *Source:* Willy Shih.

The episode illustrates a broader point: cabotage policies rarely stop trade, but they can shape where trade is organized, influencing the rise of gateway ports and the geography of global supply chains (Notteboom and Rodrigue 2005; Brooks and Pallis 2012).

Local Content Rules: A Major Nontariff Barrier

Local content requirements are among the most significant nontariff barriers to trade, and one of the fastest-growing. Rather than taxing imports directly, they work by mandating that a specific share of the inputs or labor used in production must be sourced domestically. The effect on supply chains can be just as distorting as a tariff and often more so, because the costs are less visible and harder to quantify. Governments are increasing the use of such rules as they are a more politically palatable form of protectionism. The costs are diffuse and buried in supply chain decisions, while the benefits accrue to specific domestic industries and workers. A conservative estimate puts the reduction in global trade attributable to these restrictions at around $93 billion (Hufbauer and Schott 2013).

An example of the effect of local content rules involves lithium-ion batteries. John Goodenough, working at the University of Oxford, discovered in 1980 that lithium cobalt oxide could serve as a high-energy-density cathode material, effectively doubling battery capacity. He wrote to battery companies in the United States, the United Kingdom, and continental Europe hoping to find a corporate partner but found no takers. Oxford declined to pay for a patent, and Goodenough ultimately turned to the UK's Atomic Energy Research Establishment at Harwell, which agreed to fund the patent only on the condition that he sign away his financial rights (Murray 2023).

After further work by Isao Kuribayashi at Asahi Chemical, Sony produced the first commercial lithium-ion battery using Goodenough's cobalt oxide cathode in 1991 (Murray 2023). Initially it used it in its Handycam video cameras before the technology spread to billions of mobile phones and laptops. Goodenough, who shared the 2019 Nobel Prize in Chemistry for this work, received nothing from the commercialization.

By the early 2000s, Japanese and Korean manufacturers had come to dominate lithium-ion battery production. I visited LG Chem's facilities in Korea in 2004, where the company had built a highly automated battery manufacturing line inside a huge temperature and humidity controlled dry room. Needless to say, they didn't allow me to take any pictures, but they told me that on the vast adjacent tract of vacant land, they intended to build exact copies of that factory all in a nice row.

Fast-forward to 2016 when I had an opportunity to visit the people at BYD, the Chinese company that today is the global leader in electric vehicles. BYD was a battery manufacturer founded by Wang Chuanfu in 1995. They told me that when the company got started, it eschewed automation and had people on the process line winding batteries by hand (remember how we talked about the capital versus labor trade-off in Chapter 4)!

The manager I was interviewing told me, "Lots of people [were] providing similar products to the market, the competition was getting tough . . . that's why the pricing pressure from the market definitely required aggressive cost reductions."

The turning point for BYD was when they started supplying batteries to Motorola, then a market leader for mobile phones in China. The BYD manager formerly worked at Motorola, and he explained: in China, in the beginning, there was a local content requirement. The Chinese government wanted to set a sales quota for cellular phones and pagers that would be sold to the Chinese market. The condition was that you had to increase the local content. That meant you had to buy as many components as you can. So this actually gave the manager a chance, as head of the sourcing organization, starting from zero, to develop more than 700 suppliers in China.

And one of those companies was BYD. They started by sourcing batteries and then other components like housings, injection molded plastic parts, surface decoration, and ultimately even assembly work. Motorola also had a program called early supplier involvement, which aimed to improve the quality of their suppliers' components and inputs to its own production. He told me, "Motorola quality standards [were] the military standard, especially for this kind of product. That's why [BYD] actually learned a lot."

I visited the BYD showroom and saw displays of their products and a model of the enormous battery factory next door. If I remember correctly, the factory was producing 15 GWh that year, the same year that Tesla's Gigafactory in Nevada only began mass production.

Sanitary and Phytosanitary Standards: Another Variation on Nontariff Barriers

Sanitary and phytosanitary (SPS) measures are government regulations designed to protect human, animal, and plant health and covering everything from pesticide residue limits in food to requirements that livestock come from disease-free regions. On their face, such measures serve legitimate public health purposes, and the WTO's Agreement on the Application of Sanitary and Phytosanitary Measures, which came into force in 1995, explicitly requires that they be grounded in science and applied no more broadly than necessary. In practice, however, SPS standards are among the most powerful and frequently used nontariff barriers in agricultural trade, and the line between genuine health protection and disguised protectionism is often kind of fuzzy.

Unlike tariffs, SPS barriers do not show up as a line item in a trade agreement or a customs schedule, which makes them harder to negotiate away and easier to deploy without triggering formal retaliation. For supply chains, the practical consequence is that meeting the SPS requirements of a target market can determine not just the price of entry but whether entry is possible at all.

For example, all countries set their own standards on food safety and animal and plant health based on their own assessments of acceptable levels of risk. If everyone uses different standards, trade becomes a lot more challenging. In January 1995, as part of the Uruguay Round of the General Agreement on Trade and Tariffs (GATT), countries signed the Sanitary and Phytosanitary (SPS) Agreement, which stated that countries would use common international standards. But it also recognized that countries had the right to set stricter standards if they could justify them based on science or by wanting to set a lower level of acceptable risk to their population, assuming that did not selectively target imports in a discriminatory fashion (Johnson and Hanrahan 2010). Because SPS requirements are usually enforced at a border where customs clearance and market entry take place, these measures can have significant impacts on where stuff comes from or doesn't come from (United States Office of the U.S. Trade Representative 2010).

One of the longer-running trade disputes between the United States and the European Union is over hormone-treated beef. Beginning in the 1980s, the EU imposed a ban on imports of beef treated with certain growth-promoting hormones on alleged food safety grounds (European Commission n.d.). U.S. and Canadian producers who use these hormones have effectively been shut out of the EU beef market. After dispute settlement proceedings at the World Trade Organization (WTO) under the SPS Agreement, the United States and Canada challenged the ban as inconsistent with the requirement that SPS measures be based on a scientific risk assessment.

After seemingly endless WTO consultations, panel decisions, and appeals, both the United States and the European Union claim vindication of their respective positions. Although the WTO has questioned the validity of the ban, the EU has repeatedly voted to maintain it, citing consumer worries, questions of animal welfare, meat quality, and effects of hormones on the EU's beef and milk sectors (United States Office of the U.S. Trade Representative 2010).

In retaliation, the U.S. imposed 100% tariffs on carefully selected products meant to exert maximum pain on influential constituencies. So goose pâté, Roquefort cheese, truffles, Dijon mustards, French chocolates, and jams got dragged into the fight. The two sides eventually agreed to de-escalate and allow duty-free quotas for high-quality beef from cattle raised without the banned hormones into the European Union and the United States agreeing to suspend most retaliatory tariffs, although tensions continue.

Tariff and Nontariff Barriers Distort Supply Chains

Tariffs and nontariff barriers are the primary instruments through which governments shape where things come from. Although tariffs are the most visible because they are so easy to implement, their economic effects are often misunderstood. Nontariff barriers are at least as consequential, and in many sectors more so.

The cases in this chapter share a common thread: trade barriers, whether tariffs, cabotage rules, local content requirements, or SPS measures, rarely stop trade entirely. What they do is redirect it, often in ways that persist long after the original rationale has faded. They influence where things are made, where they are shipped through, who makes them, and who gets to sell them. As we can see, the geography of supply chains is shaped as much by government policy as by the economics of production and logistics.

CHAPTER 11

Industrial Policy and the Geography of Production

Why do Botox and other pharmaceuticals come from Ireland? Why do so many commercial aircraft and aerospace components come from France? And why is China the source of so much of the world's batteries, solar cells, televisions, flat-panel displays, and rare earth minerals—and, increasingly, of so much else?

The answer in every case is the same: these are industries that received sustained, strategic support from their governments. That support goes by the name of industrial policy, and its influence on the global map of production is the subject of this chapter. We could write volumes on this subject, but we're going to narrow our focus to a few examples that had a significant impact on where things are made: commercial aircraft in Europe, pharmaceuticals in Ireland, semiconductors in Taiwan, and flat-panel displays in China.

A Definition and a Brief History of Industrial Policy

Industrial policy is broadly defined as government efforts to shape the structure of economic activities by targeting specific industries through subsidies, tax incentives, protective regulations, preferential procurement, and research support. It is hardly a modern invention. From the sixteenth through the eighteenth centuries, European policymakers embraced what economists later would call *mercantilism*: the belief that national power depended on controlling trade, promoting domestic production, encouraging exports, minimizing imports, and limiting reliance on foreign suppliers. Countries tried to accumulate monetary reserves through a positive balance of trade. Mercantilist policies encouraged domestic processing of raw materials and the development of "national champions."

Industrial Policy in the United States in the 1700s and 1800s

The United States itself was a practitioner of industrial policy at its founding. We saw in Chapter 10 that tariffs can have a major impact on where things are made, and that has been an industrial policy tool used by the United States since its founding days. Alexander Hamilton's "Report on Manufactures," delivered to Congress in December 1791, laid out a comprehensive program of tariffs, bounties, and public investment to develop American manufacturing and reduce dependence on British imports, drawing explicitly on the mercantilist traditions of Colbert's France and Elizabethan England (Carey 1827). Though Hamilton's specific proposals were not enacted in full, his tariff recommendations were largely put in place within five months, and his broader framework became the intellectual foundation for what Henry Clay would later formalize as the "American System"—a program of protective tariffs, a national bank, and federally funded "internal improvements" (infrastructure) that shaped U.S. economic policy through much of the nineteenth century (Wilentz 2005).

The Lincoln administration accelerated this tradition dramatically: the Morrill Tariff Act (1861) raised import duties to protect northern industry, the Pacific Railway Acts (1862–64) provided massive federal land grants to subsidize transcontinental railroad construction, and the Morrill Land-Grant College Act (1862) used public land to endow state universities focused on agriculture and engineering (Morrill Land-Grant College Act 1862; Stathis 2009). The Morrill Act was one of the earliest attempts by any government to use public investment in applied research and technical education as an instrument of industrial development.

Between the Civil War and the 1930s, tariffs on dutiable goods routinely averaged 40 to 50%, and the federal government played an active role in shaping the sectoral composition of the American economy (Guzik 2024). The idea that the United States rose to industrial supremacy through free markets and minimal government was, as the economic historian Richard Sylla has observed, a mythology that obscured a reality of sustained, deliberate state support for industry from the republic's earliest years (Sylla 2024).

Industrial Policy Around the Globe After World War II

Yet the decades following the Second World War marked a qualitative shift in both the ambition and the tools of state intervention in industry. Governments across Western Europe, East Asia, and eventually the developing world concluded that competitive advantage in key sectors could be engineered, not merely inherited. The consequences of those decisions reverberate today in the global map of production: in which countries make advanced aircraft, who dominates semiconductor fabrication, where the world's batteries are assembled, and who controls the raw materials that make the green economy possible (Agarwal 2023).

The early postwar decades were dominated by European, particularly French and British efforts to catch up with American industrial power and to preserve what policymakers conceived as strategic economic sovereignty. While short-term goals were simply to repair the damage from the war, the bigger challenge was to raise productivity closer to U.S. levels.

- France pursued what Elie Cohen at CNRS called "offensive protectionism." The state created national champions through subsidies, preferential public procurement, and government-directed mergers, shielding favored firms from foreign competition while funneling resources into major projects in aerospace, nuclear power, and telecommunications (Cohen 2007).
- Britain attempted similar interventions, though with less consistency and more spectacular failures, spending heavily on national champions in computers, steel, and automobiles that largely failed to compete internationally.

West Germany, by contrast, intervened far less directly, relying instead on horizontal policies—a strong competition framework, a world-class vocational training system, and the Fraunhofer network linking applied research to industry. It achieved the strongest industrial performance of the three (Owen 2012).

The lesson that emerged haltingly from this era was that governments are far better at creating conditions for competitiveness than at picking specific winners and that the costs of industrial policy failures fall heavily on taxpayers while the gains accrue unevenly.

Airbus and European Aerospace: The Grand Projet Par Excellence

One of the most successful industrial policy "Grand Projets," to use the French term, has been Airbus Industrie. The Airbus consortium was born out of European alarm at American dominance in the commercial aviation market. By the late 1960s, Boeing commanded roughly 60% of the global market for large passenger jets, while McDonnell Douglas and Lockheed shared most of the rest. Britain had been the pioneer with the first commercial passenger jet, the ill-fated de Havilland Comet that first flew in 1949 and had its commercial debut in 1952, and the French company Sud Aviation's Caravelle that entered service in 1959. But between 1960 and 1967, British and French manufacturers saw a 50% collapse in aircraft deliveries, and London had even contemplated the forced nationalization and merger of its entire aerospace industry (Francis and Pevzner 2006).

Building the Consortium

European governments concluded that no single national industry could mount a credible challenge and that survival depended on pooling resources across borders. In July 1967, France, West Germany, and Britain signed a memorandum of understanding to develop a twin-engine wide-body jetliner capable of carrying 250–300 passengers at an estimated cost of $532 million (roughly $4.7 billion today).

Three years later, Airbus Industrie was formally incorporated as a *groupement d'intérêt économique* under French law (or an economic interest group), with France's state-owned Aérospatiale and Germany's Deutsche Airbus each holding a 50% stake (New York Times 1967). Spain's CASA joined in 1971 with a 4.2% share. Britain, after the government's withdrawal from the formal partnership in 1969 over Rolls-Royce engine disputes, returned in 1979 when British Aerospace took a 20% stake.

The geography of production was extremely political as governments sought work shares based on their contributions. This led to a modularization of the airframe with sections built in different countries, and then everything shipped initially to Toulouse for final assembly. France built the cockpit and lower fuselage; Germany made the forward and rear fuselage sections; Britain produced the wings, which were the most technically demanding component; and Spain manufactured the horizontal stabilizer and tail section. Each partner was simultaneously a shareholder in and a subcontractor to the consortium, a structure that preserved national industrial employment but built in chronic tensions over transfer pricing and production efficiency.

The A300, the world's first twin-aisle, twin-engine wide-body, flew on October 28, 1972, and entered commercial service in 1974. Its early years were a study in the patience that industrial policy requires. Sales started out extremely slowly, with airlines, particularly American ones, deeply skeptical of a European manufacturer with no track record in large commercial jets. The back-to-back oil shocks of 1973 and 1979 devastated airline finances just as Airbus was trying to establish itself. By 1976 the consortium had accumulated more unsold aircraft than orders. Criticism from Boeing, which dismissed Airbus as "just another European jobs program," seemed well-founded at the time (Hamilton 2021).

A Watershed Moment

The turning point came in 1977, when Eastern Airlines agreed to take four A300s on a no-cost lease evaluation, a deal the U.S. International Trade Commission briefly considered investigating whether this constituted unfair trade practices. Eastern was sufficiently impressed to place a firm order for 23 aircraft (Witkin 1978), which cracked open the American market and demonstrated the A300's central commercial proposition: its twin-engine efficiency and lower operating costs gave airlines a significant economic advantage over the four-engine Boeing 747 and DC-10 on medium-haul routes, particularly after fuel prices spiked. WTO proceedings would later determine that European governments had provided approximately €15 billion in "launch aid," which took the form of repayable loans whose terms functioned more like equity than debt. This was repeated for successive aircraft programs since the 1970s, with findings of $18 billion in specific advantages as of 2011 (WTO 2011).

The A320, launched in 1984 with service entry in 1988, was a technological leap that transformed Airbus from a viable competitor into a genuine threat to Boeing. It was the first commercial aircraft equipped with a full digital fly-by-wire flight control system, replacing conventional mechanical linkages with computers that interpreted pilot inputs and commanded control surfaces. This innovation, which had been pioneered on the American F-16 fighter jet, reduced weight, cut maintenance costs, and enabled envelope protection that prevented pilots from inadvertently overstressing the airframe (Favre 1994). The innovation also enabled Airbus to implement a common cockpit architecture across all Airbus aircraft, allowing airlines to train pilots on one type and qualify them to fly others with minimal additional instruction.

The A320 family became the best-selling narrow-body aircraft in history, with more than 20,000 orders to date, and it was the A321neo that forced Boeing into the defensive, hastily re-engined 737 MAX, a response that culminated in two fatal crashes, a 20-month global grounding, and a reputational crisis whose full consequences are still unfolding.

The Consortium Making Its Case

The case for the government support of Airbus rests on the idea that in industries with large economies of scale and high barriers to entry, government subsidies can be crucial to enabling an industry to compete. That was probably the logic that European policymakers were depending on, whether or not they framed it that way at the time (Brander and Spencer 1985).

The Airbus story is perhaps the biggest success story for an industrial policy. The distributed production geography, with wings made in Britain, fuselages made in France and Germany, tail sections in Spain, and final assembly at first in Toulouse (but now at multiple locations), was a political compromise, and it generated real inefficiencies that the consortium spent decades trying to overcome. But it also meant that the political coalition supporting Airbus across four governments was broad and durable enough to sustain the program through many challenging years.

By 2019, Airbus had displaced Boeing as the world's largest aerospace company by revenue, and the subsidy dispute it had provoked became, in retrospect, one of the longest-running trade conflicts in WTO history, resolved only in 2021 when both sides agreed to suspend mutual tariffs and acknowledge that neither Boeing nor Airbus had competed on purely market terms. It's also why so many airplanes you fly these days were manufactured in Europe (though Airbus has a final assembly line in Alabama, many of the components still come from Europe).

Tax Incentives and the Development of the Pharmaceutical Sector in Ireland

The roots of Ireland's transformation into a manufacturing hub can be traced to the late 1950s, when a protectionist and economically stagnant Ireland, watching the rest of Western Europe achieve growth rates approaching 6% per annum, concluded that some big changes were necessary.

The government introduced a zero tax rate on profits that originated from manufactured exports, while simultaneously liberalizing laws governing foreign ownership of companies (Barry 2004). The subsequent inflow of foreign direct investment (FDI) over subsequent decades reshaped the Irish economy beyond recognition. The Industrial Development Authority (IDA) identified the pharmaceutical sector as a strategic priority from the 1960s onward and proactively pursued companies who had the potential to make large investments (Hannon et al. 2011).

The corporate tax regime that Ireland constructed over the following decades became a powerful instrument in the country's FDI strategy. After pressure from the European Commission, the zero rate on export profits was replaced by a special 10% corporation tax rate for the manufacturing sector in 1978, which gave way to a harmonized economy-wide rate of 12.5% in 2003. This was still the lowest effective corporate tax rate in the European Union (Barry 2004).

The government invested heavily in education from the mid-1960s, with a particular emphasis on science and engineering disciplines. Vocationally oriented institutes of technology were established and provided the pharmaceutical sector with a steady supply of practically trained graduates, while the proportion of Irish post-secondary graduates in the natural sciences was consistently among the highest in the EU (Eurostat and Tertiary Education Graduates: What Are Their Subject Areas? 2020).

Ireland also saw the progressive upgrading of capabilities that pharmaceutical manufacturers brought to the country. Starting with fine chemicals, companies turned to the bulk manufacture of active pharmaceutical ingredients (APIs) and then in turn to the final formulation and packaging of products. The IDA focused on deepening and strengthening the presence of individual firms. By 2007 there were 83 pharmaceutical firms in Ireland with six of the top 10 products in the world manufactured there (Hannon et al. 2011).

The town of Westport in County Mayo became home to AbbVie's facility that manufactures the world's entire supply of Botox, a product that generated $2.72 billion in cosmetic net revenues and $3.3 billion in therapeutic net revenues for AbbVie in 2024 (Webber and Kuchler 2025). The facility also produces eyecare pharmaceuticals, and it sends approximately 70% of its output to the United States. AbbVie invested a further €160 million ($182 million in 2020) in a second biologics facility in Westport in 2020, reflecting confidence in the Irish operating environment.

Similar concentrations of pharmaceutical employment exist across rural Ireland, with the sector serving as the primary economic anchor for communities that would otherwise have limited access to high-wage, high-skill employment. Pharmaceutical exports have become the dominant engine of the Irish goods economy. In 2024, medical and pharmaceutical products accounted for nearly €100 billion in exports, which was 45% of all Irish goods exports. That made Ireland the world's third largest pharmaceutical exporter, ahead of countries many times its size (Central Statistics Office [Ireland] 2025).

Ireland has also attracted significant manufacturing investment outside of pharmaceuticals, including a factory that reported to me in Youghal, County Cork (see Figure 11.1). The IDA also spent a decade courting Intel to locate its first European fab in Leixlip, which represents more than $18 billion in investment today (Intel Newsroom 2024).

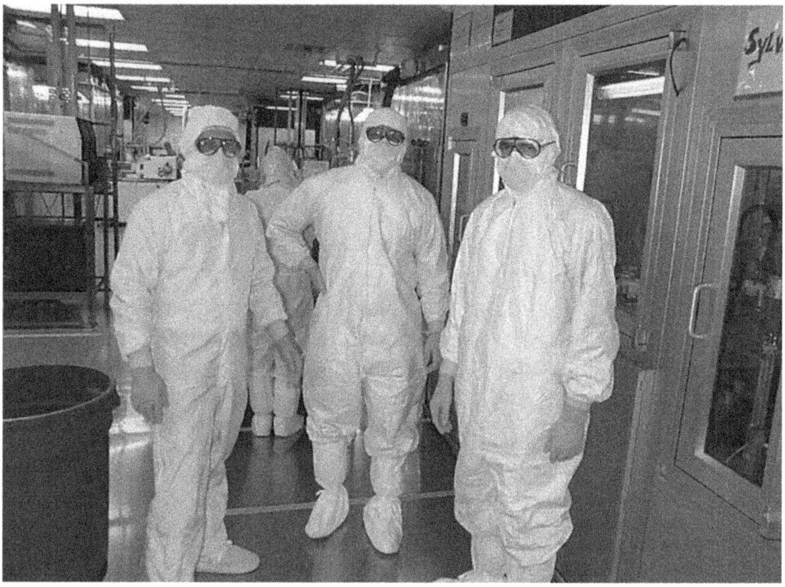

FIGURE 11.1 In the cleanroom at Kodak factory in Youghal, County Cork, Ireland, circa 1998. *Source:* Willy Shih.

Producing Semiconductors in Taiwan

Taiwan's postwar industrial trajectory began not with semiconductors but with survival. The ruling Kuomintang, chastened by its defeat on the mainland and the hyperinflation that had helped bring it about, committed itself to fiscal discipline and private-sector-led growth in a way that distinguished Taiwan from its more statist neighbors.

The Industrial Technology Research Institute

The economy of the 1960s and early 1970s was dominated by small and medium-sized enterprises (SME), many of them family-run, producing textiles, shoes, and plastic goods for export. In 1961, nearly 60% of manufacturing firms employed fewer than 100 workers, and the SME bias persisted through subsequent decades (Chu 1999). That structure had real consequences for industrial upgrading: no firm had the scale or the time horizon to invest in major research programs, and domestic capital markets were too thin to fill the gap. As Jung-Chiou Hwang, a senior Ministry of Economic

Affairs (MOEA) official, later recalled of that era, "At that time, Taiwan and mainland China, we were in a big struggle. And people would say, 'If I invest in this company, within three years we better earn our money back.' Nobody said 5 or 10 years later." (Shih and Wang 2008).

The institutional answer was the Industrial Technology Research Institute (ITRI), founded in 1973 under the patronage of Y.S. Sun, an electrical engineer who had risen to become minister of economic affairs and would later serve as premier. Sun's approach drew on a recommendation by Pan Wen-Yuan, an overseas Chinese engineer at RCA in New Jersey, who argued that Taiwan should focus on semiconductors, acquire the technology from abroad, and create a dedicated state agency to execute the plan. The government's total investment in the initial program was estimated at around $12 million over four years, which was a controversial sum in the economic climate of the time, but one that Sun, who treated the project as his personal priority, was able to push through over objections (Chang et al. 1994).

In 1976, 40 engineers, including a young Chintay Shih who would eventually become ITRI's president, traveled to New Jersey to study RCA's CMOS process which it had licensed. They returned to Taiwan in 1977, and the first successful product came out of ITRI's pilot facility that December. The technology choice, RCA's mature seven-micron CMOS process, selected partly because it offered stability and comprehensive documentation suited to people with limited prior experience, proved prescient. CMOS ultimately became the dominant semiconductor device architecture (Shih and Wang 2008).

The next phase was commercialization, and it generated a tension that would recur repeatedly over the following two decades. ITRI was a government research institute, not a business. When its pilot line began producing sellable products, the government "was not very happy with this," as Shih recalled, because the accounting was awkward and the state did not wish to absorb operating losses (Shih and Wang 2008). The resolution was to spin the technology out as a public-private company.

In 1982, ITRI spun off the United Microelectronics Corporation (UMC), initially 44% state-owned, transferring product designs, process technology, and trained personnel. UMC reached break-even rapidly and ranked first for profitability among Taiwan's top 500 corporations in its first year. The spin-off model also established a physical anchor: the Hsinchu Science-Based Industrial Park sited deliberately between ITRI and two engineering universities. The Park offered standard factory space, tax holidays of near-zero effective rates, duty-free equipment imports, and low-interest loans to attract firms (Shih and Wang 2008). The park became the nucleus of what would grow into the world's most important semiconductor cluster.

The Rise of TSMC

The founding of Taiwan Semiconductor Manufacturing Company (TSMC) in 1987 represented both the culmination of the ITRI model and its most consequential departure. By the mid-1980s, ITRI's Very Large Scale Integration (VLSI) project had pushed Taiwan's process technology within striking distance of American leaders, but the results faced resistance from private firms that feared ITRI-funded competition.

The immediate trigger for TSMC's creation was embarrassment. Technology co-developed by ITRI found its way to a Korean company after Taiwanese firms declined to invest in the necessary manufacturing capacity. Morris Chang, recruited from Texas Instruments to run the new venture, proposed a solution that was radical at the time—a "pure foundry" that would manufacture chips exclusively to the designs of outside customers, without competing with them in product markets. The foundry concept, which Chang presented as a "controlled kitchen" in which customers brought recipes, but the kitchen was managed entirely by TSMC, solved two problems at once. It gave the fragmented ecosystem of Taiwanese and overseas-Chinese fabless design firms a reliable manufacturing partner, and it allowed TSMC to concentrate on process excellence without the distractions of product development.

TSMC opened in February 1987 as a joint venture. The Taiwan government held 49% through its Development Fund, Philips of the Netherlands contributed 27% along with manufacturing technology and intellectual property cross-licenses, and private Taiwanese investors provided the remainder (Shih and Wang 2008).

TSMC's rise from that starting point to its current position—manufacturing the majority of the world's most advanced logic chips at three nanometers and below—is a story of compounding technological advantage reinforced by government support, diaspora talent, and the competitive structure of the foundry model itself. Because TSMC competed for customers rather than against them, the world's best chip designers, companies like Nvidia, Qualcomm, Broadcom, AMD, MediaTek, and eventually Intel, flocked to Hsinchu, generating revenues that funded each successive next generation of process investment.

The X + Y = 65 rule at ITRI, under which researchers whose years of service plus age totaled 65 could retire with full pensions and then move into the private sector, channeled accumulated institutional knowledge outward, seeding the Hsinchu Science Park with experienced engineers at exactly the moment start-ups needed them (Shih and Wang 2008). Between UMC's founding in 1982 and the late 1990s, the number of semiconductor design shops in Taiwan grew from 4 to more than 115, and the ecosystem extended across fabrication, packaging, testing, and mask-making (Tung 2001).

Lessons Learned in Taiwan

Several features of the Taiwan case deserve emphasis in comparative perspective.

- First, the government's institutional design was deliberately structured to avoid both the pathologies of Soviet-style planning and the scale concentration that characterized Korea's chaebol system. ITRI was a pilot agency, not a planner. It acquired technology, proved it at laboratory scale, and transferred it to private firms rather than attempting to run production itself. The SME bias of the economy, frustrating as it seemed to officials in the 1960s, ultimately produced a more distributed, resilient industrial structure than Korea's—one in which more than 30 global leaders emerged across semiconductors, flat-panel displays, notebook computers, LEDs, and machine tools, rather than the dominance of Samsung and LG that characterized Korean electronics (Shih and Wang 2008).
- Second, and critically, the government was willing to take equity stakes, absorb early losses, and backstop technology transfer, but it consistently pushed commercialization risk toward private actors as soon as viable partners existed.
- Third, the diaspora connection, exemplified by Pan Wen-Yuan's founding recommendation, the forty engineers trained at RCA, and an external science and technology advisory board that included senior figures from Texas Instruments, Bell Labs, and IBM, gave Taiwanese technocrats access to frontier knowledge that could not have been developed domestically at affordable cost.

The same concentration that made Taiwan's semiconductor industry a strategic triumph has also made it a strategic risk. TSMC now manufactures chips that no other facility in the world can replicate at comparable yield and cost. Disruption of its operations, whether from military conflict, natural disaster, or supply chain failure, would halt production of everything from smartphones to fighter aircraft across every major economy. The geopolitical response has been substantial. The CHIPS and Science Act in the United States directed $39 billion toward domestic semiconductor manufacturing, and Japan and the European Union launched parallel programs, with TSMC itself constructing fabs in Arizona, Kumamoto, Japan, and Dresden, Germany under various subsidy arrangements.

Whether these investments will produce genuinely competitive alternatives or merely expensive insurance policies remains to be seen. What is not in doubt is that the geography of advanced semiconductor manufacturing, concentrated on a politically precarious island, has become one of the central strategic facts of the current era.

The 863 Program and Why Your TV Comes from China

No country has pursued industrial policy more systematically or at greater scale than China. Beginning in the late 1980s with the explicit adoption of Japan's "state-led market economy" model as a template, China progressively built an industrial policy architecture spanning Five-Year Plans, sectoral promotion catalogues, state investment funds, and coordinated R&D programs (Fu et al. 2026).

Among these, the National High Technology Research and Development Program, universally known as the "863 Program" for the month and year of Deng Xiaoping's personal authorization of it in March 1986, stands as perhaps the most consequential early instrument.

The Legacy of the 863 Program

Proposed by leading scientists who warned that China risked falling dangerously behind the United States, the Soviet Union, Japan, and Europe in strategic technologies, the 863 Program initially broke sharply from established bureaucratic practice: it placed credentialed scientists, not party cadres, in charge of funding allocations across seven priority high-technology sectors including information technology, biotechnology, new materials, and energy (Zhi and Pearson 2017).

The program's early phases succeeded in narrowing the technology gap, establishing merit-based funding procedures, and creating a norm of expert involvement in R&D governance that, though subsequently eroded by ministerial politics, left an enduring imprint on China's science and technology system (Zhi and Pearson 2017).

Later iterations of 863 broadened into civilian industrialization and, eventually, into the development of new energy vehicles (NEVs), a priority that laid the groundwork for China's eventual global dominance in that sector. The program was wound down in 2016, its mission absorbed into a broader landscape of national science and technology initiatives, but its legacy is visible in the industrial capabilities China now deploys across semiconductors, civil aviation, batteries, and beyond.

A Boom in LCD Flat-Panel Displays

One of the technological wonders of our day is the flat-panel liquid crystal display (LCD) screen, which is the key component of televisions, computer monitors, smartphones, and a vast range of gadgets that display information electronically. There is also a newer technology, organic light-emitting diodes (OLEDs), that was invented by Ching Tang at Eastman Kodak (he even reported to me for a while).

Back in 2018 I was invited to tour BOE Technology Group's Gen 10.5 factory in Hefei, the capital of China's Anhui Province. This was the third factory, or "fab" that Beijing-based BOE built in Hefei alone, and in terms of capability, at the time it was the most advanced in the world. BOE has a total of 12 fabs in Beijing, Chongqing, and several other major cities across China.

The displays are manufactured by assembling a sandwich of two thin sheets of glass. On one of the sheets are transistor "cells" where you build millions of precisely shaped transistor parts. On the other sheet of glass, you make an array of millions of red, green, and blue dots in a black matrix, called a color filter array (CFA). This is how you produce the colors when you shine light through it. Then you drop tiny amounts of liquid crystal material into the cells on the first sheet and glue the two sheets together, aligning them with a precision of a few microns in each direction anywhere on the sheet. The sandwich is then covered with sheets of polarizing film, and the sheets are cut into individual "panels"—a term that is used to describe the subassembly that actually goes into a TV.

For the sake of efficiency, you would like to make as many panels on a sheet as possible, within the practical limitations of how big a sheet you can handle. The first modern LCD Fabs built in the early 1990s made sheets the size of a single notebook computer screen, and the size grew over time. A Gen 5 sheet, from around 2003, is 1,100 × 1,300 mm, while a Gen 10.5 sheet is 2,940 × 3,370 mm (9.6 × 11 ft) (see Figure 11.2). The sheets of glass are only 0.7 mm or 0.5mm thick or even thinner, so as you can imagine they are extremely fragile and can only be handled by robots. The Hefei Gen 10.5 fab is designed to produce the panels for either eight 65-inch or six 75-inch TVs at a time. If you wanted to make 110-inch TVs, you could make two of them at a time. The fab itself is 1.3 km long and has hundreds of thousands of square meters of cleanroom (see Figure 11.3).

When I arrived, I asked the company chairman why the fab was in Hefei. Hefei is a nice place, the capital of Anhui Province, but it is far away from Shanghai and Beijing, where a lot of people like to live. He told me that the company only built fabs where the local government would provide a subsidy. The Hefei fab cost around $6 billion to build and equip, so I asked how much was the subsidy. A lot—most of the cost; they probably don't want me to say. But that's why the Koreans, the Taiwanese, and the Japanese have gotten squeezed out of the business.

On opening day, the Hefei fab shipped panels to Sony, Samsung, LG, Vizio, and Haier. The Chinese display industry's world market share rose from negligible in 2005 to become dominant by the early 2020s. Korean producers Samsung Display and LG Display have largely exited the commodity LCD business in response, pivoting to OLED and higher-margin segments.

FIGURE 11.2 Gen 10.5 "Mother Glass" on display at BOE Hefei Fab. *Source:* Willy Shih.

FIGURE 11.3 BOE Hefei Gen 10.5 Fab. *Source:* Willy Shih.

Now you would think with that level of government support, life is good for companies like BOE. Actually, no. Other regional governments subsidize the company's competitors, firms like TCL China Star Optoelectronics Technology (CSOT) and others at similar or even higher levels. I had lunch with the chairman and founder of a big electronics manufacturer who seemed a bit surprised that BOE's subsidy was as low as it was. As a consequence of the subsidy race, the companies are in dog-eat-dog competition in what has become a commoditized market where the way you win is by investing more to get the latest technology, best yields, and economies of scale. And the prize for winning is you get to play again.

Setting that aspect aside, the Hefei government has actually done a remarkable job transforming an inconspicuous inland provincial capital into a high-tech hub, not only for displays, but electric vehicles, quantum computing, fusion research, and deep space exploration (**English.scio.gov.cn** 2023).

Questions to Ponder

Two features of the flat-panel case are worth underlining for the broader argument.

- First, this was not a sector in which China possessed any initial technological advantage or obvious factor endowment. It succeeded through sustained state financing that allowed BOE and its rivals to absorb losses across multiple investment cycles while climbing the technology curve.
- Second, the beneficiaries of that climb were not only Chinese consumers and Chinese firms: the collapse of LCD panel prices that followed Chinese overcapacity has lowered the cost of televisions and monitors globally, raising a genuine question about who gains and who loses from industrial policy interventions in sectors with substantial consumer benefits. The answer is not straightforward, but it does explain why all of your TVs and computer displays will eventually come from China.

Deliberate Policy Choices

What unifies all of these episodes, from postwar Europe's *grand projets*, through Ireland's deliberate construction of a pharmaceutical hub, Taiwan's foundry ecosystem, and China's patient displacement of established leaders in displays, is the underlying insight that where things are made is not simply an outcome of comparative advantage and market forces. It is also the product of deliberate policy choices: choices about which industries to nurture, which firms to support, and which dependencies to tolerate or to eliminate.

The cases surveyed here differ enough in their particulars to resist a single clean lesson, but several recurring patterns are worth mentioning.

Supporting a Sector Is a Long Game

The most successful interventions shared a common structure: governments identified sectors with large economies of scale, high barriers to entry, and significant positive spillovers, industries where getting in early and sustaining support through the learning curve could lock in durable competitive advantages.

Airbus would not have survived its first decade on commercial terms alone, nor would TSMC have emerged without the ITRI incubator and the Taiwanese Development Fund's equity commitment. Ireland's pharmaceutical cluster required decades of consistent tax and education policy before it became self-sustaining. BOE required subsidies covering a substantial portion of capital costs across multiple generations of fabs before it achieved the scale to displace Korean and Japanese competitors on price.

Market Forces Still Play a Major Role

A second pattern is that institutional design mattered, often more than the level of spending.

- The French model of state-directed national champions produced Airbus but also many expensive failures in computers, steel, and consumer electronics.
- What distinguished Taiwan's approach was a deliberate choice to use the state as incubator rather than operator. ITRI developed technology, proved it at pilot scale, and transferred it to private firms that bore the commercial risk. The result was an ecosystem of competing firms rather than a single national champion, and it proved more resilient because competition within it was not suppressed.
- Ireland's IDA similarly functioned less as a funder of specific firms and more as a tireless recruiter and matchmaker, letting the tax and education environment do the heavy lifting.

Not a Zero-Sum Game

A third pattern, perhaps the most consequential for the world economy, is that industrial policy success in one country frequently imposes costs on others. But those costs are not always straightforward losses. The collapse of LCD panel prices driven by Chinese overcapacity lowered costs for every consumer who bought a television or a monitor. The creation of Airbus improved the terms on which airlines everywhere could acquire aircraft, breaking a near-monopoly and driving Boeing to produce better planes.

The logic of strategic trade policy, formalized in the work of Brander and Spencer (1985) and Krugman (1986), predicts exactly this. In oligopolistic industries, a government subsidy can shift profits toward domestic firms at the expense of foreign rivals—but the importing country's consumers often benefit too. Industrial policy is not a zero-sum game, even when it is explicitly designed to be one.

Success Depends on a Complex Mix of Factors That May Be Hard to Replicate

What none of these cases can resolve is the question of whether the conditions that made each intervention successful can be replicated elsewhere, or whether they depended on particular windows of opportunity that have since closed. Taiwan's foundry model required a confluence of diaspora talent, SME flexibility, fortuitous technology choices, and a geopolitical environment in which the United States was a tolerant and cooperative partner rather than a competitor. Ireland's pharmaceutical cluster required decades of stable policy and the beneficial structure of the European single market.

These are not easily exported templates. Industrial policy can reshape the geography of production—the evidence reviewed in this chapter makes that much clear—but it cannot reliably predict, let alone guarantee, which industries will become the commanding heights of the next economy.

CHAPTER 12

The Road Ahead

Throughout this book, we have been trying to explain the logic behind the world's supply chains—why your cashews were grown in West Africa, why your salmon detoured through China, why the name on the label so rarely matches the company that actually made what's inside. In each case, we ended up with the same kind of answer: there were good reasons. Labor costs, specialization, the economics of scale, the geography of clusters, the weight of accumulated expertise. The system was not an accident; it was the cumulative outcome of millions of decisions, each of which made sense on its own terms. This final chapter is about what happens when the world decides that "makes sense on its own terms" is no longer enough.

When Supply Chain Visibility Suddenly Mattered

The wake-up calls came in quick succession. The COVID-19 pandemic was the first and, for most people, the most visceral. Suddenly, the invisibility of supply chains, the quality we noted at the start of this book, the way they only reveal themselves when something goes wrong, became a source of genuine alarm. Shelves were bare. Hospitals were short of masks and medicines. Car plants sat idle for want of microchips. For millions of people, it was the first time they had consciously registered that the things they depended on were made somewhere else, likely far away, by someone they had never thought about, in a system they did not understand and could not control.

Russia's invasion of Ukraine in February 2022 hit differently, but the lesson was related. The disruption to grain supplies and energy markets was severe, but the deeper shock was psychological: if a major power could simply decide to invade a neighbor and hold Europe's gas supply hostage in the process, what did that mean for other dependencies on other powers in other places? The question that nobody wanted to say out loud, but everyone was thinking, was obvious. If Russia could do this, what would happen if China moved on Taiwan?

That question had barely been posed when Donald Trump returned to the American presidency and offered his own answer: tariffs. Trump's worldview on trade seems to be, at its core, about two things: bilateral merchandise trade deficits, which he treats as a kind of national scoreboard where any deficit is a loss, and strategic competition with China, which he frames as an existential contest that the United States has been losing. The tariffs that followed were sweeping, often applied to allies and rivals alike, and deeply disruptive to the supply chain strategies that companies had spent decades building. Whatever one thinks of the policy logic, the practical effect was to force a reckoning that efficiency-minded supply chain managers had been deferring for years.

China, meanwhile, was not a passive actor in all this. Its trade surpluses have reached extraordinary scale, its companies have achieved global leadership in electric vehicles, batteries, solar panels, and an expanding list of advanced technologies, and its Dual Circulation strategy has made explicit what was already implicit in its industrial policy: China wants the world to depend on it, while it depends on no one. That is not a posture that invites complacency from trading partners.

The United States had long maintained, at least formally, an aversion to state intervention on the grounds that government attempts to direct resource allocation toward favored industries causes distortions and inefficiencies that outweighed any strategic benefits. That thinking has gone out the window. Even Europe, long the most committed champion of commercial engagement with Beijing, and the part of the world most invested in the idea that trade builds peace, has grown uneasy. The word that European policymakers now reach for is not decoupling but "de-risking," a distinction they insist upon but whose practical implications are, day by day, looking more similar than different.

The conflict that erupted between the United States, Israel, and Iran in 2026 added another dimension to this. Damage to the liquefied natural gas (LNG) production infrastructure in Qatar, oil production infrastructure around the Persian Gulf, and effective closure of the Strait of Hormuz brought a shock to the economies of Japan, South Korea, India, and Southeast Asia that Europe had felt three years earlier. A lot of other assumptions in those parts of the world are likely to go out the window as well.

Taken together, these forces—a pandemic that exposed hidden fragility, wars that made dependencies feel dangerous, a trade war that rewrote the economics of global sourcing, and a rising power that has openly declared its intention to be indispensable—have brought the era of frictionless globalization to something that looks very much like a turning point. Whether what comes next is better or worse, more stable or less, fairer or not, is genuinely uncertain. But it will be different. The rest of this chapter tries to make sense of how.

How We Got Here: The Forces That Remade Global Trade

The economic forces described in the preceding chapters—labor arbitrage, specialization, the logic of clusters, the relentless pressure to reduce costs—all pushed in the same direction: toward concentrating production in the places that could do it most cheaply and most efficiently. In a well-functioning trading system, those forces would eventually generate their own corrections. A country that exports far more than it imports should, in theory, see its currency appreciate, making its goods gradually more expensive for foreign buyers and gradually restoring balance. Adam Smith and David Ricardo, for all their enthusiasm about the gains from trade, assumed that something like this adjustment would operate in the background, keeping the system from drifting too far out of equilibrium.

What actually happened over the past three decades is that the forces driving concentration operated freely, while many of the forces that should have pushed back and corrected were constrained or simply did not function as the textbook said they would.

The clearest example is the exchange rate. For much of the period when manufacturing was flowing most rapidly toward China, Beijing actively managed the renminbi (China's official currency) to keep it undervalued relative to what a freely floating market would have produced. This was not a minor technical footnote. It was a substantial and sustained suppression of the price signal that should, in theory, have made Chinese exports progressively less competitive over time.

The surplus dollars that China accumulated didn't recirculate in ways that bid up Chinese wages or the currency; they were recycled into U.S. Treasury bonds, which had the paradoxical effect of keeping American borrowing costs low and American consumers well-positioned to keep buying. The circuit that classical trade theory assumed would close stayed stubbornly open. The arbitrage opportunity never competed itself away. And so the concentration that market forces set in motion continued far longer, and reached far greater depths, than the underlying theory would have predicted.

Against that backdrop, China's rise to manufacturing dominance was not simply the outcome of good policy or hard work, though it was both of those things too. It was also the product of a system in which the accelerators were working and the brakes were not.

China's Rise to Manufacturing Dominance

China's emergence as the dominant force in global manufacturing is one of the most consequential economic transformations in modern history. When

China joined the World Trade Organization in 2001, it was already a significant exporter. What followed, however, exceeded almost every projection at the time. By the mid-2010s, China accounted for roughly 28% of global manufacturing output, more than the United States, Germany, and Japan combined. In sector after sector, from consumer electronics and textiles to steel, solar panels, and advanced industrial components, Chinese producers achieved a combination of scale, cost, and speed that competitors in other countries found nearly impossible to match.

This dominance was built on a foundation of clearly thought through industrial policy: preferential financing for strategic industries, state-directed investment in infrastructure, a disciplined approach to technology acquisition, and the mobilization of a vast and increasingly skilled labor force. Over time, China moved steadily up the value chain, from assembling products designed elsewhere to engineering and manufacturing them, and ultimately to setting global standards in industries such as telecommunications equipment, electric vehicles, and battery technology. For multinational corporations, China became not just the lowest-cost option but, in many cases, the only practical option. It was *the* place with the suppliers, the capacity, the logistics networks, and the ecosystem depth that no other country could replicate at comparable speed or scale. If you talk to people running manufacturing operations today who touch China, they will tell you that. There is nowhere else like it.

The concentration of productive capacity that has resulted is staggering. By the early 2020s, China produced the majority of the world's smartphones, laptops, and solar modules; was the dominant global supplier of active pharmaceutical ingredients; and controlled significant shares of the global output of critical minerals processing, rare earth elements, and advanced battery materials. Global supply chains had not merely incorporated China; in many cases, they had become structurally dependent on it in ways that became fully visible only when disruption struck.

The U.S.–China Strategic Competition

For decades, the dominant framework in Washington, DC, held that economic integration with China would gradually produce political liberalization and, ultimately, a stable partner in the international order. By the mid-2010s, that hypothesis had been largely abandoned. What replaced it was the recognition—slow at first, then rapid—that the United States and China were engaged in a long-term strategic competition across multiple dimensions: economic, technological, military, and ideological. This reframing has reshaped American trade and industrial policy more fundamentally than any development since the end of the Cold War.

The first Trump administration's imposition of sweeping tariffs on Chinese goods beginning in 2018 marked the decisive break. Tariffs covering hundreds of billions of dollars in annual trade—first at 10%, then 25% on a broad range of categories, and ultimately far higher on specific strategic goods—fundamentally altered the economics of China-based sourcing for American companies. The Biden administration largely maintained these tariffs while layering on an additional architecture of export controls, investment screening, and semiconductor restrictions designed to slow China's advance in technologies deemed critical to national security. The Trump administration that returned to office in 2025 escalated further still, deploying tariffs as both an economic weapon and a negotiating instrument across a far wider range of trading partners, triggering retaliatory measures and raising serious questions about the long-term architecture of the multilateral trading system.

For the business community, the effect was a forced reckoning with supply chain geography that efficiency calculations alone would never have prompted. Companies that had built sophisticated, deeply optimized China-centric supply chains found themselves facing a new and unanticipated variable: the cost of geopolitical exposure. The tariff shock did not immediately produce a wholesale exodus from China—the ecosystem advantages were too significant, and the transition costs too high, for that—but it decisively launched a process of diversification, duplication, and strategic repositioning that continues to reshape global investment patterns today.

China's Dual Circulation Strategy

China's response to the intensifying strategic pressure was itself a strategic reorientation of historic significance. In 2020, Beijing formally articulated the "Dual Circulation" development strategy, which has since become the organizing framework for Chinese economic policy. The concept is straightforward in its outlines: China would continue to engage with global markets (the "external circulation") while simultaneously strengthening the internal drivers of growth and technological self-sufficiency that would insulate the Chinese economy from external pressure (the "internal circulation"). The strategy is, in essence, a systematic effort to reduce China's own vulnerabilities to the kind of supply chain weaponization that the United States has demonstrated is available and willing to deploy. In an October 2020 speech to the Chinese Communist Party's (CCP's) Central Financial and Economic Affairs Commission, Xi Jinping said China must "tighten international production chains' dependence on China, forming powerful countermeasures and deterrent capabilities against foreigners artificially cutting off supplies" (The Economist 2020; Hart 2023).

In practice, Dual Circulation has meant an intensified push for domestic semiconductor development, accelerated investment in advanced manufacturing capabilities, a drive to reduce dependence on foreign technology in critical systems, and efforts to build out Chinese consumer demand as an alternative engine of growth less subject to the volatility of export markets. It has also entailed a more assertive approach to controlling China's own critical resource chokepoints, most visibly through export restrictions on gallium, germanium, and other materials central to semiconductor and defense manufacturing, signaling that Beijing is prepared to use its supply chain leverage symmetrically.

The Dual Circulation strategy has profound implications for multinational corporations operating in and with China. It signals that Beijing's long-term intent is to make the Chinese economy progressively less dependent on foreign technology, components, and expertise while simultaneously maintaining access to foreign markets for Chinese exports. For foreign companies that have built business models premised on serving as technology or component suppliers to Chinese industry, this trajectory poses an existential strategic question: how long does the window of market access remain before it narrows from the inside?

Europe's Reckoning with Strategic Dependency

If the United States' reassessment of China was driven primarily by security competition, Europe's was driven by a more painful lived experience. The continent that had built its postwar prosperity on open markets and economic interdependence found itself, in the early 2020s, confronting two devastating lessons in the risks of strategic dependency.

- First came the near-collapse of European industry when pandemic-era supply chain disruptions exposed the depth of reliance on Asian, particularly Chinese, manufacturing.
- Second was the energy crisis triggered by Russia's invasion of Ukraine, which demonstrated with brutal clarity what happens when a major economy becomes dependent on a single supplier for a critical input, especially when that supplier might not be in friendly hands.

Germany's experience was particularly instructive. The Federal Republic had built the most successful export economy in Europe on a model that, in retrospect, carried structural vulnerabilities it had chosen not to examine too closely: cheap Russian energy as the feedstock for industrial competitiveness, and deep integration with Chinese markets as the demand engine for its automotive, mechanical engineering, and chemical industries. For years, German business and political leaders resisted pressure—from Washington, from Central and Eastern European partners, from within the European Union—to reduce these dependencies, arguing that commercial engagement was itself a form of stability. The events of 2022 rendered that argument untenable.

The European Union's policy response has been substantial: the Critical Raw Materials Act, the Net-Zero Industry Act, the European Chips Act, and the broader "de-risking" framework articulated by European Commission President Ursula von der Leyen all reflect a new political consensus that strategic dependencies must be identified, mapped, and systematically reduced. This is not decoupling in the American sense. Europe's economic ties with China remain deep, and its political appetite for confrontation is more limited. But it represents a genuine shift in how European governments and major corporations approach supply chain decision-making. The era in which lowest-cost sourcing was justification is over.

A Transitional Phase: Circumventing New Trade Barriers

One of the central lessons of Chapter 10 is that trade barriers rarely stop trade. They reduce tradability, but they also redirect it. When the first wave of U.S. tariffs on Chinese goods hit in 2018, the initial response from businesses was not to fundamentally restructure their supply chains unless you were in politically sensitive goods like communications and networking equipment. That is expensive, can take time, and can be quite disruptive.

The first response was to find workarounds. Some of this took the form of China+1 strategies. I know companies that moved U.S.-destined production from China to Vietnam, which worked fine until the pandemic, when for much of the time Chinese factories stayed in operation while ones in Vietnam shut down. What followed was a period that might be called the great rerouting: a globally distributed exercise in regulatory arbitrage, creative logistics, and financial engineering, all in the service of preserving supply chain relationships that new trade policy was nominally designed to unwind. Understanding why that phase is now exhausting itself is essential to understanding why the more fundamental restructuring described in the rest of this chapter is finally, genuinely underway.

Trans-Shipment and the Geography of Evasion

The most visible workaround was trans-shipment: routing Chinese-origin goods through a third country to change the declared country of origin and avoid the tariff. Solar panels became the emblematic case. Faced with anti-dumping duties on Chinese solar products, manufacturers and importers discovered that panels could be shipped to Malaysia or Vietnam for minimal additional processing, sometimes little more than repackaging, and re-exported to the United States as Malaysian or Vietnamese goods at far lower duty rates (Dvorak and Mollica 2024; Iyoha et al. 2025).

The same pattern appeared in aluminum, steel, and a wide range of manufactured products. For a period, imports from Vietnam, Malaysia, Thailand, and Mexico surged in almost perfect correlation with the categories of Chinese goods facing the highest tariffs. That was something that was not lost on U.S. trade investigators.

The U.S. response was to extend the tariff net. The Commerce Department broadened its scope for finding that goods processed in third countries retained their Chinese origin if the "substantial transformation" standard had not been met. By 2024, tariffs on solar panels were extended to cover imports from Cambodia, Malaysia, Thailand, and Vietnam, essentially following the supply chain as it tried to escape. The game of regulatory arbitrage was not over, but the window for simple trans-shipment as a durable strategy had narrowed considerably.

Front-Running and the Inventory Surge

A second workaround required no geography at all—just timing. When tariff announcements gave companies advance notice of impending duty increases, the rational response was to accelerate imports before the new rates took effect: to front-run the tariff by building inventory. The pattern appeared first in 2018 and 2019, as companies scrambled to pull forward orders ahead of successive rounds of U.S.–China tariff escalation. It reappeared, at far greater scale, in early 2025, when the announcement of sweeping new tariffs under the second Trump administration triggered one of the largest inventory buildups in recent memory. Port traffic surged, and ocean container rates on the main trade lanes to the United States spiked. Warehouses filled. Companies that had the balance sheet to stockpile months of inventory did so; those that did not faced a painful competitive disadvantage. In March 2025, U.S. imports of both capital goods and consumer goods hit all-time records, as did imports from Mexico, the United Kingdom, Ireland, Germany, Italy, India, and Vietnam. Imports from Ireland alone reached $30.7 billion in the month, which was probably a lot of pharmaceuticals (see Chapter 11), which are highly tradable (see Chapter 1).

Front-running is, of course, a temporary fix that contains the seeds of its own reversal. The bullwhip effect, which we discussed in Chapter 8, applies with particular force when the signal is a tariff deadline rather than a genuine demand surge. The inventory glut that follows a front-running episode depresses orders for months afterward, creating exactly the kind of volatility that supply chains are designed to minimize. And as tariff policy became more unpredictable, announced, suspended, reinstated, and modified on timelines that outpaced corporate planning cycles, even the calculus of front-running became unworkable. Stockpiling inventory against a tariff that might be negotiated away before it takes effect is an expensive bet.

Tariff Engineering and the Fine Print of Trade

A more technically sophisticated response was tariff engineering: modifying a product, its components, or its classification to qualify for a more favorable duty treatment. This is not new; as Chapter 10 showed, companies have been navigating the fine print of tariff schedules since tariff schedules first existed. The chicken tax that kept foreign light trucks out of the American market for six decades spawned an entire genre of engineering workarounds, from Ford and its Transit Connect vans to various manufacturers adjusting the precise specifications of products to land on the more favorable side of a tariff line. The post-2018 environment simply generated a new wave of the same practices, as trade lawyers and customs specialists found themselves among the most sought-after professionals in global commerce.

Changes in trade terms offered a related avenue for financial engineering. The shift from free on board (FOB) to delivered duty paid (DDP) pricing, in which the seller, rather than the buyer, assumes responsibility for duties, did not reduce the tariff cost, but it changed who bore it (even though the ultimate buyer remains responsible), how it was accounted for, and how it appeared in transaction records. For some companies, particularly those selling into markets where price transparency was limited, absorbing duty costs into the landed price and presenting a single DDP number to customers offered a way to manage the commercial impact of tariffs without making them visible as a line item. This too was a workaround rather than a solution, but in an environment of tariff uncertainty it provided a degree of contractual flexibility that FOB terms did not.

Why the Workarounds Are Running Out of Road

Workarounds are rational responses to trade barriers, and they will always exist in some form. But several forces are converging to make the workaround phase of the current trade disruption less viable than it once was.

- The first is enforcement. Customs authorities around the world but especially in the United States have become more sophisticated in detecting trans-shipment and origin fraud, and the political pressure to close loopholes has rarely been higher.

- The second is scale. The tariff increases of 2025 were, in many categories, simply too large to engineer around. A 145% tariff on Chinese goods cannot be absorbed, reclassified, or front-run into commercial viability. At that level, the economics of the supply chain have to change.
- The third, and perhaps most important, force is strategic clarity. For the first several years of the increased tariff era, many executives clung to the hope that the disruption was temporary and that a negotiated settlement would restore something close to the pre-2018 trading environment. Wait it out and hope things revert to the way they were. That hope has faded. The bipartisan consensus in the United States on competition with China, the embedding of supply chain resilience into industrial policy on both sides of the Atlantic, and the sheer duration of the disruption have collectively shifted the corporate calculus from "How do we get around this?" to "What does our supply chain need to look like for the world as it actually is?" It is that shift that defines the current moment.

The Rewiring of Global Trade

The era of seamless globalization is giving way to something more fragmented, more managed, and more political. Economists have begun using the term "slowbalization" to capture the deceleration of cross-border integration (The Economist 2019), but the reality is more nuanced: globalization is not retreating so much as it is being rewired.

Friend-Shoring and the Politics of Trade Routes

The concept of "friend-shoring," directing trade and investment toward politically aligned partners, has moved from think-tank whitepapers to the explicit language of finance ministers and trade negotiators. The United States, European Union, Japan, and a growing set of middle powers are actively building preferential trade corridors that prioritize geopolitical reliability alongside price competitiveness. This does not mean the end of global supply chains; it means that geography, governance, and alliance structures are becoming as important as comparative advantage.

The practical consequences are already visible. New investment in semiconductor fabrication is flowing to the United States, Japan, and Europe not because of lower costs but because of strategic necessity. Pharmaceutical supply chains that once ran almost entirely through Asian hubs are being diversified to include domestic and allied-nation production. Critical mineral agreements are being signed with an urgency that echoes the energy diplomacy of the 1970s.

One underappreciated consequence of geopolitical fragmentation is the growing power of countries that sit at the intersections of competing blocs. Mexico, Vietnam, India, Poland, and Morocco, among others, are emerging as critical nodes in the rewired global economy, attracting investment from multinationals seeking to maintain access to both Western and Asian markets without the exposure of operating directly in contested territories. This "connector economy" phenomenon is reshaping foreign direct investment patterns in ways that will have lasting consequences for development trajectories across the Global South.

Technology as a Shaper

Technology has always restructured trade. As we have described throughout this book, the steam engine, refrigeration, and containerization had dramatic impacts on where things came from. But the restructuring has never been as clean or as fast as the advocates promised at the time. The current wave of digital transformation is likely no different.

Genuine gains over the short term will most likely be at the execution layer. Warehouse automation has materially reduced labor intensity and error rates in fulfillment operations. Visibility tools, knowing where a container actually is, rather than where the booking system says it should be, have real value, even if "real-time visibility" is a more modest achievement than it sounds. Demand forecasting has improved, meaningfully in some sectors, incrementally in most. The digitization of what used to be paper, phone calls, and fax machines has made freight forwarding faster and less opaque. These are real improvements. They are also, mostly, improvements to how supply chains execute rather than transformations of what supply chains are.

The more ambitious claims have had a rougher time. The venture capital wave that flowed into supply chain technology after the COVID-19 pandemic produced a generation of companies, some of which no longer exist in the form they were funded, that raised enormous sums on the premise that software-first approaches would disrupt traditional logistics the way software disrupted media or retail. The results have been more complicated.

Flexport's struggles illustrated a recurring lesson: freight forwarding is a relationship and execution business, and algorithmic elegance does not substitute easily for the human judgment, local knowledge, and organizational trust that make complex logistics work. The vision of AI systems that autonomously reoptimize supply chains in real time, anticipating disruptions before they materialize and rerouting flows dynamically, remains considerably more aspirational than practice for most companies. Also, the organizations best positioned to benefit from these tools are large and sophisticated enough to have the data infrastructure and integration capability to deploy them. AI may be widening the gap between multinationals and their suppliers rather than democratizing capability, the opposite of what the marketing usually promises.

Additive manufacturing deserves its own honest accounting. 3D printing has genuinely restructured specific pockets of industrial supply chains. Here I am thinking tooling and fixtures, spare parts for low-volume high-complexity components, medical devices where customization to individual anatomy justifies the cost premium, and certain aerospace and defense applications where the alternative is an expensive machining setup for a part ordered in the dozens. These are real and growing use cases. The recurring prediction that additive manufacturing would decentralize the production of consumer goods, printing products locally rather than shipping them from China, has not materialized and shows little sign of doing so at the economics that make mass manufacturing work. That vision has been approximately 5 years away for about 15 years. The technology is useful, but for different things than the hype might suggest.

Climate Change and the Physical Reordering of Trade

Of all the forces shaping the road ahead, climate change may prove to be one of the most consequential. And it operates on a timeline that business planning horizons struggle to accommodate. Its effects on global trade are both direct, through the physical disruption of trade infrastructure, and indirect, through the policy frameworks being erected in response.

The world's trade infrastructure was built for the climate of the twentieth century, not the one emerging in the twenty-first. Low-lying port facilities face rising sea levels and intensifying storm surges. River systems that serve as inland freight corridors—the Rhine, the Mississippi, the Yangtze—are experiencing both unprecedented flooding and historically low water levels that restrict barge traffic. The cascading effects of a single chokepoint failure, as demonstrated by drought-reduced water levels in the Panama Canal in 2023 and 2024, can ripple through global commodity markets for months.

The European Union's Carbon Border Adjustment Mechanism, now moving through its transitional phase, represents the most significant attempt yet to internalize the climate costs of internationally traded goods. It will not be the last. As major economies put price signals on carbon-intensive production, the comparative advantage calculations that have driven global sourcing decisions for decades will shift. Industries and countries that have built export competitiveness on cheap, dirty energy face a structural reckoning. Those that invest early in clean production processes and lower-emission logistics networks will find themselves with an advantage that compounds over time. Though the United States has been pulling back from global engagement and has derailed the International Maritime Organization's plans for a carbon price on seaborne shipping, we should remember that 85% of global trade does not involve the United States. The decarbonization of global shipping, which carries approximately 80% of world trade by volume, represents perhaps the most complex technological and commercial challenge in the history of the industry and it is now underway in earnest. Even as the United States walks away from its ability to influence it, it will continue.

The Human Dimension

We want high-paying jobs, and we love having a wide choice of inexpensive products that were made (or harvested) with low-cost labor. These two desires are in tension, and acknowledging that tension honestly is the precondition for thinking clearly about what comes next.

The math is not complicated. In a high-cost country, the only sustainable path to competitive manufacturing is high productivity, and that means producing more value per worker than lower-wage competitors can match. And in the current technological moment, high productivity means automation: robots on the factory floor, AI in the logistics network, software replacing the coordination work that once required armies of clerks and planners. There is no other mechanism. Labor costs in the United States or Germany or Japan are not going to fall to Vietnamese or Bangladeshi levels. The gap closes only if output per worker rises dramatically, and that means machines.

This creates a political bind that most elected officials have found it more rewarding to obscure than to confront. The same voters who want manufacturing brought home often resist, with entirely understandable anxiety, the automation that would make that manufacturing viable. The promise that tariffs and reshoring will restore the factory jobs of a previous generation is, in most cases, technically incoherent. The factories that come back will be highly automated, and they will employ far fewer people than the ones that left. A semiconductor fabrication plant employs hundreds of engineers and technicians, not thousands of assembly workers. An automated fulfillment center replaces a warehouse floor that once required hundreds of people with a fleet of robots managed by a much smaller, much more technically skilled team.

None of this means that automation is bad or that reshoring is pointless or that policy has no role to play. It means the honest version of the conversation is harder than the political version. The question is not "how do we get the old jobs back?" It is "what do we do for the people whose skills don't match what the new supply chain requires, and how do we build the education and retraining infrastructure to close that gap over time?" Those are tractable questions—but only if we stop pretending the contradiction doesn't exist.

As I hope you have found reading this book, global trade is, at its core, also a story about work. Who does it, where, under what conditions, and with what skills. Getting this right will determine not just corporate performance but the political sustainability of the broader transition.

We have already seen that the rapid automation of warehousing, freight sorting, and last-mile delivery is displacing a significant volume of routine physical labor while creating demand for a different skill profile: workers who can program, maintain, and collaborate with robotic systems. This transition is happening faster than workforce development institutions in most countries are equipped to manage. The result is high-value logistics roles that command good wages and face acute talent shortages, alongside displaced workers whose skills do not match what new supply chains require.

Simultaneously, a new generation of supply chain due diligence legislation in Germany, France, Norway, and at the EU level is extending corporate accountability beyond direct operations to suppliers, subsuppliers, and service providers. The Uyghur Forced Labor Prevention Act in the United States has demonstrated that sourcing from regions with documented labor rights violations can trigger import bans with significant commercial consequences. This represents a fundamental shift. Labor standards are becoming a supply chain risk category alongside delivery reliability and price.

Strategic Imperatives

Against this complex backdrop, what does sound strategy look like? The honest answer is that there is no single blueprint. The right configuration depends on industry, geography, competitive position, and risk appetite. But several strategic imperatives appear robust across a wide range of scenarios.

- **Build for resilience, not just efficiency.** The most important shift in supply chain strategy over the coming decade will be the rebalancing of efficiency and resilience. This does not mean abandoning lean principles or accepting unnecessary cost. It means recognizing that a supply chain optimized purely for cost minimization in stable conditions is, in effect, an undiversified bet on stability, a bet that the last several years have shown to be a loser. Resilient supply chains hold strategic inventory for critical inputs, maintain redundant supplier relationships, invest in visibility tools that surface risk early, and have tested contingency plans for plausible disruption scenarios.

- **Invest in supply chain visibility as a strategic asset.** Many organizations still lack basic visibility beyond their first-tier suppliers. They cannot answer with confidence where critical components originate, which subsuppliers are single points of failure, or which parts of their network are concentrated in climate-vulnerable or in geopolitically exposed locations. Closing these visibility gaps, through supplier mapping and real-time monitoring partnerships, is among the highest-return investments available to supply chain leaders today.
- **Treat geopolitical risk assessment as a core business function.** For most of the globalization era, geopolitical risk was a specialized concern, handled by government affairs teams on the periphery of operational decision-making. And that risk was unpriced, so we didn't build it into our models. That model is no longer adequate. Trade policy, sanctions regimes, export controls, and investment screening are now moving rapidly enough that they require ongoing monitoring and integration into strategic planning cycles. Leading organizations are building cross-functional capabilities combining trade policy expertise, scenario planning, and operational agility to navigate this environment. Those that treat geopolitical risk as an episodic external shock rather than a structural feature of the operating environment will repeatedly find themselves caught off guard.
- **Accelerate the transition to sustainable supply chains.** The decarbonization of global supply chains is moving from a reputational consideration to a commercial and regulatory necessity. Carbon pricing is spreading. Customer and investor scrutiny of Scope 3 emissions is intensifying. Due diligence legislation is creating legal exposure for environmental harms in upstream operations. Organizations that are still treating supply chain sustainability as a reporting exercise rather than an operational transformation will face mounting pressure from regulators, customers, lenders, and talent markets. Those investing now in lower-emission logistics, circular supply chain models, and clean-energy sourcing are building durable competitive advantages.

Embracing Productive Uncertainty

There is a temptation, in writing about the road ahead, to project false confidence onto an inherently uncertain future. The honest assessment is that the transformation of global trade and supply chains is still in its early stages. The geopolitical landscape will continue to shift in ways that are difficult to anticipate. Technologies will mature faster or slower than current trajectories suggest. Climate impacts will intensify, but their precise spatial and temporal patterns are not yet known. Policy environments will evolve in response to domestic political pressures that are themselves in flux.

What is clear is that the organizations, countries, and communities that will fare best in this environment are those that build adaptive capacity alongside technical capability—that invest not just in the ability to execute a supply chain strategy, but in the ability to recognize when that strategy needs to change and to change it quickly. The competitive advantage of the next era will belong not to the most efficient supply chains, but to the most intelligent ones: networks that sense the world, learn from it, and respond faster than the disruptions they face.

The road ahead in trade and supply chains is not a straight line. It is a landscape of branching paths, some well-marked and many still obscure. Navigating it will require rigor, imagination, and a willingness to hold competing possibilities in mind simultaneously. The chapters that preceded this one have mapped the terrain as it exists today. The work of building supply chains worthy of the challenges that lie ahead belongs to every leader, policymaker, and practitioner who carries this analysis forward into action.

And that will change where a lot of your stuff comes from.

References

Abernathy William & Kenneth Wayne. (September/October 1974). "Limits of the Learning Curve," *Harvard Business Review* 52: 109–19.

Acemoglu Daron, & Pascual Restrepo. 2020. "Robots and Jobs: Evidence from US Labor Markets." *The Journal of Political Economy* (Chicago) 128(6): 2188–244. **https://doi.org/10.1086/705716**.

adidas Group. "adidas Annual Report 2024." **adidas-Group.Com**. adidas Group. Accessed January 24, 2026. **https://report.adidas-group.com/2024/en/_assets/downloads/annual-report-adidas-ar24.pdf**.

Agarwal Ruchir. "Industrial policy and the growth strategy trilemma." *IMF Finance and Development*, March 2023.

Agrilinkage. "Where Are Blueberries Produced? Complete Guide to Blueberry Producers & Regions [2026]." Agrilinkage (blog), February 4, 2026. **https://www.agrilinkage.com/post/blueberries-producers-countries-guide#:~:text=to%20your%20table.-,China%3A%20The%20Rapid%20Rise%20to%20Production%20Dominance,in%20the%202024%2D2025%20season**.

Ahmad Majeed. "Malaysia's semiconductor journey spanning half a century." *EDN Asia*. October 6, 2023. **https://www.ednasia.com/malaysias-semiconductor-journey-spanning-half-a-century/**.

Al S. 2012. *Factory towns of South China 華南工廠城: An Illustrated Guidebook 圖示旅遊書*. Hong Kong University Press.

Alberts Bruce, Rebecca Heald, Alexander Johnson, David Morgan, Martin Raff, Keith Roberts, & Peter Walter. 2022. *Molecular Biology of the Cell: Seventh International Student Edition with Registration Card*. New York: W.W. Norton & Company.

Allen Robert C. 1994. "Agriculture During the Industrial Revolution." In *The Economic History of Britain Since 1700*, Vol. 1., edited by Roderick Floud and Paul Johnson, 96–116, Cambridge University Press.

AMNH. "Ruby Land: The Gems and Geology of Myanmar's Mogok Stone Tract." **AMNH.org**, August 11, 2014. Accessed February 21, 2026. **https://www.amnh.org/explore/news-blogs/ruby-land-gems-geology#:~:text=The%20Mogok%20Stone%20Tract%20is,gem%20pockets%20inside%20other%20rocks**.

Anderson Cynthia D., Michael D. Schulman, & Phillip J. Wood. 2001. "Globalization and Uncertainty: The Restructuring of Southern Textiles." *Social Problems* 48(4): 478–98. **https://doi.org/10.1525/sp.2001.48.4.478**.

Anderson R. 2012. "One Yeast or Two? Pure Yeast and Top Fermentation." *Brewery History* 149: 30–8.

Aquafeed Media & Aquafeed Media SLU. (2025, July 22). "China releases 2024 National Fishery Economic Statistics Bulletin." *Aquafeed*. **https://www.aquafeed.com/newsroom/reports/china-releases-2024-national-fishery-economic-statistics-bulletin/**.

Arias Edgar, Henry Quesada, & Robert L Smith. 2020. "Competitive Strategies for International Marketing of Hardwood Products Based on the Mining of Open Questionnaire Data." *Bioresources* (Raleigh) 15(4): 7872–92. **https://doi.org/10.15376/biores.15.4.7872-7892**.

Arrow Kenneth, Hollis B. Chenery, Bagicha S. Minhas, & Robert M. Solow. (1961). "Capital-Labor Substitution and Economic Efficiency." *Review of Economics and Statistics*.

Asche Frank, Bixuan Yang, Jessica A. Gephart, Martin D. Smith, James L. Anderson, Edward V. Camp, Taryn M. Garlock, David C. Love, Atle Oglend, & Hans-Martin Straume. 2022. "China's seafood imports—Not for domestic consumption?" *Science (American Association for the Advancement of Science)* 375(6579): 386–8. **https://doi.org/10.1126/science.abl4756**.

Asia News Monitor (Bangkok). 2015. "Thailand: Gems & Jewelry." January 6.

Associated Press. (2019, March 13). 1st Transpacific Fiber-Optic Cable links U.S., Japan – Los Angeles Times. *Los Angeles Times*. **https://www.latimes.com/archives/la-xpm-1989-04-18-fi-2297-story.html#:~:text=1st%20Transpacific%20Fiber%2DOptic%20Cable,More%20to%20Reas**.

Australian Mining Review. "Asserting Australia's Iron Ore Supremacy," December 12, 2025. **https://australianminingreview.com.au/issue/2025/11/asserting-australias-iron-ore-supremacy/**.

Autor David H., David Dorn, & Gordon H. Hanson. 2013. "The China Syndrome: Local Labor Market Effects of Import Competition in the United States." *American Economic Review* 103(6): 2121–68.

Autor David, Frank Levy, & Richard Murnane. 2003. "The Skill Content of Recent Technological Change." *Quarterly Journal of Economics* 118(4): 1279–333.

Baldwin Carliss Y. & Kim B. Clark 2000. *Design Rules*. MIT Press.

Barry Frank. 2004. "Export-Platform Foreign Direct Investment: The Irish Experience." EIB Papers 9(2): 8–37.

Bassett Thomas J. 2001. *The Peasant Cotton Revolution in West Africa: Côte d'Ivoire, 1880-1995*. Cambridge University Press.

Bassett Thomas J, Moussa Koné, & Nathan R Pavlovic. 2018. "Power Relations and Upgrading in the Cashew Value Chain of Côte d'Ivoire." *Development and Change (Oxford)* 49(5): 1223–47. **https://doi.org/10.1111/dech.12400**.

Baunsgaard Thomas & Michael Keen. 2010. "Tax Revenue and (or?) Trade Liberalization." *Journal of Public Economics* 94(9–10): 563–77.

Beiser Vince. "The Ultra-Pure, Super-Secret Sand That Makes Your Phone Possible." *WIRED*, August 7, 2018. **https://www.wired.com/story/book-excerpt-science-of-ultra-pure-silicon/#:~:text=The%20processor%20that%20makes%20your,from%20this%20obscure%20Appalachian%20backwater**.

Bennett Jeff. "Quake Spurs Supplier—Japan Paint Shortage Has Tiny Gage Products in Demand." *Wall Street Journal*. March 31, 2011. **https://www.wsj.com/articles/SB10001424052748703712504576232980626319082**.

Berkowitz H., H. Dumez, & i3-CRG, École Polytechnique, CNRS, Université Paris-Saclay. 2016. The Gribeauval system, or the issue of standardization in the 18th century. In *GÉRER & COMPRENDRE—ENGLISH LANGUAGE ONLINE SELECTION*. Retrieved October 12, 2025, from **https://annales.org/gc/GC-english-language-online-edition/2016/BERKOWITZ-DUMEZ.pdf**.

Bettis Richard A., Stephen P. Bradley, & Gary Hamel. 1992. "Outsourcing and Industrial Decline." *Academy of Management Perspectives* 6(1): 7–22. **https://doi.org/10.5465/ame.1992.4274298**.

Bintsis Thomas & Photis Papademas. 2022. "The Evolution of Fermented Milks, from Artisanal to Industrial Products: A Critical Review." *Fermentation* 8(12): 679.

Blake Hannah. “A History of . . . Novo Nordisk.” *Pharmaphorum*, February 27, 2013. **https://pharmaphorum.com/views-and-analysis/a_history_of-_novo_nordisk?utm**.

Braidwood Robert J., Jonathan D. Sauer, Hans Helbaek, Paul C. Mangelsdorf, Hugh C. Cutler, Carleton S. Coon, Ralph Linton, Julian Steward, & A. Leo Oppenheim. 1953. “Symposium: Did Man Once Live by Beer Alone?” *American Anthropologist* 55(4): 515–26.

Brander James A. & Barbara J. Spencer. 1985. “Export Subsidies and International Market Share Rivalry.” *Journal of International Economics* (Amsterdam) 18(1): 83–100. **https://doi.org/10.1016/0022-1996(85)90006-6**.

Bray David. 2005. *Social Space and Governance in Urban China: The Danwei System from Origins to Reform*. Redwood City: Stanford University Press. **https://doi.org/10.1515/9781503624924**.

Brooks Mary R. & Athanasios A. Pallis, eds. 2012. The Handbook of Maritime Economics and Business. 2nd edn. London: Lloyd’s List.

Brown Vivienne. 1997. “‘Mere Inventions of the Imagination’: A Survey of Recent Literature on Adam Smith.” *Economics and Philosophy*, 13(2): 281–312. **https://doi.org/10.1017/S0266267100004521**.

Buehlmann Urs, Omar Espinoza, Matthew Bumgardner, & Bob Smith. 2010. “Trends in the US Hardwood Lumber Distribution Industry: Changing Products, Customers, and Services.” *Forest Products Journal* (Madison) 60(6): 547–53. **https://doi.org/10.13073/0015-7473-60.6.547**.

Butler, Ed. “Ghana Wants More for Its Cashews, but It’s a Tough Nut to Crack,” February 5, 2025. **https://www.bbc.com/news/articles/cg5y1r189m0o?**

Calvin Linda, Philip M Martin, Skyler Simnitt, & United States. Department of Agriculture. Economic Research Service issuing body. 2022. *Supplement to Adjusting to Higher Labor Costs in Selected U.S. Fresh Fruit and Vegetable Industries: Case Studies. Economic Research Service*, U.S. Department of Agriculture.

Cang Alfred & Katharine Gemmell. “Rio, Fortescue Change Benchmark Used for China Iron Ore Pricing.” **Bloomberg.Com**, December 29, 2025. **https://www.bloomberg.com/news/articles/2025-12-29/rio-fortescue-change-benchmark-used-for-china-iron-ore-pricing**.

Carey Mathew. 1827. Alexander Hamilton’s Report on the Subject of Manufactures, Made in His Capacity of Secretary of the Treasury, on the Fifth of December, 1791. 6th edn. Printed by William Brown.

Casey Christopher. “Imports and the Section 321 (De Minimis) Exemption: Origins, Evolution, and Use.” Congress.Gov. Congressional Research Service, January 31, 2025. Accessed February 26, 2026. **https://www.congress.gov/crs-product/R48380**.

Casey G. P. 2020. “Yeast Selection in Brewing.” In *Yeast Strain Selection*, edited by Chandra J. Panchal, pp. 65–111. Boca Raton: CRC Press.

Center for Automotive Research. 2015. *Contribution of the Automotive Industry to the Economies of All Fifty States and the United States*. Ann Arbor, MI: Center for Automotive Research.

Central Statistics Office (Ireland), Goods Exports and Imports, December and Annual 2024 (February 2025), reported in Euronews, “Irish Exports Hit Record High with Pharmaceuticals Showing Major Boost,” February 17, 2025; IDA Ireland, “Key Players in Ireland’s Pharmaceutical Manufacturing Space,” **idaireland.com**.

Chacholiades Jagdish. 1973. *The Pure Theory of International Trade.* Aldine Publication Co.

Chakrabarti Meghna. "Henry Ford's Assembly Line Turns 100," *NPR* (October 16, 2013). **https://www.npr.org/transcripts/235602439?storyId=235602439#:~:text=EISENSTEIN:%20They%20found%20inspiration%20in,faster%20process%20than%20ever%20before**.

Chang Pao-Long, Chintay Shih, & Chiung-Wen Hsu. 1994. "The Formation Process of Taiwan's IC Industry: Method of Technology Transfer." *Technovation* 14(3): 161–71.

CheeseScience. "What Is Fermentation-produced Chymosin?," 2008. **http://www.cheesescience.net/2008/07/what-is-fermentation-produced-chymosin.html**.

Chen Dene-Hern. "Pandora Expands Manufacturing in Thailand." *WWD*, May 7, 2018. **https://wwd.com/accessories-news/jewelry/pandora-expands-manufacturing-in-thailand-1202665352/**.

Chow Andrew R. "The Tax Loophole That Helps Temu and Shein Keep Prices so Low." TIME, February 16, 2024. **https://time.com/6695469/temu-shein-de-minimis/**.

Chu Wan-wen. 1999. "Industrial Growth and Small and Medium-sized Enterprises: The Case of Taiwan." Working Paper, Sun Yat-Sen Institute for Social Sciences, Academia Sinica, Taipei.

Coe Sophie D. 2013. *The True History of Chocolate.* 3rd edn. London: Thames & Hudson.

Cohen Elie. 2007. "Industrial Policies in France: The Old and the New." *Journal of Industry, Competition and Trade* 7(3): 213–27.

Cohen Stanley N., Annie C. Y. Chang, Herbert W. Boyer, & Robert B. Helling. 1973. "Construction of Biologically Functional Bacterial Plasmids In Vitro." *Proceedings of the National Academy of Sciences* 70(11): 3240–4.

DARPA. "Innovation Timeline | DARPA," n.d. **https://www.darpa.mil/about-us/timeline/mosis**.

Das Raya, Sanchit Gupta, & Ashok Gulati. 2025. *India's Shrimp Exports: Coping with US Tariffs.* Policy brief, Indian Council for Research on International Economic Relations (ICRIER). **https://icrier.org/pdf/pb50_India-s-Shrimp-Exports_Coping-with-US-Tariffs.pdf**.

De Gier H. G. (2016). *Capitalist Workingman's Paradises Revisited: Corporate Welfare Work in Great Britain, the USA, Germany and France in the Golden Age of Capitalism, 1880–1930* 1st edn. Amsterdam University Press.

De Vries Jan. 1974. *The Dutch rural economy in the Golden Age, 1500–1700.* Yale University Press.

Delbridge Timothy. 2021. "Robotic Strawberry Harvest Is Promising but Will Need Improved Technology and Higher Wages to Be Economically Viable." *California Agriculture* 75(2): 57–63. **https://doi.org/10.3733/ca.2021a0009**.

Dell Technologies. "Public Supplier List." **Dell technologies.com**. Accessed January 12, 2026. **https://www.delltechnologies.com/asset/en-us/solutions/business-solutions/briefs-summaries/dell-public-supplier-list.pdf?utm**.

Dennard Robert H., Fritz H. Gaensslen, Hwa-Nien Yu, V. Leo Rideout, Ernest Bassous, & Andre R. LeBlanc. 1974. "Design of Ion-Implanted MOSFET's with Very Small Physical Dimensions." *IEEE Journal of Solid-State Circuits* 9(5): 256–68. **https://doi.org/10.1109/JSSC.1974.1050511**.

Dennis Neil. 2024. Apple and Ford Settle Fraud Allegations, Deny Wrongdoing in Separate Cases. In *Benzinga Newswires.* Southfield: Accretive Capital LLC d/b/a Benzinga.

Department of Foreign Affairs and Trade. 2012. *Australia's Coal and Iron Ore Exports 2001 to 2011.* Canberra: Commonwealth of Australia. **https://www.dfat.gov.au/sites/default/files/australias-coal-and-iron-ore-exports-2001-to-2011.pdf.**

Dhillon Sohita. 2018. "Semaglutide: First Global Approval." *Drugs* 78(2): 275–84.

Donnel Jessica. "Harvest CROO Robotics Gains Patent for Pitzer Wheel Strawberry Robot." **andnowuknow.com**, July 11, 2016. Accessed February 14, 2026. **https://www.andnowuknow.com/headlines/harvest-croo-robotics-gains-patent-pitzer-wheel-strawberry-robot-wish-farms/jessica-donnel/50156.**

Dornbusch Rudiger, Stanley Fischer, & Paul Anthony Samuelson. 1977. "Comparative Advantage, Trade, and Payments in a Ricardian Model with a Continuum of Goods." *The American Economic Review* 67(5), 823–39.

Drysdale Peter. 1970. "Minerals and Metals in Japanese-Australian Trade." *Developing Economies* 8(2): 198–218.

Duffy Siobain. 2021, January 27. *Small formats' big future in retail.* Progressive Grocer. Retrieved December 23, 2025, from **https://progressivegrocer.com/small-formats-big-future-retail.**

Dvorak Phred & Andrew Mollica. "Can the U.S. Break China's Grip on Solar?" *The Wall Street Journal,* February 12, 2024.

Dyer Jeffrey H. 2000. *Collaborative Advantage: Winning through Extended Enterprise Supplier Networks.* New York: Oxford University Press.

Eble Philipp & Henk de Vries. 2018. "How One of the World's Oldest Food Safety Standards Approaches Expiration." In *EURAS Proceedings 2018 – Standards for a Smarter Future* 5–15. Aachen: Wissenschaftsverlag Mainz.

Ebling Jennifer. "Emil Christian Hansen: The Botanical Genius Who Saved Your Beer." *The Daily Gardener,* March 26, 2025, **https://thedailygardener.org/otb20190508/.**

Eck Peter. 2013. "Recombinant Technologies in Food." In *Biochemistry of Foods,* 3rd edn. edited by N.A. Michael Eskin & Fereidoon Shahidi. London: Academic Press.

Economic Research Service. 2025. "U.S. H-2A (Temporary Agricultural Employment of Foreign Workers) Positions Certified by State, Fiscal Years 2005–24 | Economic Research Service," n.d. **https://www.ers.usda.gov/data-products/chart-gallery/chart-detail?chartId=86844.**

English.scio.gov.cn. "Behind 'Hefei model': How reforms reshape China's emerging tech hub," December 19, 2023. Accessed March 1, 2026. **http://english.scio.gov.cn/m/in-depth/2023-12/19/content_116888781.htm.**

European Commission. "Hormones in Meat." Accessed February 5, 2026. **https://food.ec.europa.eu/food-safety/chemical-safety/hormones-meat_en?utm.**

Eurostat. "Tertiary Education Graduates: What Are Their Subject Areas?," January 24, 2020, **https://ec.europa.eu/eurostat/web/products-eurostat-news/-/EDN-20200124-1** (data year: 2017).

Fajgelbaum Pablo D., Amit Khandelwal, National Bureau of Economic Research, Viyaleta Farysheuskaya, Davin Chor, Lydia Cox, Gary Hufbauer, Martin Rotemberg, Pete Schott, & John Sturm Becko. "The Value of De Minimis Imports." National Bureau of Economic Research, 2024. **https://www.nber.org/system/files/working_papers/w32607/w32607.pdf.**

FAO. 2025. *Fishery and Aquaculture Statistics – Yearbook 2023.* FAO Yearbook of Fishery and Aquaculture Statistics. Rome. **https://doi.org/10.4060/cd6788en**.

FAO (Food and Agriculture Organization). 2023. FAOSTAT Trade Data. Rome.

Favre Christian. 1994. "Fly-by-Wire for Commercial Aircraft: The Airbus Experience." *International Journal of Control* 59(1): 139–57. **https://doi.org/10.1080/00207179408923072**.

Felix Sharon, Gregg Gildemann, Tom Hoang, Calvin Jin, Diego Rodriguez, Wendy Sowers, Aaron Tayler, Diane Tchakirides, & Boeing Air Cargo Market Analysis. "World Air Cargo Forecast 2024–2043," 2024. **https://www.boeing.com/content/dam/boeing/boeingdotcom/market/assets/downloads/Boeing-WACF-2024.pdf**.

Ferdows Kasra, Michael A. Lewis, & Jose A.D. Machuca. 2004. "Rapid-Fire Fulfillment." *Harvard Business Review* (Boston).

Fielden Sandy. "Slow Train Coming – The Decline and Fall of East Coast Crude by Rail." RBN Energy LLC, March 13, 2016. **https://rbnenergy.com/daily-posts/blog/slow-train-coming-decline-and-fall-east-coast-crude-rail**.

Fisher Marshall L. 1997. "What Is the Right Supply Chain for Your Product?" *Harvard Business Review* (Boston).

Fonrouge Gabrielle, Melissa Repko, & Annie Palmer. "Retail Panic: What the End of the 'de Minimis' Exemption Means for Brands Across the Globe." CNBC, September 8, 2025. **https://www.cnbc.com/2025/08/29/retail-impact-de-minimis-exemption-ends-globally.html#:~:text=Tailoring%20supply%20chains,into%20the%20country%20each%20day**.

Food and Agriculture Organization of the United Nations (2025) – with major processing by Our World in Data. "Cashew nut production – UN FAO" [dataset]. Food and Agriculture Organization of the United Nations, "Production: Crops and livestock products" [original data]. Retrieved January 25, 2026 from **https://archive.ourworldindata.org/20260119-235736/grapher/cashew-nut-production.html** (archived on January 19, 2026).

Food Ingredients Online. "DuPont Launches POWERPasta&Trade; Enzymes to Help Food Manufacturers Offer Products with Improved Appearance and 'Bite' at Reduced Cost," 2019. **https://www.foodingredientsonline.com/doc/dupont-launches-powerpasta-enzymes-products-and-bite-at-reduced-cost-0001**.

Ford Motor Company Archives, The Reminiscences of Mr. Max F. Wollering 1955. **https://cdm15889.contentdm.oclc.org/digital/collection/p15889coll2/id/19600/**.

Ford R. C. 2005. The Springfield Armory's Role in Developing Interchangeable Parts. *Management Decision* 43(2): 265–77. **https://doi.org/10.1108/00251740510581966**.

Fox P. F., T. Uniacke-Lowe, P. L. H. McSweeney, & J. A. O'Mahony. 2015. "Milk Proteins." In *Dairy Chemistry and Biochemistry*, pp. 145–239. Cham: Springer International Publishing.

Francis John G. & Alex F. Pevzner. 2006. "Airbus and Boeing: Strengths and Limitations of Strong States." *Political Science Quarterly* (Oxford, UK) 121(4): 629–51. **https://doi.org/10.1002/j.1538-165X.2006.tb00584.x**.

Friedman Jeffrey M. 2024. "The discovery and development of GLP-1 based drugs that have revolutionized the treatment of obesity." *Proceedings of the National Academy of Sciences* 121(39): e2415550121.

Frittelli John. "Shipping Under the Jones Act: Legislative and Regulatory Background." Congress.Gov. Congressional Research Service, November 21, 2019. Accessed February 22, 2026. **https://www.congress.gov/crs-product/R45725**.

Frittelli John, Anthony Andrews, Paul Parfomak, Robert Pirog, Jonathan Ramseur, & Michael Ratner. "U.S. Rail Transportation of Crude Oil: Background and Issues for Congress." Congress.Gov. Congressional Research Service, December 4, 2014. Accessed February 22, 2026. **https://www.congress.gov/crs-product/R43390**.

Fu Xiao, Ping Lin, & Gaofen Ye. 2026. "Industrial Policy in China: Its Development and Ongoing Transformation." *International Journal of Industrial Organization* 104 (January): 103229. **https://doi.org/10.1016/j.ijindorg.2025.103229**.

George Henry, Tom Loftin Johnson, William Joel Stone, Joseph E. Washington, George W. Fithian, Thomas Bowman, and Jerry Simpson. 1892. Protection or Free Trade? Govt. Print. Off.

Geoscience Australia. "Australian Mineral Facts." Geoscience Australia, October 29, 2025. **https://www.ga.gov.au/education/minerals-energy/australian-mineral-facts#:~:text=Australia%20is%20one%20of%20the,elements%2C%20uranium%2C%20and%20zinc**.

Gereffi Gary, John Humphrey, & Timothy Sturgeon. 2005. "The Governance of Global Value Chains." *Review of International Political Economy: RIPE (London)* 12(1): 78–104. **https://doi.org/10.1080/09692290500049805**.

Gilley K. Matthew & Abdul Rasheed. 2000. "Making More by Doing Less: An Analysis of Outsourcing and Its Effects on Firm Performance." *Journal of Management* 26(4): 763–90. **https://doi.org/10.1016/S0149-2063(00)00055-6**.

Godfrey M. 2020, May 14. "China shifting aquaculture production to higher-value species," *SeafoodSource*. **https://www.seafoodsource.com/news/aquaculture/china-shifting-aquaculture-production-to-higher-value-species**.

Graff Michelle. "Pandora Announces Plans to Build Third Factory, First Outside Thailand." *National Jeweler*, December 6, 2022. **https://nationaljeweler.com/articles/10900-pandora-announces-plans-to-build-third-factory-first-outside-thailand**.

Gross Michael. 2018. "On the Origins of Cheese." *Current Biology* 28(20): R1171–3.

Grossman Gene M. & Elhanan Helpman. 1994. "Protection for Sale." *American Economic Review* 84(4): 833–50.

Guinee T. P. & B. O'Brien. 2010. "The Quality of Milk for Cheese Manufacture." In *Technology of Cheesemaking*, pp. 1–67. Oxford: Wiley-Blackwell.

Guzik Erik. 2024. "Tariffs Are Back in the Spotlight, but Skepticism of Free Trade Has Deep Roots in American History." *The Conversation: Economy + Business* (Boston), October 31.

Hamilton Scott. Air Wars: The Global Combat Between Airbus and Boeing, 2021.

Hanisch Manfred. 2023. "Robert Shea Terrell, *A Nation Fermented: Beer, Bavaria, and the Making of Modern Germany*." Oxford University Press. Reviewed in *Historische Zeitschrift* 320(2025): 754–6.

Hannon Enda, Kathy Monks, Edel Conway, Grainne Kelly, Patrick Flood, Katie Truss, and Michele Mastroeni. 2011. "The State and Industrial Policy in Ireland: A Case Study of the Irish Pharmaceutical Sector." *International Journal of Human Resource Management* 22(18): 3692–710.

Hansen, Emil C. "Recherches sur la physiologie et la morphologie des ferments alcooliques. XII." *Comptes Rendus des Travaux du Laboratoire Carlsberg* 5(1902): 68.

Harboe M., M. L. Broe, & K. B. Qvist. 2010. "The Production, Action and Application of Rennet and Coagulants." In *Technology of Cheesemaking*, pp. 98–129. Oxford: Wiley-Blackwell.

Harpers Ferry National Historical Park. Harpers Ferry Armory and Arsenal – Harpers Ferry National Historical Park (U.S. National Park Service). n.d. **https://www.nps.gov/hafe/learn/historyculture/harpers-ferry-armory-and-arsenal.htm?simple=True**.

Hart Brian. "Will the Dual Circulation Strategy Enable China to Compete in a Post-Pandemic World? | ChinaPower Project." ChinaPower Project, November 9, 2023. **https://chinapower.csis.org/china-covid-dual-circulation-economic-strategy/**.

Hayami Yujiro & Vernon W. Ruttan. 1985. *Agricultural Development: An International Perspective*. Johns Hopkins University Press.

Hegde Narayan G. 2022. "Value Chain Development for Improving the Income of Cashew Growers (October 1, 2022)." *Journal of Rural Advancement* 10(02). **https://ssrn.com/abstract=4407115**.

Helper Susan & Mari Sako, 2010. "Management Innovation in Supply Chain: Appreciating Chandler in the Twenty-First Century." *Industrial and Corporate Change* 19(2): 399–429.

Henry Ford Heritage Association. "Henry Ford – an Impact Felt – Henry Ford Heritage Association," March 16, 2016. **https://hfha.org/the-ford-story/henry-ford-an-impact-felt/#:~:text=He%20called%20it%20vertical%20integration,all%20in%20a%20single%20place**.

Hidalgo César A. & Ricardo Hausmann. 2009. "Building Blocks of Economic Complexity." *Proceedings of the National Academy of Sciences – PNAS* (United States) 106(26): 10570–75. **https://doi.org/10.1073/pnas.0900943106**.

Hieber Ralf & Ingo Hartel. 2003. "Impacts of SCM Order Strategies Evaluated by Simulation-Based 'Beer Game' Approach: The Model, Concept, and Initial Experiences." *Production Planning & Control* 14(2): 122–34. **https://doi.org/10.1080/0953728031000107680**.

Hirtenstein Anna & Alfred Cang. "China's Massive Simandou Iron Mine in Africa Threatens to Upend Iron Ore Market." *Bloomberg*, November 3, 2025. **https://www.bloomberg.com/news/features/2025-11-03/china-s-massive-iron-mine-in-africa-threatens-to-upend-a-market**.

Hochheiser S. & S. Hochheiser. (2022, May 16). *Your Engineering Heritage: Fiber Optics*. IEEE-USA InSight. **https://insight.ieeeusa.org/articles/your-engineering-heritage-fiber-optics/#:~:text=For%20example%2C%20the%20last%20copper,;%20and%202000s%20fiber%2C%20terabits**.

Hoffman Carter. "History of Tariffs: From Ancient Times to the Modern Day." Trade Treasury Payments, June 2, 2025. Accessed February 8, 2026. **https://tradetreasurypayments.com/articles/history-of-tariffs-from-ancient-times-to-the-modern-day**.

Høiby Niels. 2024. "Louis Pasteur and the Birth of Microbiology in Denmark." *APMIS* 132(1): 43–52.

Hoke D. 1990. *Ingenious Yankees: The Rise of the American System of Manufactures in the Private Sector*. Columbia University Press.

Home of Carlsberg. "Five of the Most Significant Discoveries from the Carlsberg Research Laboratory." 2025 **https://homeofcarlsberg.com/stories/five-of-the-most-significant-discoveries-from-the-carlsberg-research-laboratory**.

Hounshell D. 1984. *From the American System to Mass Production, 1800–1932: The Development of Manufacturing Technology in the United States*. JHU Press.

Henry Ford to the editor, *Automobile* 14(1906): 107–19, quoted in John B. Rae, ed., Henry Ford, cited by David Hounshell, 1984b. *From the American System to Mass Production, 1800–1932* Baltimore: Johns Hopkins University Press, p. 218.

Hufbauer Gary C. & Jeffrey J. Schott. 2013. *Local Content Requirements: A Global Problem*. Peterson Institute for International Economics.

Hughes Richard W. 1997. *Ruby & Sapphire: A Gemologist's Guide*. Boulder, CO: RWH Publishing.

Hurst Luke. 2015. "The Development of the Asian Iron Ore Market: A Lesson in Long-Run Market Contestability." *Resources Policy* 46: 22–29. **https://doi.org/10.1016/j.resourpol.2015.08.001**.

Intel Newsroom. 2024. "Intel and Apollo Agree to Joint Venture Related to Intel's Fab 34 in Ireland." Newsroom, June 4, 2024. **https://newsroom.intel.com/corporate/co-invest-program-news-2024**.

Irwin Douglas A. 2017. *Clashing over Commerce: A History of US Trade Policy*. Chicago: University of Chicago Press.

Iron Knob. "Our History - Iron Knob," n.d. **https://ironknob.org/our-history/**.

Iyoha Ebehii, Edmund Malesky, Jaya Wen, & Sing Ju Wu. "Exports in Disguise?: Trade Rerouting during the US-China Trade War." Harvard Business School Working Paper 24–072, March 2025.

Jacobsen N. B. 2006. Industrial Symbiosis in Kalundborg, Denmark: A Quantitative Assessment of Economic and Environmental Aspects. *Journal of Industrial Ecology* 10(1–2): 239–55. **https://doi.org/10.1162/108819806775545411**.

Janzen Bernd G., Matthew R. Nicely, Yujin Kim McNamara, Devin S. Sikes, Daniel M. Witkowski, Julia K. Eppard, Yuzhe PengLing, Sydney Stringer, Paul S. Bettencourt, Jooyoun Jeong, Sung Un K. Kim, Ruby Rodriguez, & Sarah P. Tinaphong, "New Anti-dumping Duty Petition on Fresh Winter Strawberries from Mexico." Akin Gump, n.d. **https://www.akingump.com/en/insights/alerts/new-antidumping-duty-petition-on-fresh-winter-strawberries-from-mexico**.

Jefferson T. & J. P. Boyd. 2018. *Papers of Thomas Jefferson. 15, The Papers of Thomas Jefferson, Volume 15; March 1789 to November 1789*. Princeton University Press.

Johnson M. E. 2017. "A 100-Year Review: Cheese Production and Quality." *Journal of Dairy Science* 100(12): 9952–65.

Johnson Renee & Charles E. Hanrahan. 2010. "The U.S.-EU Beef Hormone Dispute." In Congressional Research Reports for the People, Dec 6 2010, p. 31.

Kalecki Michał. 1944. *Studies in Economic Dynamics*. Farrar & Rinehart, Inc.

Kanigel R. (1997). *The One Best Way: Frederick Winslow Taylor and the Enigma of Efficiency*. Viking.

Kaplan G. 1987. "Special report: On good design," *IEEE Spectrum* 24(5): 27–8. **https://doi.org/10.1109/MSPEC.1987.6447920**.

Kastner Jens & Dimitri Simes. "China Tariff on Australia's Barley Reshapes Global Trade." Nikkei Asia. March 19, 2021. **https://asia.nikkei.com/business/agriculture/china-tariff-on-australia-s-barley-reshapes-global-trade**.

Kaufman Nicolas. "Shein, Temu, and Chinese e-Commerce: Data Risks, Sourcing Violations, and Trade Loopholes." U.S.-China Economic Security and Review Commission, April 14, 2023. Accessed February 26, 2026. **https://USCC.gov**.

Kilby Jack S. "Miniaturized Electronic Circuits," issued June 23, 1964. **https://patentimages.storage.googleapis.com/30/d5/b4/ac7134ecd78946/US3138743.pdf**.

Kim Dong-Hyeon, Dana Jeong, Kwang-Young Song, & Kun-Ho Seo. 2018. "Comparison of Traditional and Backslopping Methods for Kefir Fermentation Based on Physicochemical and Microbiological Characteristics." *LWT* 97: 503–7.

Klein Benjamin, Robert G. Crawford, & Armen A. Alchian. 1978. "Vertical Integration, Appropriable Rents, and the Competitive Contracting Process." *The Journal of Law & Economics* (Chicago) 21(2): 297–326. **https://doi.org/10.1086/466922.**

Klier Thomas & James Rubenstein. 2008. *Who Really Made Your Car? Restructuring and Geographic Change in the Auto Industry*. W.E. Upjohn Institute.

Koistinen David. 2002. "The Causes of Deindustrialization: The Migration of the Cotton Textile Industry from New England to the South." *Enterprise & Society* 3(3): 482–520. **http://www.jstor.org/stable/23699718.**

Kragh Helge. 2015. "From Ørsted to Bohr: The Sciences and the Danish University System, 1800–1920." In *Sciences in the Universities of Europe, Nineteenth and Twentieth Centuries: Academic Landscapes*, pp. 31–47. Dordrecht: Springer.

Kresge Naomi & Michelle Fay Cortze. "Novo Advances After US Clears Wegovy for Liver Disease." Business Week, August 18, 2025. **https://www.bloomberg.com/news/articles/2025-08-18/novo-advances-after-us-clears-wegovy-for-liver-disease?cmpid=081825_marketsdaily&utm_medium=email&utm_source=newsletter&utm_term=250818.**

Kreymann Bernard, M. A. Ghatei, G. Williams, & S. R. Bloom. 1987. "Glucagon-like Peptide-1 7-36: A Physiological Incretin in Man." *The Lancet* 330(8571): 1300–4.

Krizan William G. 2009. "Ford's Transit Connect Van Will Find Use in Construction." ENR 262(18): 18.

Kroeber Arthur. "The Hot Zone." *Wired Magazine* 10.11 2002.

Krugman Paul. 1991. "Increasing Returns and Economic Geography." *The Journal of Political Economy* (Chicago) 99(3): 483–99. **https://doi.org/10.1086/261763.**

Krugman Paul. 1992. *Geography and Trade*. MIT Press.

Krugman Paul R. 1986. "Introduction." In *Strategic Trade Policy and the New International Economics*, edited by Paul R. Krugman, 1–22. Cambridge: MIT Press.

Kuchler Hannah. 2025. "Obesity drug sales surge at Novo Nordisk." *Financial Times*, February 5. **https://www.ft.com/content/b97c13c9-c08c-4d52-9915-f9d4477e6f2c.**

Kuenzel David J. 2024. "Non-Tariff Measures vs. Tariffs: A Fresh Look at the Evidence." *Economics Letters* 237:111669. **https://doi.org/10.1016/j.econlet.2024.111669.**

Lacy Robert. "*The Rise and Sudden Decline of North Carolina Furniture Manufacturing*." Econ Focus, Federal Reserve Bank of Richmond, Q4 2020. **https://www.richmondfed.org/publications/research/econ_focus/2020/q4/economic_history.**

Landgraf Wolfgang & Juergen Sandow. n.d. "Recombinant Human Insulins – Clinical Efficacy and Safety in Diabetes Therapy." *European Endocrinology* 12(1): 12–7.

Laursen Keld. 1996. "Horizontal Diversification in the Danish National System of Innovation: The Case of Pharmaceuticals." *Research Policy* 25(7): 1121–37.

Lawson Lynda. 2019. "Women Working in the Thai Coloured Gemstone Industry: Insights from Entrepreneurial Ecosystems." *The Extractive Industries and Society* 6(4): 1066–74. **https://doi.org/10.1016/j.exis.2019.08.002.**

Lee David. 2013. "The Establishment of Iron Ore Giants: Hamersley Iron and the Mount Newman Mining Company, 1961–1969." *Journal of Australasian Mining History* (Crawley, W.A) 11: 61–77.

Lee Hau L. 2002. "Aligning Supply Chain Strategies with Product Uncertainties." *California Management Review* 44(3): 105–19.

Lee Hau L., V. Padmanabhan, & Seungjin Whang. 1997. "The Bullwhip Effect in Supply Chains." *Sloan Management Review* 38(3): 93–102.

Leonardi Marco & Elena Meschi. 2024. "Non-Tariff Barriers to Trade." *Journal of Law, Economics, & Organization* 42: 188–220. **https://doi.org/10.1093/jleo/ewae023**.

Levinson, Marc. 2008. *The Box: How the Shipping Container Made the World Smaller and the World Economy Bigger*. Princeton University Press.

Lewis Andrew L., Nicholas McEntee, Justin Holland, & Asma Patel. 2022. "Development and Approval of Rybelsus (Oral Semaglutide): Ushering in a New Era in Peptide Delivery." *Drug Delivery and Translational Research* 12(1): 1–6.

Lewis Leo. 2018. "Japan Whisky Drought Offers Bitter Aftertaste of Corporate Caution." **FT.Com** (London).

Liu Li, Jiajing Wang, Danny Rosenberg, Hao Zhao, György Lengyel, & Dani Nadel. 2018. "Fermented Beverage and Food Storage in 13,000 Y-Old Stone Mortars at Raqefet Cave, Israel: Investigating Natufian Ritual Feasting." *Journal of Archaeological Science: Reports* 21: 783–93.

Livingston S. 2025. The new challenge of Communist corporate governance. **https://www.csis.org/analysis/new-challenge-communist-corporate-governance**.

Locke R.M. (2003) The promise and perils of globalization: The case of Nike. In: Kochan T.A., Schmalensee R.L. (eds) *Management: Inventing and Delivering Its Future*, edited by T.A. Kochan, R.L. Schmalensee, pp. 39–70. Cambridge: MIT Press.

Lü H., & Perry, E. J. (1997). *Introduction: The Changing Chinese Workplace in Historical and Comparative Perspective* Danwei (1st edn.), edited by E. J. Perry and X. Lü, pp. 3–17 Routledge. **https://doi.org/10.4324/9781315700014-.1**.

Luppold William, Matthew Bumgardner, & T. Eric McConnell. 2014. "Impacts of Changing Hardwood Lumber Consumption and Price on Stumpage and Sawlog Prices in Ohio." *Forest Science* (Oxford, UK) 60(5): 994–99. **https://doi.org/10.5849/forsci.13-706**.

Man Joyce Yanyun, Siqi Zheng, & Rongrong Ren. 2011. "Housing Policy and Housing Markets: Trends, Patterns, and Affordability." *China's Housing Reform and Outcomes*. 3–18.

Marcom John Jr. (May 02 1985). "IBM Introduces Line of Printers for Computers — Move Is Seen as Challenge to Japanese Dominance of Lucrative U.S. Market." *Wall Street Journal* Eastern edition, 1. **https://search.proquest.com/newspapers/ibm-introduces-line-printers-computers-move-is/docview/397913906/se-2**.

Martin Philip. 2017. "Immigration and Farm Labor: From Unauthorized to H-2A for Some?" *Applied Economic Perspectives and Policy* 39(3): 418–32.

Massot Pascale. "China Moves to Regain Iron Ore Market Power." *East Asia Forum*, December 12, 2025. **https://eastasiaforum.org/2025/12/12/china-moves-to-regain-iron-ore-market-power/**.

McCabe Carol. 2001. "The Mill Girls of Lowell." *Early American Life* 32: 34–7.

McGee Patrick. 2025. *Apple in China: The Capture of the World's Greatest Company*. Simon and Schuster.

McLaughlin Raoul. 2014. *The Roman Empire and the Indian Ocean: The Ancient World Economy and the Kingdoms of Africa, Arabia and India*. Barnsley, UK: Pen & Sword Maritime.

McWilliams Gary. 2005. "In Electronics, U.S. Companies Seize Momentum from Japan." *Wall Street Journal* 245(48): 1.

Metchnikoff Élie. 2004. *The Prolongation of Life: Optimistic Studies*. New York: Springer Publishing Company.

MINING.COM. "Xi's Giant Iron Ore Trader Is Shaking Up a $130 Billion Market - **MINING.COM**," June 19, 2025. **https://www.mining.com/web/xis-giant-iron-ore-trader-is-shaking-up-a-130-billion-market/**.

Mobley Grant. "The Complete History of Diamond Cutting." Only Natural Diamonds, November 4, 2025. **https://www.naturaldiamonds.com/historic-diamonds/diamond-cutting-history/**.

Modlin Irvin M. & Mark Kidd. 2001. "Ernest Starling and the Discovery of Secretin." *Journal of Clinical Gastroenterology* 32(3): 187–92.

Mojsov Svetlana, Gerhard Heinrich, Ira B. Wilson, Mariella Ravazzola, Lelio Orci, & Joel F. Habener. 1986. Preproglucagon Gene Expression in Pancreas and Intestine Diversifies at the Level of Post-Translational Processing. *Journal of Biological Chemistry* 261(25): 11880–9.

Moore Gordon E. 1965. "Cramming More Components onto Integrated Circuits." *Electronics Magazine*.

Morrell Peter S. 2018. *Moving Boxes by Air: The Economics of International Air Cargo*. 2nd edn. Routledge, Taylor & Francis Group.

Morrill Land-Grant College Act. Legislative History of 12 Stat. 503, Chap. 130. 1862.

Morse Philip McCord & George Elbert Kimball. 1962. *Methods of Operations Research*. MIT Press.

Müller T. D., B. Finan, C. Clemmensen, R. D. DiMarchi, & M. H. Tschöp. 2017. "The New Biology and Pharmacology of Glucagon." *Physiological Reviews* 97(2): 721–66.

Murray Charles J. "Who really invented the rechargeable lithium-ion battery?" *IEEE Spectrum* 30 2023.

National Geographic. "Road Trip Follows Strawberries Across the U.S. | National Geographic," October 23, 2014. **https://www.youtube.com/watch?v=a3T-uSJpxOg**.

National Marine Fisheries Service, Alaska Fisheries Science Center, Resource Ecology and Fisheries Management, and Stephen Kasperski. "Alaska Seafood Snapshot," 2024. **https://www.fisheries.noaa.gov/s3/2024-10/ak-seafood-industry-snapshot-10-31-2024-afsc.pdf**.

National Museum Australia. "Iron Ore Exports." Accessed February 28, 2026. **https://www.nma.gov.au/defining-moments/resources/iron-ore-exports**.

Naughton B. 1997. Danwei: The Economic Foundations of a Unique Institution. In *Danwei* 1st edn. edited by X. Lü and E. J. Perry. pp. 169–94. Routledge. **https://doi.org/10.4324/9781315700014-11**.

New York State Cheese Manufacturers Association. 2020. *146 Years of Cheese Manufacturing*. **https://nyscheesemakers.com/wp-content/uploads/2020/07/NYCM-March-2-Presentation.pdf**.

New York Times (New York, NY). 1967. "London, Paris and Bonn Agree to Develop a Huge Jet Airbus." July 26.

New York Times (New York). 2012. "How Zara Grew into the World's Largest Fashion Retailer."

Ngai Pun, & Chris Smith. 2007 Putting Transnational Labour Process in Its Place: The Dormitory Labour Regime in Post-socialist China. *Work, Employment and Society* 21(1): 27–45. **https://doi.org/10.1177/0950017007073611**.

Nike Inc. "Nike Inc Form 10-K." (July 17, 2025) **https://www.sec.gov/ix?doc=/Archives/edgar/data/320187/000032018725000047/nke-20250531.htm**.

NOAA Fisheries. "NOAA Fisheries Foreign Trade." Accessed January 17, 2026. **https://www.fisheries.noaa.gov/foss/f?p=215:2:11813278711831**.

Notteboom Theo & Jean-Paul Rodrigue. 2005. "Port Regionalization: Towards a New Phase in Port Development." *Maritime Policy & Management* 32(3): 297–313.

Novo Nordisk. 2020. Novo Nordisk Annual Report. **https://www.novonordisk.com/content/dam/nncorp/global/en/investors/irmaterial/annual_report/2020/Novo-Nordisk-Annual-Report-2019.pdf**.

NPR. "Trump Ends China's De Minimis Trade Loophole for Low-Cost Goods. What Is It?" February 5, 2025. **https://www.npr.org/2025/02/05/g-s1-46670/de-minimis-trade-china-temu-shein-trump**.

Ohashi Hiroshi. 2002. "Anticipatory Effects of Voluntary Export Restraints: A Study of Home Video Cassette Recorders Market, 1978–86." *Journal of International Economics* 57(1): 83–105. **https://doi.org/10.1016/S0022-1996(01)00136-2**.

Ohno Taiichi. 1988. *Toyota Production System: Beyond Large-Scale Production*. Boca Raton: Productivity Press **http://dx.doi.org/10.4324/9780429273018**.

Opoku S.Y., R. Bhattacharjee, M. Kolesnikova-Allen, J.C. Motamayor, R. Schnell, I. Ingelbrecht, L. Enu-Kwesi, & Y. Adu-Ampomah. 2007. "Genetic Diversity in Cocoa (*Theobroma Cacao L.*) Germplasm Collection from Ghana." *Journal of Crop Improvement* 20(1–2): 73–87. **https://doi.org/10.1300/J411v20n01_04**.

Owen Geoffrey. Industrial policy in Europe Since the Second World War: What Has Been Learnt? No. 1/2012. ECIPE occasional paper, 2012.

Parisis Vassilis, Rafael da Gama Ferreira, Nikiforos Misailidis, & Demetri Petrides. "Production of Semaglutide." 2025.

Park YoungWon, Paul Hong, & James Jungbae Roh. 2013. "Supply Chain Lessons from the Catastrophic Natural Disaster in Japan." *Business Horizons* 56(1): 75–85. **https://doi.org/10.1016/j.bushor.2012.09.008**.

Pasteur Louis. 1857. "Mémoire sur la fermentation appelée lactique." *Comptes Rendus Chimie* 45: 913–916.

Pasteur Louis. *Studies on Fermentation – The Diseases of Beer, Their Causes, and the Means of Prevention*. Translated by Frank Faulkner and D. Constable Robb. London: MacMillan & Co., 1879. Project Gutenberg. **https://www.gutenberg.org/files/63355/63355-h/63355-h.htm**.

Patton Phil. "Harvest Season for the '08 Car Colors." *New York Times*, June 13, 2005. **https://www.nytimes.com/2005/06/13/automobiles/harvest-season-for-the-08-car-colors.html**.

Pershey Edward Jay. 1990. "Lowell and the Industrial City in Nineteenth-Century America." *OAH Magazine of History* 5(2): 5–10.

Pham Vu & Nguyen, T. 2023, June 17. Millions of industrial park workers in need of housing. theinvestor.vn. **https://theinvestor.vn/millions-of-industrial-park-workers-in-need-of-housing-d5437.html**.

Pisano G. P. & W. C. Shih. 2009. "Restoring American Competitiveness." *Harvard Business Review* 87(7, 8): 114.

Port of Corpus Christi. "Outbound Crude Oil – Domestic and Export Markets." Accessed February 22, 2026. **https://portofcc.com/outbound-crude-oil/**.

Porubcan Randolph S. & Robert L. Sellers. "*Preparation of Culture Concentration for Direct Vat Set Cheese Production*." U.S. Patent 4,115,199, filed May 4, 1977, and issued September 19, 1978.

Postgate J. N. 1992. *Early Mesopotamia: Society and Economy at the Dawn of History*. London: Routledge.

Pou Chen Group. 2026. "Pou Chen Group-About PCG," **https://www.pouchen.com/index.php/en/investor-relations/faq/8-pcc/1-about**.

Prahalad C. K. & Gary Hamel. 1990. *The Core Competence of the Corporation. Harvard Business Review*. Vol. 68. Boston: Harvard Business Review.

Prince Marcelo & Willa Plank. 2012. "A Short History of Apple's Manufacturing in the U.S." *Wall Street Journal*, **https://www.wsj.com/articles/BL-DGB-25630**.

Pun Ngai & Xiaomin Yu. 2008. "When Wal-Mart and the Chinese Dormitory Labour Regime Meet: A Study of Three Toy Factories in China." *China Journal of Social Work* 1(2): 110–29. **https://doi.org/10.1080/17525090802086356**.

Quianzon Celeste C. & Issam Cheikh. 2012. "History of Insulin." *Journal of Community Hospital Internal Medicine Perspectives* 2(2): 18701.

Quinn James Brian, Thomas L. Doorley, & Penny C. Paquette. 1990. "Technology in Services: Rethinking Strategic Focus." *Sloan Management Review* 31(2): 79.

Raitano Lucy & Danilo Masoni. "Novo Nordisk briefly overtakes LVMH as Europe's most valuable company." *Reuters*, September 1, 2023. **https://www.reuters.com/markets/europe/drugmaker-novo-nordisk-briefly-overtakes-lvmh-europes-most-valuable-company-2023-09-01/**.

Rappaport Andrew S. & Shmuel Halevi. 1991. "The Computerless Computer Company." *Harvard Business Review* (Boston).

Reisch Marc S. "DuPont to Buy Danisco for $6.3 Billion." *Chemical & Engineering News*, January 10, 2011. **https://cen.acs.org/articles/89/web/2011/01/DuPont-Buy-Danisco-63-Billion.html**.

Renshaw Jarrett. "Phillips 66 says Algerian crude cheaper than U.S. shale." *North American Energy News*. April 20, 2016. **https://theamericanenergynews.com/phillips-shuns-domestic-oil-imports-algerian-crude-bayway-refinery-new-jersey/**.

Ricardo David. 1817. *On the Principles of Political Economy and Taxation*. London: John Murray.

Richards Timothy J. 2018. "Immigration Reform and Farm Labor Markets." *American Journal of Agricultural Economics* (Malden) 100(4): 1050–71. **https://doi.org/10.1093/ajae/aay027**.

Riis Thomas. 2012. "The Story of Emil Chr. Hansen." *The Journal of European Economic History* 41(1): 159.

Riordan Michael H., & Oliver E. Williamson. 1985. "Asset Specificity and Economic Organization." *International Journal of Industrial Organization* (Amsterdam) 3(4): 365–78. **https://doi.org/10.1016/0167-7187(85)90030-X**.

Robertson R. Paul. 2023. "Brief Overview: Glucagon History and Physiology." *Journal of Endocrinology* 258(2).

Rouay Limsuwan. 2019. "The Gemstone and Jewelry Industry in Thailand: A Brief Report on the Changes and Challenges from Upstream to Downstream." 社会地質学会誌 = Geo-Pollution Science, *Medical Geology and Urban Geology* 15(1–2): 17–21.

Rural Migration News. "Alternatives to Hand Labor in Strawberries—Rural Migration Blog | Migration Dialogue," n.d. **https://migration.ucdavis.edu/rmn/blog/post/?id=2504**.

S&P Global Commodity Insights. "Iron Ore Industry Challenges Simandou's 'Pilbara Killer' Status." S&P Global, January 5, 2026. **https://www.spglobal.com/energy/en/news-research/latest-news/metals/010526-iron-ore-industry-challenges-simandous-pilbara-killer-status**.

Sanger David. "IBM Making Its Own PC Printers." *New York Times,* May 2, 1985. **https://www.nytimes.com/1985/05/02/business/ibm-making-its-own-pc-printers.html**.

Savage Susannah & Madeleine Speed. 2025. "Record Cocoa Prices Prompt Buyers to Delay Orders, Says Swiss Chocolate Maker." **FT.Com**, 2025.

Schurmann Franz. 1966. *Ideology and Organization in Communist China*. Berkeley: University of California Press.

SCI Systems—Company History. "SCI Systems, Inc.—Company History," n.d. **https://www.company-histories.com/SCI-Systems-Inc-Company-History.html**.

Secrest Fred G. 1981. "The American Automobile Industry and the Japanese Challenge." In *The Japanese Automotive Industry: Model and Challenge for the Future?*, edited by Robert E. Cole, pp. 41–50. University of Michigan Press. **http://www.jstor.org/stable/10.3998/mpub.18647.10**.

Shauk Zain. "North Dakota Crude Bound for New Jersey." Houston Chronicle. January 9, 2013. **https://www.houstonchronicle.com/business/article/north-dakota-crude-bound-for-new-jersey-4180685.php**.

Shih Willy. 2014. "Living Proof: Are we a technology company or a beauty company?" HBS Case No. 614-013. (Boston) Harvard Business School Publishing.

Shih Willy C. & Sen Chai. 2013. *Novozymes: Establishing the Cellulosic Ethanol Value Chain. (Case No. 614-001)*. Boston: Harvard Business School Publishing.

Shih Willy C. & Sen Chai. 2015. "What to Know About Locating in a Cluster." *MIT Sloan Management Review* 57(1): 8.

Shih Willy & Veronica Chua. "Trump's Trade and Deportation Plans Could Be Disastrous for the U.S. Food Supply." **hbr.org**. Harvard Business Publishing, January 22, 2025. Accessed January 31, 2026. **https://hbr.org/2025/01/trumps-trade-and-deportation-plans-could-be-disastrous-for-the-u-s-food-supply**.

Shih Willy & Jyun-Cheng Wang. 2008. "Upgrading the Economy: Industrial Policy and Taiwan's Semiconductor Industry." Harvard Business School Case No. 609-089. Boston: Harvard Business School Publishing.

Shih Willy & Jyun-Cheng Wang. "Upgrading the Economy: Industrial Policy and Taiwan's Semiconductor Industry." *Harvard Business School Case Study*. Harvard Business Publishing, 2009. **https://www.hbs.edu/faculty/Pages/item.aspx?num=36951**.

Sikri Richa G. "Why Bangkok Is the Go-To Spot for Colored Stones." *Rapaport*, January 24, 2024. **https://rapaport.com/magazine-article/why-bangkok-is-the-go-to-spot-for-colored-stones/**.

Slack Brian. 1999. Across the Pond: Container Shipping on the North Atlantic in the Era of Globalisation. *GeoJournal* 48(1): 9–14. **https://doi.org/10.1023/A:1007080517715**.

Smith Adam. 1776. *An Inquiry into the Nature and Causes of the Wealth of Nations.* London: W. Strahan and T. Cadell.

Smith Andrew F. 2012. *American Tuna: The Rise and Fall of an Improbable Food* 1st ed. Vol. 37. University of California Press. **https://doi.org/10.1525/9780520954151**.

Smith Chris & Ngai Pun, 2006. "The Dormitory Labour Regime in China as a Site for Control and Resistance1." *International Journal of Human Resource Management*, 17(8): 1456–70. **https://doi.org/10.1080/09585190600804762**.

Smith M. R. 1973. John H. Hall, Simeon North, and the Milling Machine: The Nature of Innovation among Antebellum Arms Makers. *Technology and Culture*, 14(4): 573–91. **https://doi.org/10.2307/3102444**.

Solinger D. J. 1997. The Impact of the Floating Population on the Danwei: Shifts in the Pattern of Labor Mobility Control and Entitlement Provision. In *Danwei* 1st edn. edited by X. Lü and E. J. Perry, pp. 195–222. Routledge. **https://doi.org/10.4324/9781315700014-12**.

Solow Robert M. 1956. "A Contribution to the Theory of Economic Growth." *The Quarterly Journal of Economics* (Cambridge, Mass. [etc.]) 70(1): 65–94. **https://doi.org/10.2307/1884513**.

Sorenson Niels Henrik. "*A Method for Processing of Hides or Skins into Leather, Comprising Enzymatic Treatment of the Hide or Skin with a Trypsin Acting Microbial Protease*." European Patent EP 0 784 706 B1, filed September 22, 1995, and issued January 12, 1999.

Sotheby's. "Complete Guide to the Rare and Often Record Breaking Pigeon Blood Ruby." **Sothebys.com**, June 5, 2025. **https://www.sothebys.com/en/articles/complete-guide-to-the-rare-and-often-record-breaking-pigeon-blood-ruby**.

Spencer Sally. 2016. "Building a Future for American Hardwoods." *Timber Trades Journal* (Tonbridge), no. 6799: 35.

Srinivasan T. N. & Anne Krueger. 2005. Information-Technology-Enabled Services and India's Growth Prospects [with Comment and Discussion]. *Brookings Trade Forum 2005*(1): 203–40. **https://doi.org/10.1353/btf.2006.0023**.

Stathis Stephen W. 2009. "Pacific Railroad Act * 1862." In *Landmark Debates in Congress: From the Declaration of Independence to the War in Iraq*. CQ Press. **https://doi.org/10.4135/9781452240145.n18**.

Steensels Jan & Kevin J. Verstrepen. 2014. "Taming Wild Yeast: Potential of Conventional and Nonconventional Yeasts in Industrial Fermentations." *Annual Review of Microbiology* 68: 61–80.

Sturgeon Timothy J. 2002. "Modular Production Networks: A New American Model of Industrial Organization." *Industrial and Corporate Change* 11(3): 451–96. **https://doi.org/10.1093/icc/11.3.451**.

Sturgeon Timothy J., Johannes Van Biesebroeck, & Gary Gereffi. 2008. "Value Chains, Networks and Clusters." *Journal of Economic Geography* 8(3): 297–321.

Suh Neville N, & Ernest L Molua. 2022. "Cocoa Production under Climate Variability and Farm Management Challenges: Some Farmers' Perspective." *Journal of Agriculture and Food Research* 8:100282. **https://doi.org/10.1016/j.jafr.2022.100282**.

Sukagawa Paul. 2010. "Is Iron Ore Priced as a Commodity? Past and Current Practice." *Resources Policy* 35(1): 54–63. **https://doi.org/10.1016/j.resourpol.2009.09.001**.

Sylla Richard. 2024. "Alexander Hamilton's Report on Manufactures and Industrial Policy." *The Journal of Economic Perspectives* 38(4): 111–30. **https://doi.org/10.1257/jep.38.4.111**.

Tabassum Juveria. "Walmart, Best Buy, Nike's Major Supply Hubs in Asia." *Reuters.* April 3, 2025. **https://www.reuters.com/business/retail-consumer/walmart-best-buy-nikes-major-supply-hubs-asia-2025-04-03/**.

Tamime A. Y. 1993. "Modern Cheesemaking: Hard Cheeses." In *Modern Dairy Technology: Volume 2, Advances in Milk Products*, pp. 49–220. Boston: Springer US.

Tamm Ditlev. 2020. *The Carlsberg Story*. Cham: Springer International Publishing.

Tano Assi Maxime. 2012. "Crise cacaoyère et stratégies des producteurs de la sous-préfécture de Meadji au sud-ouest ivoirien."

Taylor F. W. 1911. *The Principles of Scientific Management*. Harper.

Terlep Sharon. "Americans Have Too Much Toilet Paper. Finally, Sales Slow." *Wall Street Journal*. April 13, 2021. **https://www.wsj.com/business/retail/americans-have-too-much-toilet-paper-it-is-catching-up-to-companies-11618306200?mod=Searchresults&pos=1&page=1**.

The Economist. "The Steam Has Gone Out of Globalisation." January 24, 2019. **https://www.economist.com/leaders/2019/01/24/the-steam-has-gone-out-of-globalisation**.

The Economist. "China's 'Dual-circulation' Strategy Means Relying Less on Foreigners." November 5, 2020. **https://www.economist.com/china/2020/11/05/chinas-dual-circulation-strategy-means-relying-less-on-foreigners**.

The Straits Times. 2025. "Foxconn workers faced tough conditions during rush to make iPhone 17, labour group says," November 2, 2025. **https://www.straitstimes.com/world/foxconn-workers-faced-tough-conditions-during-rush-to-make-iphone-17-labour-group-says**.

TJX.com. "The TJX Companies, Inc. Form 10-K." **tjx.com**, March 21, 2025. Accessed February 20, 2026. **https://www.tjx.com/docs/default-source/investor-docs/quarterly-results/tjx-fourth-quarter-fiscal-year-2025-form-10-k.pdf**.

Tolchin Martin. "Gene-Altered Item Approved by F.D.A." *New York Times*, March 25, 1990.

Tschöp Matthias H. & Jeffrey M. Friedman. 2023. "Seeking Satiety: From Signals to Solutions." *Science Translational Medicine* 15(723): eadh4453.

Tung An-Chi. 2001. "Taiwan's Semiconductor Industry: What the State Did and Did Not." *Review of Development Economics* 5(2): 266–88.

U.S. Govt. Print. Off., 1789. "The Avalon Project : Statutes of the United States," n.d. **https://avalon.law.yale.edu/18th_century/qw08.asp**.

U.S. International Trade Commission. 2026. "Investigation No. 731-TA-1770 (Preliminary) Fresh Winter Strawberries from Mexico; Institution of Antidumping Duty Investigation and Scheduling of Preliminary Phase Investigation." *Federal Register* 91(3): 380.

U.S. National Park Service. n.d. "The Mill Girls of Lowell—Lowell National Historical Park (U.S. National Park Service)." **https://www.nps.gov/lowe/learn/historyculture/the-mill-girls-of-lowell.htm**.

Unger Richard W. 2004. *Beer in the Middle Ages and the Renaissance*. Philadelphia: University of Pennsylvania Press.

United States Trade Representative. "China – Measures Affecting Imports of Automobile Parts (WT/DS340)," March 13, 2007. **https://ustr.gov/sites/default/files/uploads/agreements/morocco/pdfs/dispute_settlement/ds340/asset_upload_file677_11099.pdf**.

United States. Office of the U.S. Trade Representative, issuing body. 2010. Report on Sanitary and Phytosanitary Measures. Washington, DC: Office of the United States Trade Representative, Executive Office of the President.

USCIS.gov. "H-2A Temporary Agricultural Workers." Accessed February 16, 2026. **https://www.uscis.gov/working-in-the-united-states/temporary-workers/h-2a-temporary-agricultural-workers**.

USDA Agricultural Marketing Service. 2021. *World's leading cheese coagulant portfolio from Chr. Hansen*. **https://www.ams.usda.gov/sites/default/files/media/FMMO_Select_8.pdf**.

USDA Economic Research Service. 2024. "Agricultural Trade." Washington, DC. Accessed May 24, 2026. **https://www.ers.usda.gov/data-products/ag-and-food-statistics-charting-the-essentials/agricultural-trade**.

Utah State University. "An Overview of the Cut Flower Industry." USU, January 4, 2024. **https://extension.usu.edu/apec/research/cut-flower-industry#:~:text=As%20many%20as%2080%25%20of,2016;%20Tegethoff%2C%202023**.

Valencia C. & N. Paulson. "The Growing Role of H-2A Workers in U.S. Agriculture." Farmdoc Daily, July 10, 2025. **https://farmdocdaily.illinois.edu/2025/07/the-growing-role-of-h-2a-workers-in-us-agriculture.html**.

Walsh John. 1972. "Carlsberg Laboratory: Ferment over Future of Copenhagen Lab." *Science* 175(4025): 973–4.

Wang James J. & Brian Slack. 2000. "The Evolution of a Regional Container Port System: The Pearl River Delta." *Journal of Transport Geography* 8(4): 263–75.

Webber Jude & Hannah Kuchler. "Trump Tariffs Bring Furrowed Brows to Ireland's Botox Town." *Financial Times*, April 19, 2025.

Weerathilake W. A. D. V., D. M. D. Rasika, J. K. U. Ruwanmali, & M. A. D. D. Munasinghe. 2014. "The Evolution, Processing, Varieties and Health Benefits of Yogurt." *International Journal of Scientific and Research Publications* 4(4): 1–10.

Weinswig Deborah. 2019. "US Retailer Survey: Revealing the Hidden Costs of Poor Inventory Management," February 6, 2019. **https://production-wordpress-cdn-dpa0g9bzd7b3h7gy.z03.azurefd.net/wp-content/uploads/2019/02/US-Retailer-Survey-Revealing-the-Hidden-Costs-of-Poor-Inventory-Management-Feb-6-2019.pdf**.

Whitehurst Clinton H. 1986. *The U.S. Shipbuilding Industry: Past, Present, and Future*. Naval Institute Press.

Whittington Hunter D., Suzanne F. Dagher, & José M. Bruno-Bárcena. 2019. "Production and Conservation of Starter Cultures: From 'Backslopping' to Controlled Fermentations." In *How Fermented Foods Feed a Healthy Gut Microbiota: A Nutrition Continuum*, pp. 125–38. Cham: Springer International Publishing.

Wilentz Sean. 2005. *The Rise of American Democracy: Jefferson to Lincoln*. W.W. Norton.

Witkin Richard. 1978. "Eastern accepts $778 Million Deal to Get 23 Airbuses: Approval From Airline's Lenders Is Required—Borman Indicates This Will Be—Granted External Financing Arranged Eastern Leasing 4 Aircraft Eastern Accepts Deal for Airbuses." *New York Times* (New York, N.Y), April 7.

Wolff Michael F. 1976. "Retrospective: The Genesis of the Integrated Circuit." *IEEE Spec*trum. **https://doi.org/10.1109/MSPEC.1976.6369299**.

Womack J. P., Jones, D. T., & Roos, D. 1990. *Machine That Changed the World*. Simon and Schuster.

World Trade Organization. "China—Measures Affecting Imports of Automobile Parts (AB-2008-10)" Report. Reports of the Appellate Body, November 15, 2008. **https://www.wto.org/english/tratop_e/dispu_e/339_340_342abr_e.pdf.**

Wrege C. D., & Greenwood, R. G. 1991. *Frederick W. Taylor, the Father of Scientific Management: Myth and Reality*. Business One Irwin.

WTO. "European Communities and Certain Member States – Measures Affecting Trade in Large Civil Aircraft." **Wto.Org.** World Trade Organization, May 18, 2011. Accessed March 1, 2026. **https://www.wto.org/english/tratop_e/dispu_e/cases_e/ds316_e.htm.**

Yeh D. Adeline, Jaclyn Kramer, Linda Calvin, & Catharine Weber. 2023. *The changing landscape of U.S. strawberry and blueberry markets: Production, trade, and challenges from 2000 to 2020* (Report No. EIB-257). U.S. Department of Agriculture, Economic Research Service. **https://doi.org/10.32747/2023.8134359.ers.**

Yeong Choy Leng. "NW salmon sent to China before reaching U.S. tables," July 16, 2005. **https://www.seattletimes.com/business/nw-salmon-sent-to-china-before-reaching-us-tables/.**

Zadeh John. "Dalian Iron Ore Futures Surge 3.67% Amid Cautious Trading." Discovery-Alert.au, July 10, 2025. Accessed February 28, 2026. **https://discoveryalert.com.au/dalian-iron-ore-futures-market-dynamics-trading-strategies/.**

Zhang Xilin, Yi Meng, Eugene P. Deess, NJBIA, & NJIT, Office of Institutional Effectiveness. "Economic Impact Analysis Report for Bayway Industrial Complex." NJBIA/NJIT IMPACT REPORT, 2023. **https://njbia.org/wp-content/uploads/2025/11/2025-Bayway-Project-FINAL.pdf#:~:text=does%20this%20facility%20make%20to,their%20effects%20extend%20far%20beyond%E2%80%94.**

Zhi Qiang & Margaret M. Pearson. 2017. "China's Hybrid Adaptive Bureaucracy: The Case of the 863 Program for Science and Technology," *Governance* 30(3): 408–12.

Acknowledgments

Many people made this book possible—almost too many to count. But some of those I worked for during my 28 years in industry made far more of a difference than they probably realized at the time. Several individuals stand out. Richard (Dick) Schwemm hired me out of graduate school at the University of California – Berkeley to join IBM, and he had an outsized impact on my future path: he gave me the space to learn and to make mistakes but also to recover from them. Jack Kuehler, whom I worked for in Armonk when he was the president of IBM, did the same, signing me up for audacious projects like working with Apple on microprocessors, something that was almost unthinkable at the time.

The years I learned the most were my seven years at Eastman Kodak, where I led the consumer digital operations. George Fisher, the chairman and CEO who brought me in, was probably the finest leader one could hope for when a company finds itself in such dire straits as Kodak was when I arrived. Under him and his successor Dan Carp, I had a front-row seat on globalization and the accelerating movement of production to Asia. George was a pioneering thinker on these trends, and Dan gave me the space and support to explore them. During those years I saw and absorbed more than I could have ever imagined, and you'll find much of that learning woven throughout this book. My time at Kodak ended in something of a train wreck—but I couldn't have come away with more lasting lessons.

That brings me to all the people who reported to me and taught me things. In today's complex world, it is impossible to be the best at everything. You need to hire the best people you can find and then be willing to learn from them. Throughout my career in industry, some of my most important lessons came from people who worked for me. I was fortunate to hire some of them but even more fortunate to inherit many of them. I am grateful for their teamwork and the trust they put in me.

I also want to thank the executives and team members at Flex, Inc., led by Revathi Advaithi, whose board I served on for 15 years. The breadth and scope of the company's manufacturing and supply chain services is a wonder to behold, and I learned a great deal from people at every level—from the CEO and fellow board members to the operators on shop floors stretching from China to India, Hungary to Mexico, and across the United States. Particular thanks to Paul Baldassari, who guided me through so many remote corners of the company.

My time at Harvard Business School has given me an unmatched opportunity to observe and study operations firsthand. It has opened doors to businesses around the world—from cacao plantations in the jungles of

Côte d'Ivoire to the most advanced semiconductor fabs on Earth; from the baggage-sorting operations beneath one of the world's busiest airports to a palm oil plantation in Sumatra. I am deeply grateful to the school for that privilege and to the late Clayton Christensen for recruiting me to teach with him here. The school has a network of Global Research Centers that has supported my field work and case writing. Nancy Dai, the director of the Harvard Center Shanghai, her team, and I have explored businesses and supply chains all over China since I first arrived at the school. The other centers around the world have similarly been a great help in expanding my horizons.

Through its Executive Education programs, I have met people from different parts of the world who have been an immense aid to my learning. I worked with Carsten Orth Garn Larsen and Trine Abo Andersen on a multiyear program with companies from Denmark, which introduced me to the outsized role that fermentation plays in the Danish industrial cluster, as well as world-leading firms like LEGO, A.P. Møller–Mærsk, Grundfos, and Novo Nordisk. Thanks also to Nigel Edmonson of the Manufacturing Academy of Denmark, who opened so many doors across Denmark, and to Dr. Michael Kaschke at Carl Zeiss in Oberkochen, Germany, who opened his company to me—where I learned about everything from the optical engines inside extreme ultraviolet lithography tools to progressive-lens eyewear. The Division of Research and Faculty Development has generously funded my work, as has the family of Robert and Jane Cizik, whose endowed chair I have been honored to hold.

Finally, I want to thank my wife Julie and daughters Kathryn and Anna, who have unconditionally supported every job change and every improbable venture I decided to pursue. That included moving seven times within one 42-month period. Anna has been urging me for years to write this book, and I'm glad I finally listened. Their support has been indispensable.

About the Author

Willy C. Shih is the Robert and Jane Cizik Baker Foundation Professor of Management Practice in Business Administration at the Harvard Business School, where he teaches and writes about operations management, global supply chains, manufacturing strategy, and industrial competitiveness. His research examines how supply chains are structured and why they matter—for the competitive position of firms and for the economic strength of nations. A direct consequence of that work has been unusually detailed first-hand knowledge of where the world's goods are made and why production ends up where it does.

Before joining Harvard Business School (HBS) in 2007, Shih spent 28 years in industry, leading technology and manufacturing businesses with global operations at companies including IBM, Digital Equipment, Silicon Graphics, and Eastman Kodak. Concurrently with his time at HBS, he served as a director at Flex, Inc., one of the world's largest contract manufacturers, from 2008 to 2022. Together, these experiences—building, sourcing, and scaling production across multiple continents during one of history's great waves of globalization—inform everything he researches and teaches.

His work sits at the intersection of business strategy and public policy. He has advised the U.S. government on supply chain resilience and the implementation of the CHIPS and Science Act, and he writes and speaks regularly on how corporate decisions and national industrial policy together shape long-term competitiveness.

Shih is a firm believer that you cannot truly understand production from a spreadsheet. Over the course of his career, he has visited more than 1,000 factories, toured container ports and air cargo hubs, and traced supply chains across five continents—convinced that real insight comes from seeing how things are actually made. *Where Does My Stuff Come From?* reflects that conviction, bringing together theory, practice, and decades of firsthand observation to illuminate the hidden logic of global production.

Index

Q

R

S

U

V